D1553669

The Missile Gap:
A STUDY OF THE FORMULATION
OF MILITARY AND POLITICAL POLICY

The Missile Gap:

A STUDY OF THE FORMULATION
OF MILITARY AND POLITICAL POLICY

Edgar M. Bottome

Fairleigh Dickinson

Rutherford • Madison • Teaneck
FAIRLEIGH DICKINSON UNIVERSITY PRESS

© 1971 by Associated University Presses, Inc.
Library of Congress Catalogue Card Number: 77-129964

Associated University Presses, Inc.
Cranbury, New Jersey 08512

ISBN: 0-8386-7734-7
Printed in the United States of America

To My Parents

CONTENTS

PREFACE

THIS BOOK TRACES AND ANALYZES THE COMPLEX AND OFTEN contradictory factors which led to a popular belief in the United States that the Soviet Union possessed a commanding superiority over the United States in intercontinental ballistic missiles* during the period 1958-1961. This illusion of a "missile gap" was created by the numerous Americans who feared that this Soviet superiority would lead to a devastating attack on United States retaliatory forces. The factors and forces which nurtured and maintained this belief constitute the subject matter of this book.

The thesis of this study is that a multitude of interacting forces combined to give rise to the illusion of an American ICBM inferiority. The possibility of a missile gap was debated in the United States by politicians, military men, members of the press, and many concerned citizens. This debate created the belief in the missile gap. However, this writer's purpose is to go beyond this and demonstrates that the origins of this phenomenon are deeply rooted both in American political and military policy making procedures and in the underlying assumptions and attitudes of policy formulation in the United States and the Soviet Union.

In approaching the missile gap period, this writer has chosen to present a chronological unfolding of information as it was presented to the public at the time. This is intended to give the reader an unobstructed appreciation and understanding of the diversity of forces involved, and

---

* Hereafter referred to as ICBM.

the role played by each of these forces in the creation and destruction of the missile gap myth.

The reliability of source material is handled with honest skepticism, since in many cases the degree of built-in bias of the author was either not known, or known well enough to discredit the authenticity of the information published; a single source rarely could be accepted as authoritative. For this reason, much of the analysis of the subject matter was possible only when later information became available, and the various sources could be compared with more authoritative and corroborative information. The classified nature of much of the material also left unanswered questions; these are noted in the text.*

A note about terms is relevant here. The distinction is made between a possible "missile lag" which would not have endangered the security of the United States, and a possible "deterrent gap" which could have threatened American security. A missile lag would have meant simply that the Soviet Union had more missiles than the United States. A deterrent gap would have meant that the Soviet Union possessed the ability to destroy United States retaliatory installations in a first strike, and thereby effectively remove the American ability to deter. Throughout this book, for the most part, the term missile gap has been used to mean a deterrent gap, since the public advocates of a missile gap stated or implied that the term meant a deterrent gap. Belief in a simple missile lag would hardly have warranted the concern and controversy which surrounded the missile gap.

This study is divided into three basic sections. The first is a single chapter providing an abbreviated survey of the relevant background information on United States defense policy from the end of World War II to 1956. The following five chapters trace the unfolding and eventual destruction of the missile gap myth. The final chapter pre-

* See "Note on Source Materials" at the end of this study.

sents the analysis of the subject matter, and it is here that this writer's opinions and calculated speculations are found, based on the total evidence available in retrospect.

The aim of this study is to present the concerned reader with a clear picture of a confusing period in recent American defense policy. The process of policy formation is always more complex than the resulting policy, and the missile gap period provides a good example of how much confusion and misunderstanding can surround United States governmental policy and action. This period also demonstrates how areas of political and military influence, conceivably separate, can become deeply intertwined. It is hoped that the complexities surrounding the missile gap illusion will encourage students of politics to examine basic policy questions more closely in terms of the roles played by the component parts in policy evolution. It is hoped that policy makers themselves might better understand influences around them by becoming more aware of how dependent each question is on a seemingly almost unlimited number of interrelated factors.

The author would like to express his thanks to the many previous military analysts who have attempted to unravel some of the mysteries of American defense policy and thus made this study possible. A sincere debt of gratitude is owed to Dr. Ruhl Bartlett for his initial guidance in formulating this work and to Dr. Howard Zinn for his constant encouragement and assistance. Finally, a special note of thanks is due to Estelle Bottome for her invaluable editorial assistance.

1

NUCLEAR WEAPONS AND UNITED STATES STRATEGY: 1945-1956

THE UNITED STATES EMERGED FROM WORLD WAR II WITH THE largest Air Force in the world and with a monopoly on atomic weapons. There appears to have been a great deal of initial confusion in the United States government as to what should be done with this unprecedented amount of power. It was decided to establish, if possible, an international agreement to control the manufacture and use of atomic weapons. After the failure of these efforts it became necessary for the United States to establish an effective doctrine for the use of atomic weapons in its defense policy.

By 1948, the leaders of the United States believed that they were faced with an aggressive and expansionist Soviet foreign policy. A policy of containing this perceived Soviet expansion had begun to develop following World War II, and by 1948 the policy of containment had achieved wide acceptance among the policy makers in the United States. However, the reduction in United States conventional armaments following the war had left this country in a position where its monopoly on the atomic bomb and the means of delivering it were the principle means of implementing the policy of containment. With the United States limited to a nuclear response to any aggressive Soviet act, the problem of how to implement the policy of containment became acute.[1] It became obvious that the United States needed a more clearly defined military strategy to enforce containment of perceived Soviet aggression within its existing boundaries.

The foundation of the United States policy of containment was the evolving concept of deterrence. According to this idea, the decisive task of the military leaders was no longer to vanquish in war, but to deter the enemy from precipitating an attack. The United States needed to develop the military capability necessary to convince the Soviet Union that it would not gain as much by aggression as it would lose. It was realized that the threat of force, even an apparently superior force, had often failed to prevent the outbreak of hostilities. The formulation and implementation of the strategy of containment through deterrence became the major problem of United States defense policy from the late 1940s through the period of the alleged "missile gap."

The initial phases of defining United States military policy following World War II were hectic and assumed no clearly discernible pattern. The goal of containment had been stated and accepted by the vast majority of American policy makers by 1950, but the military power to be used to implement this policy had not been defined clearly, much less put into effect. The United States was inhibited in its military planning by its doctrinal heritage of thinking in terms of conventional weapons and by the pressure of domestic demands upon scarce resources. These two factors combined to produce a serious gap between military policy and foreign policy.[2] The United States was not willing to use atomic weapons to prevent an aggressive Communist power from attempting to ad-

---

1. Bernard Brodie, "The Atomic Bomb as Policy Maker," *Foreign Affairs*, Vol. 27 (October 198) , p. 20.

2. Samuel P. Huntington, *The Common Defense: Strategic Programs in National Politics* (New York: Columbia University Press, 1961) , p. 47.

vance in Iran, Greece, Turkey, Czechoslovakia, Berlin, China, and eventually in Korea.

The Soviet announcement in August 1949 of its first atomic test caused many Americans, both military and civilian, to scrutinize carefully the ill-defined nuclear strategy of the United States. Even at this early date, the Military Editor of *The New York Times* stated that due to the Soviet explosion it should be the goal of the United States ". . . to find a substitute for the atomic bomb as a deterrent to Russian aggression."[3] Although the Soviet explosion of a nuclear device served as a catalyst to the debate over defense policy, the argument centered around two other major aspects of United States policy—the development of the hydrogen bomb and the controversy surrounding the future of the newest Air Force bomber, known as the B-36.

The debate over whether the United States should attempt to develop a hydrogen bomb occupied the inner circles of the Truman Administration for about five months (September 1949 to January 1950). In January 1950, President Truman announced that the United States would proceed to develop the hydrogen bomb. The main rationale for this decision was that the United States could not allow the Soviet Union to be the first nation to possess this potentially devastating weapon. The hydrogen bomb became the crucial weapon in the emergence of a United States policy of strategic deterrence, and this shaped the evolution of American military policy for the coming decade. Without the hydrogen bomb, the intercontinental ballistic missile would have been of limited value, but with the hydrogen warhead the basis for a relatively stable nuclear stalemate was established.[4]

---

3. *The New York Times*, news article by Hanson W. Baldwin, September 25, 1949.

4. Huntington, *The Common Defense*, p. 299. Once nuclear warheads were developed, a number of President Eisenhower's military and scientific

During this period the major controversy over American defense policy essentially focused on the various Congressional hearings concerning United States military posture and the quarrel among the several military services as to the efficacy and value of the B-36 bomber. Although this argument centered around the question of development and production of the bomber, the fundamental issue was the relationship of Army, Navy, and Air Force weapons systems to the exact nature of a future war. In this initial interservice conflict, the arguments of the three branches of the armed forces began to assume the posture they maintained through the controversy over the "missile gap."

The Air Force argument for the development of the B-36 bomber was based on the belief that the next war would be fought and won by attacking the enemy from the air and destroying his cities and industrial potential. This early strategy of aerial warfare was based on an Air Force evaluation stating that atomic bombs were too scarce to be used on military targets and therefore should be used against the enemy's cities. The Air Force believed that the possession of a long-range air striking force directed against Soviet cities was the most effective means of deterring aggression.[5]

Those opposed to this Air Force doctrine, the Navy and Army, doubted the political wisdom, military efficiency, and general morality of employing strategic nuclear bombing in a war. The Navy did not believe the United States would immediately resort to nuclear weapons in the event of war, and believed that it certainly would not employ them against the large cities of the enemy. Even if this

---

advisors began to push for an expanded missile program. U.S. Congress, House, Committee on Government Operations, Organization and Management of Missile Programs, *Hearings*, 86th Cong., 1st sess. (1959), p. 70.

5. *The New York Times*, news article by Hanson W. Baldwin, October 27, 1949.

were done, the Navy spokesmen did not believe that an initial air offensive could be decisive. A final aspect of the Navy's argument was the call for the capability to meet limited aggression with land and naval forces.[6] A vigorous spokesman for the Navy's point of view was Admiral Arthur W. Radford, Naval Chief of Staff. He testified before the House Armed Services Committee and stated: "I do not believe the threat of atomic blitz will be an effective deterrent to war."[7] The Army was in fundamental agreement with the Navy and placed even greater emphasis on the need for land troops to occupy the enemy's terrain.[8] However, the arguments of the Air Force prevailed and the B-36 went into production.

One of the fundamental problems that plagued United States defense planning became evident in the course of this debate. The argument between the services illustrated that there were two answers to the question of how to fight and/or prevent the next war. The Army and Navy accepted the doctrine of "balanced forces" ("mixed forces" during the period of the alleged missile gap) ; while the Air Force refused to abandon its belief that the next war would be settled by the use of air power and air power alone.[9]

At this stage of the argument over the military posture of the United States, the Air Force appeared to have a large majority of the American people in favor of increasing the size and strength of American air power, while a smaller but still significant majority favored increases in the strength of the Army and Navy.[10]

---

6. *Ibid.*, September 25, 1949.
7. U.S. Congressional Record, 83rd Cong., 2nd sess., Vol. 100, pt. 1 (Statement by Admiral Radford before House Armed Services Committee in 1949) , p. 467.
8. Huntington, *The Common Defense*, p. 373.
9. *Ibid.*, p. 373.
10. Gabriel Almond, *The American People and Foreign Policy* (New York: Frederick A. Praeger, 1950) , p. 204. Reprint of a poll of the Ameri-

The debate over how the next war would be fought was cut short by the "police action" necessitated by the invasion of South Korea by forces from North Korea. By 1950 the United States had not yet formulated any clear application of its nuclear power to strategic policy and had failed to integrate this new force into a military strategy that could respond to anything less than an all-out attack on the United States. Once the United States decided that it would fight in South Korea, the lack of United States preparedness for this type of conflict and the complete reliance of the United States on air power became apparent. The greatest industrial nation of the world could do no better than airlift two rifle companies and a battery of artillery to meet six North Korean divisions in the initial stages of the conflict.[11]

The United States was unwilling to deter limited aggression by threatening a massive nuclear strike at a potential aggressor, while at the same time not prepared militarily to meet the limited type of warfare that occurred in Korea. The gap between technological development and military-political policy became evident when the United States chose to fight the initial stages of the Korean "police action" using the military means for which it was least prepared. Before the end of the Korean conflict, the major weakness in United States defense posture was corrected to the extent that America fought the war to a stalemate, and could have won it if the decision had been made to override political considerations.[12]

The Korean conflict heightened the controversy in the United States concerning the role of nuclear weapons in defense policy. One group opposed a policy of trusting

can Institute of Public Opinion, February 1948, that showed 63 percent of the American public favoring a larger air force, 55 percent for a larger navy, and 55 percent for a larger army.

11. Gavin, *War and Peace in the Space Age*, p. 122.
12. Huntington, *The Common Defense*, p. 65.

American security to nuclear weapons delivered by the Air Force. The influence of this group was probably enhanced by divisions of opinion among those in the government responsible for American air power. The Air Force Chief of Staff doubted the ability of the Air Force to overcome the air power of the Soviet Union,[13] but the civilian Secretary of the Air Force claimed the United States possessed the strength necessary to resist any Soviet challenge.[14]

The acrimonious debate in the United States over nuclear weapons and air power should not obscure the fact that the Soviet Union was not prepared to challenge American security during the period 1951-1952. The Soviet Union possessed only a few nuclear weapons and a limited number of Tupelov-4 bombers (the Soviet equivalent of the United States B-29 bomber, with a 2000 mile range). This force was faced by a far superior United States capability.[15]

Following the Korean conflict, there was a great deal of revulsion and frustration in the United States due to the limited application of American power in this "police action." Many Americans, aware of this nation's great nuclear strength, could not comprehend the subtle reasoning behind fighting a war other than one aimed at total victory, particularly if the United States could have won the war without the use of nuclear weapons.[16] One of the major manifestations of this frustration was the increasing demand on the new Eisenhower Administration for a

13. *Aviation Week*, Vol. 54 (June 11, 1951), p. 11, statement by General Hoyt Vandenburg; *Aviation Week*, Vol. 58 (January 5, 1953), p. 13, statement by General Hoyt Vandenburg.
14. *The New York Times*, statement by Secretary of the Air Force Finletter, November 12, 1952.
15. *The New York Times*, June 7, 1951. Leonard Bridgeman, ed., *Jane's All the World's Aircraft* (London: Sampson Low, Marston & Company Ltd., 1952), p. 18.
16. John W. Spanier, *The Truman-MacArthur Controversy* (Cambridge: The Belknap Press of Harvard University Press, 1959), p. 259.

clearly stated, applicable policy concerning use of the nuclear power of the United States to implement American
policies.

Although the doctrine of massive retaliation was not
officially stated until January 1954, its foundation and
underlying philosophy became apparent during the first
year of the Eisenhower Administration. In President
Eisenhower's State of the Union Message in February
1953, he stated that the free world could not leave to the
aggressor "the choice of the time and place and means to
cause the greatest hurt to us at the least cost to himself."[17]
He then set forth his Administration's policy for obtaining
national security without excessive defense spending:

> To amass military power without regard to our own eco-
> nomic capacity would be to defend ourselves against one
> kind of disaster by inviting another. . . . The biggest force is
> not necessarily the best.[18]

The President's goal of balancing American military
requirements and economic capacity proved to be difficult
to achieve. The Eisenhower Administration became en-
snarled in the same dilemma that frustrated the Truman
Administration; it plagued President Eisenhower throughout his whole term of office. In precise terms, that dilemma
was: how to maintain United States security and the military posture needed to conduct United States foreign policy while at the same time following a domestic policy of
solvency and expansion of essential domestic governmental programs.[19]

The old strategy of planned mobilization of manpower
and industrial resources over an extended period of time

---

17. *The New York Times,* President Eisenhower's State of the Union
Message, February 3, 1954.
18. *Ibid.*
19. *The New York Times,* news article by Hanson W. Baldwin, October
21, 1953.

appeared to be outmoded in the nuclear age, and the new
strategy of deterrence through readiness accentuated military versus nonmilitary claims on scarce resources.[20]

President Eisenhower continued to state many of the
more significant aspects of the doctrine of massive retaliation before its formal announcement. In his second State
of the Union Message, he announced that: "We shall not
be the aggressor, but we and our allies have and will maintain a massive capability to strike back."[21]

The formal announcement of the doctrine of massive
retaliation was made by Secretary of State John Foster
Dulles on January 12, 1954. The original doctrine had
two basic precepts—one dealing with the cost of deterrence
and the other with the response of the United States to
aggression. The Secretary of State said, "We want for
ourselves and for others a maximum deterrent at bearable
costs."[22] In order to secure the two goals of security and
solvency, the Eisenhower Administration initially adopted
a dual posture to prevent Soviet aggression. Strategically,
the policy of threatened massive retaliation emerged to
deter Soviet aggression. On the tactical level, especially in
Western Europe, military planning relied on smaller overseas forces and tactical atomic weapons. Both the strategic
and tactical means of deterrence were intended to succeed
in containing through deterrence. This task was to be
accomplished by giving more firepower for less money
than would have been needed under more traditional
forms of defense policy.

By publicly articulating the doctrine of massive retaliation as United States policy, Secretary Dulles introduced
this policy to open scrutiny and debate as the official

20. Huntington, *The Common Defense*, p. 25. In spite of the increased
awareness of the need for existing military preparedness, the United States
continued to plan for industrial mobilization in the event of war.

21. *The New York Times*, January 8, 1954.

22. *The New York Times*, statement by Secretary of State John Foster
Dulles before the Council on Foreign Relations, January 13, 1954.

policy of the American government. This debate was not long in coming and it illustrated that a degree of ambiguity and confusion arose from the original statements. The combination of continued debate and the subsequent Administration attempts to clarify the new doctrine continued until the concept eventually changed and was redefined.

The first express criticism of the doctrine raised the question of the President's constitutional authority to initiate massive retaliation,[23] and other critics questioned the doctrine's credibility in the mind of a potential aggressor.[24] The problem of constitutionality of the doctrine was never seriously discussed, but the question of credibility was a constant factor throughout the debate on massive retaliation.

Surrounding the whole controversy over this new doctrine was a substantial element of partisan politics. Such criticism is not always valid and is often irresponsible. Therefore, when we consider the statement of a Senate Democrat who said that the United States had been placed in the position of being a "paper tiger" and that the Secretary of State "has put political expediency before wise and courageous action,"* the political motivation behind such a statement must be considered carefully in analyzing the validity of the criticism. This element of partisanship remained important throughout the whole controversy concerning United States defense policy and became particularly acute during the period of the "missile gap."

Due to the criticism and confusion arising from the original statement in January, Secretary Dulles attempted

23. *The New York Times*, news article by James Reston, January 17, 1954.

24. U.S. Congressional Record, 83rd Cong., 2nd sess., Vol. 100, pt. 1 (January 6 to February 5, 1954), p. 467; *The New York Times*, speech by Adlai Stevenson to the Southeast Democratic Conference, March 7, 1954.

* *U.S. Congressional Record*, 80th Cong., 1st sess., Vol. 101, pt. 5 (May 5 to May 25, 1955), reprint of a speech by Senator Magnuson (Dem.-Wash.), p. 5932.

to clarify the doctrine of massive retaliation and to answer his critics in the April 1954 issue of *Foreign Affairs*. He began by restating what he believed to be the basic question concerning the maintenance of free world security; that is, "How should collective defense be organized by the free world for maximum protection at minimum cost?"[25] Mr. Dulles believed that to allow the aggressor to dictate the battle conditions that suited him, and thereby to engage the free world in a struggle involving manpower, was to encourage aggression. He thought that the aggressor would be tempted to attack in places and by means with which he could impose the greatest burden on the United States at a minimum cost to himself. If the free world responded to this strategy, it could bankrupt itself and not achieve the security required.[26] Secretary Dulles attempted to forestall any act of aggression when he stated:

> The potential of massive attack will always be kept in a state of readiness, but our program will retain a wide variety of means and scope for responding to aggression.[27]

This new policy was based on the belief that it was impossible for the free world to build up adequate conventional defense forces around the Communist perimeter. By claiming that the United States could choose the time, place, and means of warfare, there was a strong implication that local conflicts might be escalated in terms of place and methods of retaliation. The doctrine of massive retaliation implied the threat of and preparation for total war in an effort to prevent not only all-out war but also limited aggression.

Despite this clarification, the exact response of the United States to any given act of Soviet aggression remained vague. It appears that the doctrine of massive

---

25. John Foster Dulles, "Policy for Security and Peace," *Foreign Affairs*, Vol. 32 (April 1954) , p. 357.

26. *Ibid.*, pp. 357–358.

27. *Ibid.*, p. 363.

retaliation was left vague on purpose. By not stating exactly what aggressive act would initiate instant retaliation, or the exact nature of the retaliatory act, Secretary of State Dulles hoped to prevent all types of aggression.

For complete credibility, such a doctrine should have been based on a United States counterforce posture—the United States' ability to strike first at the enemy's nuclear capability and destroy enough of his delivery system to prevent an unacceptable second strike by the enemy. Unless the United States possessed this capability, it made no sense to retaliate massively against limited aggression, because the United States would suffer unacceptable damages in return. Massive retaliation could deter local aggression only as long as there existed a reasonable prospect of an immediate victory in an all-out war and as long as the potential aggressor understood this. However, the possibility did exist that the doctrine of massive retaliation, even though not supported by a known American counterforce posture, would still be an effective deterrent to limited war if a potential aggressor was convinced that American prestige and honor were so involved in a dispute that the United States would respond massively to limited aggression. Nonetheless, as Soviet nuclear strength increased, the credibility of massive retaliation weakened.

There can be no doubt that the Soviet nuclear capability was growing at a rapid rate in 1954 and Soviet secrecy surrounding its weapons systems prevented the United States from being absolutely certain of the exactness and completeness of United States intelligence estimates. It appears that the Soviet Union had some 300 to 400 nuclear or thermonuclear bombs, but still only possessed an extremely limited capacity to deliver these weapons.[28]

---

28. *The New York Times*, February 13, 1954. "How Good is Russia's Long-Range Turboprop Bear Bomber?" *Air Intelligence Training Bulletin* (published by the United States Air Force) , Vol. 9 (September 1957) , p. 39.

As it became increasingly evident that American military power could deter an all-out attack on the United States but not necessarily stop more limited aggression, the question arose as to how limited aggression could be prevented. In keeping with the desire of the Administration to provide security and solvency, the decision was made in 1954 to equip ground, air, and naval forces with tactical nuclear weapons.[29]

The controversy over the efficacy of the substitution of firepower for manpower began almost immediately and still has not been resolved. The United States initially placed a great deal of faith in the concept of the use of tactical nuclear weapons to defend against local aggression, especially in Europe. But as the weapons systems evolved and the age of nuclear plenty became a reality, the validity of this belief was opened to serious doubt. This doubt arose in response to two factors: (1) the growing belief that to defend Europe with tactical nuclear weapons would result in the destruction of the area defended;[30] and, (2) increasing evidence negating the argument that tactical nuclear weapons favored the defense over the offense.[31]

Despite the growing awareness of these startling facts, the North Atlantic Treaty Alliance did not develop an adequate conventional defense against any major attack on the main front of central Europe. The early acceptance of the idea that tactical nuclear weapons diminished the need for troops naturally tended to counteract efforts to build up a conventional shield force in Europe. As a consequence, in Europe there was very little defense and a

---

29. B. H. Liddell Hart, *Deterrence or Defense* (New York: Frederick A. Praeger, 1960) , p. 82.

30. M. O. Miksche, *The Failure of Atomic Strategy* (New York: Frederick A. Praeger, 1958) , p. 87.

31. Liddell Hart, *Deterrence or Defense*, p. 82. The question of the efficacy of tactical nuclear weapons in offensive versus defensive military operations is still being debated among military and defense leaders.

decreasingly effective deterrent.[32] As will be seen below, it was this growing dichotomy between the United States' declared intent versus its capability which, along with other critical factors, eventually led to the partial fragmentation of NATO during the period when the "missile gap" was accepted as a reality by many people at home and abroad.

Even though both aspects of the early Eisenhower Administration defense policy—massive retaliation and the threatened use of tactical nuclear weapons—came under heavy attack throughout his Administration, the fact remains that during this period Soviet aggression was extremely limited, if not stopped in the military field.*

During 1954-1955 American belief in the increase in Soviet nuclear strength continued to grow. Ex-Secretary of the Air Force Finletter predicted that by 1956 the Soviet Union would be able to destroy not only American cities, but also the ability to retaliate effectively. This warning was followed by an interesting statement that offered some insight into the assumptions behind United States intelligence estimates during the missile gap period. Mr. Finletter continued by emphasizing that United States estimates of Russian progress and capabilities should be based on the assumption that the Russians would do "substantially" better than the average prediction.[33] Early in 1955 this same theme was repeated by the Chairman of the Atomic Energy Commission when he stated that "it is unintelligent to decry their [Soviet Union's] capability."[34]

Late in 1955, the first indications of United States concern over Soviet progress in missile development began to appear, both in public and governmental sources. Presi-

---

32. *Ibid.*

* This statement is based on the assumed aggressive intent of the Soviet Union, which was accepted by most American leaders during this period.

33. Thomas K. Finletter, Eugene M. Emme, ed., in *Air Power*, (Princeton, N.J.: D. Van Nostrand, 1959), p. 647.

34. *The New York Times*, statement by Lewis Strauss, January 12, 1955.

dent Eisenhower appointed a committee headed by Dr. James Killian to make a study of the comparative progress of the United States and the Soviet Union in missile development. Although the final report remained classified, several comments from "informed sources" were reported in the press. The Soviet Union was reported to have developed an intermediate range ballistic missile with a range of 600 to 800 miles. There was also strong evidence to indicate that the Soviet Union had the technological know-how and ability to develop thermonuclear warheads that could be delivered by a ballistic missile. The "informed source" stated that the United States government was not worried about existing American security, but was very concerned about the period 1959-1961, and that the United States should take immediate steps to fill certain "gaps" in its missile program.[35]

Nonetheless, at this time the civilian and military experts within the Eisenhower Administration remained confident that the deterrent strength of the United States was sufficient to deter a nuclear attack by the Soviet Union.[36]

---

35. *The New York Times,* news article by Hanson W. Baldwin, December 19, 1955; Huntington, *The Common Defense,* p. 89. It was reported in 1957 that United States Radar stations in Turkey had been monitoring Soviet missile tests since 1955. *The New York Times,* November 21, 1957; *Ibid.,* November 24, 1957.

36. *The New York Times,* statements by Secretary of Defense Charles E. Wilson and Secretary of the Air Force Donald A. Quarles before the House Military Appropriations subcommittee, March 30, 1956; Curtis Lemay, in Eugene M. Emme, ed., *Air Power,* p. 672; Nathan Twining (Air Force Chief of Staff) , *Ibid.,* p. 470.

2

THE ORIGINS OF THE MISSILE GAP:
1956-1957

THE SOVIET UNION ANNOUNCED THE LAUNCHING OF ITS FIRST successful intercontinental ballistic missile* on August 26, 1957. In the United States, the period immediately preceding this announcement was characterized by two main features—continued military interservice rivalry and an intensified debate in the United States over the comparative strategic strength of the two super powers.

The possible missile threat by the Soviet Union implicit in the information from the "informed sources" who reported on the Killian Report, gave added impetus to the temporary lull in the controversy among the armed services in the United States. The services recognized the potential use and value of missiles and began a debate on missile programs and budget allocations which lasted throughout the initial period of the alleged missile gap.

Although the military services disagreed on the exact nature of a future war and the weapons and forces needed to fight this war, there was considerable agreement over the types of forces needed to meet any specific threat to United States security. With the development of the missile race, the services could agree on what systems were needed, but differed drastically over which service should

---

* Reference; hereafter referred to as an ICBM.

receive the responsibility and the appropriations for the development of a particular missile system.

Initially, the most significant of the many conflicts among the services occurred between the Army and the Air Force over the development of the intermediate range ballistic missile (IRBM) (approximate range 1500 miles) .* The Air Force claimed that the IRBM performed an Air Force mission and wanted appropriations to develop its *Thor* missile, while the Army made the same claim for the development of its *Jupiter C* missile.[1]

The conflict among the services became so intense that many concerned individuals feared that this disagreement seriously hampered United States missile development. In an attempt to alleviate the competition and overlapping in the missile effort among the military services, Secretary of Defense Charles Wilson published a memorandum on November 26, 1956 that established the following service responsibilities.

1. All ICBMs (over 1500 mile range) were to be the responsibility of the Air Force.

2. All land-based IRBMs (over 200 mile range) were to be the responsibility of the Air Force and all sea-based IRBMs were to be the responsibility of the Navy.

3. "Local" surface to air missiles (under 100 mile range) were to be the responsibility of the Army and "area" surface to air missiles (over 100 mile range) were to be the responsibility of the Air Force.

4. Ship-based surface to air missiles were to be the responsibility of the Navy.[2]

---

* Hereafter, this type of missile will be referred to as an IRBM.

1. Samuel P. Huntington, *The Common Defense* (New York: Columbia University Press, 1961) , p. 413; U.S. Congress, Senate, Committee on Armed Services, *Preparedness Investigating Sub-Committee*, 85th Cong., 1st and 2nd sess., Vol. 2, pt. 1 (November, 1957) , testimony by General Maxwell D. Taylor, Chief of Staff, United States Army, p. 479.

2. Charles H. Donnelly, *United States Defense Policy in 1957*, The Li-

Despite the determined effort to reduce, if not stop, the
interservice rivalry, the argument over the function of the
separate services in missile development continued for
several years. The debate centered on questions of national security and the future role of each of the services
in protecting this security. Due to the intensity and seri-
ousness of the dissension, the controversy became an object
of interest in the press and among the concerned public.

Numerous events occurred during the period from 1957
to 1961 that highlighted public interest in the developing
missile argument and increased the agitation within the
inner circle of the United States Government. One such
event was the controversy that surrounded the court-
martial of Colonel John Nickerson of the Army Ballistic
Missile Agency for releasing official secrets of the government. Colonel Nickerson was accused of circulating to
members of Congress a memorandum that criticized Secretary Wilson's decision of November 1956 to limit the
role of the Army in missile development to missiles under
200 miles in range. Colonel Nickerson went on to claim
that when the Army's *Jupiter C* was compared with the
Air Force's *Thor,* the Army's missile was superior.[3] Later
in the year, Colonel Nickerson's court-martial resulted in
a light sentence and heavy reprimand for him; then the
case was allowed to drop from view as discreetly as possible.[4] The exact impact of the Nickerson affair on the
United States missile program cannot be determined.
However, the publicity that surrounded this case added
substantially to the already growing interest of the concerned public in the coming of the missile age.[5]

brary of Congress, Legislative Reference Service, reprint of Memorandum
from the Secretary of Defense (Washington, D.C.: United States Government Printing Office, January 10, 1958), pp. 113–117.

3. *The New York Times,* news article by Jack Raymond, February 24,
1957.

4. *The New York Times,* news article by Hanson W. Baldwin, July 16,
1957.

5. *The New York Times,* February 24, 1957; *Ibid.,* July 16, 1957.

As work progressed on the Army's *Jupiter C* missile, the debate over missiles continued in the United States Congress and the various committees responsible for national defense. An examination of Congressional testimony indicated that its value to the public was limited due to the fact that information considered essential to national security was excluded from the public version. Much valuable testimony was removed as "deleted," or "off the record," or through the use of the closed hearing. Despite this handicap, in many cases the general conclusions of individuals who had had access to this classified information can be considered valid.

From the testimony available it appeared that the Army not only was involved in a struggle for an expanded missile role,[6] but also waged a fight to maintain its existing share of the military budget appropriations. The Air Force appeared to have gained control over long-range missile development, while at the same time the future usefulness of a large army was challenged by the proposed substitution of tactical nuclear weapons for manpower in the event of future hostilities. It would be an exaggeration to say that the Army was fighting for its very existence, but there was no doubt that its size and function was being seriously challenged.[7]

Coinciding with the service-oriented debate that took

6. U.S. Congress, House, Committee on Appropriations, *Hearings*, Department of Defense Appropriations for 1958, 85th Cong., 1st sess., Vol. 9, pt. 2 (February 27, 1957), testimony of General John B. Medaris, Commanding General, Army Ballistic Missile Agency; Dr. Werhner von Braun, Director of Development Operations, Army Ballistic Missile Center; and General James M. Gavin, Chief of the Army Research and Development, pp. 1502–1531; *The New York Times*, May 3, 1957; *The New York Times*, May 17, 1957.

7. The implications of this dispute go far beyond the scope of this paper. For a detailed account of this problem see: Gavin, *War and Peace in the Space Age*; Henry A. Kissinger, *Nuclear Weapons and Foreign Policy* (Garden City: Doubleday & Company Inc.), 1957; Robert Endicott Osgood, *Limited War: The Challenge to American Strategy* (Chicago: The University of Chicago Press), 1957; Maxwell D. Taylor, *The Uncertain Trumpet* (New York: Harper & Brothers, Publishers), 1959.

place in the Pentagon, the Congress, and to a limited extent in the press, was increased public concern and confusion surrounding United States missile posture early in 1957. A full eight months before the first official ICBM test was announced by the Soviet Union, the public missile debate was initiated by an article in *The New York Times* which quoted *Pravda** as having stated:

> It is common knowledge that the United States is far from being a monopolistic either in the sphere of nuclear weapons, or even less so, in the sphere of long range missiles. Here it would be more appropriate to talk of America's lag.[8]

It is worth noting that the Soviet Union's public statements during this period consistently encouraged the belief that they were far superior to the United States in missile strength; and this propaganda bluff heightened the resolve of the United States to accelerate greatly and expand its missile program. The result was a Russian missile lag or gap by 1963.[9]

The preceding Soviet statement was followed by two articles on Russian missile development in *The New York Times*. These articles stated that the Soviet Union had test fired an IRBM with a range of 1800 miles and would have operational ICBMs in two or three years, whereas it was alleged that the United States was at least five years away from an operational ICBM.[10] Then, the American press did a major about-face and stated for the next several months that the United States was not behind, but was "neck and neck" with the Soviet Union in the missile race.

---

* The official newspaper of the Communist Party of the U.S.S.R.

8. *The New York Times*, January 24, 1957.

9. *The New York Times*, November 14, 1957; *The New York Times*, December 5, 1957; *New York Times*, November 8, 1959; *Aviation Week*, text of Premier Khrushchev's speech to All Union Congress of Soviet Journalists, Vol. 31, November 30, 1959, p. 34.

10. *The New York Times*, news article by Richard Witkin, "Soviet Missiles Lead the U.S.," February 10, 1957; *Ibid.*, news article by Hanson W. Baldwin, March 17, 1957.

It also was emphasized that the United States had been galvanized by the reports that the Soviet Union was ahead with the subsequent result that the American Government had expanded the missile program and reorganized the missile effort.[11]

During this period, the whole question of a possible missile lag received wide and conflicting coverage by all facets of the American mass media. For example, such diverse publications as *Aviation Week* and *The New Republic* printed editorials that lent credence to the approach of the "missile gap." At the same time, an article in *Fortune Magazine* told the American people that the United States margin of power was widening and that the Soviet Union could not keep up the economic pace of the arms race and was in desperate economic straits.[12]

The New York Times made its final comment before the successful Russian ICBM launch when it stated that the Soviet Union was substantially behind the United States in the development of ICBMs and IRBMs.[13] From the evidence available, it appeared that during this period immediately prior to the first Soviet ICBM test the Pentagon, and particularly the United States Air Force, believed that the Strategic Air Command furnished the United States with an "over-riding deterrent" against any attack by the Soviet Union.[14]

11. *The New York Times,* news article by Hanson Baldwin, March 31, 1957; *Ibid.,* news article by Richard Witkin, April 7, 1957; *Ibid.,* news article by Jack Raymond, May 14, 1957.
12. "Beaten to the Missile Punch?" *Aviation Week,* Vol. 66 (May 20, 1957); "Air Force Cover-up," *The New Republic,* Vol. 137 (July 29, 1957); Charles J. Murphy, "America's Widening Military Margin," *Fortune,* Vol. 56 (August 8, 1957), p. 94.
13. *The New York Times,* editorial, July 14, 1957.
14. U.S. Congress, Senate, Committee on Armed Services, Preparedness Subcommittee *Hearings,* 85th Cong., 1st and 2nd sess., Vol. 2, pt. 1 (November 25 to December 17, 1957), testimony by General Thomas D. White, Chief of Staff, United States Air Force, p. 876. It also became apparent that the White House not only expected the upcoming Soviet ICBM test, but even knew the missile launching site from which the test was to be made.

With these examples of the conflicting reports received by the American people before the first ICBM had ever been launched, it came as no surprise that the period following the first ICBM test was characterized by additional confusion and an increase in the different evaluations of comparative military strength available to the public through the mass media.

On August 27, 1957 the first official announcement was made of a successful ICBM test by the Soviet Union. The Soviet announcement stated that the Soviet Union could direct rockets to any part of the world and implied that the manned aircraft of the Strategic Air Command were vulnerable to Soviet offensive rockets and to Soviet air defenses.[15]

In this initial announcement the Soviet Union made the claim that was later defined in the United States as an attempt at "nuclear blackmail" and created the fear that the retaliatory power of the Strategic Air Command and other nuclear forces could be destroyed before becoming airborne. This fear of a paralyzing surprise attack by the Soviet Union became the underlying assumption of those persons in the United States who professed belief in the existence of a missile gap.[16] These persons overlooked or downgraded an extremely significant strategic problem faced by either of the major powers which contemplated an initial counterforce strike against its opponent. This problem, stated concisely, was the near impossibility of either of the two major powers launching a surprise attack with the *certainty* that all of its opponent's retaliatory power would be destroyed. For the United States the problem was one of intelligence and uncertainty that United States forces successfully had destroyed *all* Soviet nuclear

15. "The Soviet ICBM Announcement" (text), *Current History*, Vol. 34 (January 1958), p. 47.
16. *The New York Times*, statement by Senator Lyndon B. Johnson (Dem.-Texas) comparing present United States military posture with that just prior to the attack on Pearl Harbor, December 19, 1957.

delivery vehicles. For the Soviet Union the problem was even more difficult. The Soviet Union had to be certain that they could launch a simultaneous attack against United States nuclear forces spread throughout the world with the assurance that all would be destroyed before a significant number of these delivery vehicles could go into action.[17] By August of 1957, the United States had approximately 4000 dispersed delivery vehicles capable of delivering a nuclear device (see Appendix "A"). The problem of destroying all of these delivery vehicles at the same moment in order to prevent retaliation was extremely difficult, if not impossible.[18]

Prior to the Soviet ICBM test, the missile controversy had been primarily fought among the military services. With the announcement of the first successful ICBM test, the political debate over the missile program broke into open conflict. No attempt will be made at this time to investigate whether this controversy was politically motivated or based upon a true concern for national security. This problem, a difficult one, will be dealt with in the conclusions of this study.

The assaults by political figures on the Eisenhower Administration were intensified when Senator Henry Jackson (Democrat-Washington) and Senator Stuart Symington (Democrat-Missouri) attacked various aspects of United States defense policy. Senator Jackson asked for a restoration of budget reductions for missile development and bomber production made earlier in the year and suggested that the United States lagged behind the Soviet Union in the missile race.[19] At the same time, Senator

---

17. Herman Kahn, "The Arms Race and Some of Its Hazards," in Donald G. Brennan, ed., *Arms Control, Disarmament, and National Security* (New York: George Braziller, 1961), p. 98.

18. Glen H. Snyder, *Deterrence and Defense: Toward a Theory of National Security* (Princeton: Princeton University Press, 1961), p. 69.

19. Senator Henry Jackson (Chairman of the Senate subcommittee on Nuclear Weapons), "Senator Jackson on Missiles," *Newsweek*, Vol. 50 (September 9, 1957), p. 45.

Symington wrote that the Russians were ahead of the United States in the ballistic missile field and that the American public should be given the truth about United States air power.[20] In later public statements Senator Symington claimed that the Soviet Union was ahead of the United States in every phase of military capability except surface vessels and that the military position of the free world was critical.[21] Although many key members of the Democratic Party criticized the defense policies of the Eisenhower Administration from 1957 to 1961, these two Senators were constantly strong critics of the Administration.

Added to the doubts of some politicians was the prestigious voice of *The New York Times*. In an editorial this newspaper questioned the wisdom of the defense policy of the Eisenhower Administration. Specifically, the paper questioned the Administration's position of holding the budget line and reducing the funds for missile research and development when the Russians were making such obvious progress. The Administration was also assailed for keeping under a veil of secrecy the successful 3600 mile test flight by the Army's *Jupiter C* in 1956. The editorial concluded that the Soviet Union was ahead of the United States in ICBM and IRBM development.[22]

The information received by the public from nongovernmental sources was not entirely critical. Several major periodicals took the editorial position that the military balance remained unchanged and that neither side would gain a decisive advantage in the missile race unless the United States programs failed completely.[23]

20. Senator Stuart Symington (Secretary of the Air Force under President Truman), "Let's Give the American Public the Truth about Air Power," *Aviation Week*, Vol. 40 (September 1957), p. 107.

21. *The New York Times*, September 13, 1957; *Ibid.*, October 6, 1957.

22. *The New York Times*, editorial, September 7, 1957.

23. "Intercontinental Missiles," *The New Republic* (editorial), Vol. 137 (September 9, 1957), p. 5; "How the U.S. Will Block Russia's Missiles," *U.S. News and World Report*, Vol. 43 (September 13, 1957), p. 46.

The editor of the more specialized *Aviation Week* took a more critical position of United States defense policy. In three successive issues of this weekly periodical, many of the charges against the Administration that repeatedly appeared during this period were made. The Eisenhower Administration was accused of lack of imagination, overlap and duplication in its missile effort,[24] clamping an iron curtain of secrecy solely for political effect on anything concerning missiles,[25] and, finally, of supporting the Army's efforts in the missile field to the detriment of the entire missile effort.[26] With the exception of the charge of sacrificing national security for budgetary solvency, these represented all of the charges made against the Eisenhower Administration during the early period of the missile controversy.

The missile debate barely had started when the Soviet Union launched the first earth satellite. Once again the Administration felt constrained to reassure an increasingly doubtful and confused public. The Department of Defense immediately attempted to dispel the growing belief in Soviet superiority and issued a statement to the effect that there was no evidence of Soviet superiority in missile development.[27]

President Eisenhower voiced some concern over the United States missile program and gave it top priority over the satellite program. The President ordered a speedup in the missile program, but he ordered that the buildup

---

24. Robert Hotz, "Fact and Fiction on the ICBM," *Aviation Week*, Vol. 67 (September 2, 1957), p. 21.

25. Robert Hotz, "Missile Misinformation," *Aviation Week*, Vol. 67 (September 9, 1957), p. 21.

26. Robert Hotz, "The Missile Industry Myth," *Aviation Week*, Vol. 67 (September 16, 1957), p. 21.

27. *The New York Times*, statement by William A. Holaday, Special Assistant to the Secretary of Defense for Guided Missiles, October 5, 1957; *Ibid.*, news article by John W. Finney, October 8, 1957; *Ibid.*, news article by W. H. Lawrence, October 9, 1957.

stay within the existing $38 billion defense budget in order to avoid an appropriations increase.[28]

Shortly after the Soviet satellite launch, a new American Secretary of Defense, Neil H. McElroy, was sworn into office to replace Secretary Wilson. For the next several years it was this relatively inexperienced, former executive of the Proctor and Gamble Company who had the task of formulating and defending much of the Defense policy of the Administration. Immediately upon assuming office, the new Secretary gave his opinion on the major issues faced by the Department of Defense. He began by stating that "our missile program is well along," but that the manned bomber would continue to play a major role in United States defense posture for some years to come. When questioned on interservice rivalry he indicated his belief that the competition between the services had had a beneficial effect on United States military effort and that he would allow the continued parallel development of the Army's *Jupiter C* and the Air Force's *Thor*.[29]

The orbiting of the first earth satellite increased the number of political figures who attacked the Administration missile and space programs. Added to the continued criticism of Senator Symington and Senator Jackson were the voices of numerous other Democratic leaders. The charges against the Administration during this stage of the debate were not well defined in terms of specific problems but concentrated mainly on demands for increased military spending and the restoration of research and development funds, with an occasional demand for an increased number of manned bombers.[30]

---

28. *The New York Times*, October 10, 1957; *Ibid.*, October 12, 1957; *Ibid.*, October 13, 1957.

29. *The New York Times*, news conference by Secretary of Defense Neil H. McElroy, October 10, 1957.

30. *The New York Times*, statement quoting Senator Mike Mansfield (Democrat-Montana) , October 6, 1957; *Ibid.*, statement quoting Senator Clinton P. Anderson (Democrat-New Mexico) , October 11, 1957; *Ibid.*,

The criticism of the Eisenhower Administration policies assumed an even more strongly partisan nature when 20 members of the Democratic National Committee charged the Administration with "complacency" and with not giving American scientists full support in the United States missile and space efforts. In this 2000 word indictment of President Eisenhower's defense policy, the Advisory Committee also accused the President of "leading the American people to believe that we have a national security which in fact we are rapidly losing." The report concluded by stating that the Administration had subordinated national security to domestic policies and budgetary goals. The report was approved unanimously by the Advisory Committee which meant that it had been approved by Ex-President Harry S. Truman and past Democratic presidential nominee Adlai Stevenson.[31]

The controversy that surrounded the Soviet achievements was not limited to the domestic reaction within the United States. Indications appeared that some individuals within governments of United States allies began to doubt the ability of the United States to match successfully Soviet missile and space accomplishments. Representatives of the seven member nations of the Assembly of Western European Union assembled in Strasbourg claimed that the United States had let them down. These representatives announced a lack of confidence in the United States and indicated their determination to move away from complete reliance on the United States for their defense.[32]

statement quoting Senator Mike Manroney (Democrat-Oklahoma), October 26, 1957; *Ibid.,* statement quoting Senator Lyndon B. Johnson (Democrat-Texas), November 4, 1957.

31. *The New York Times,* October 12, 1957; *Ibid.,* article by Arthur Krock, October 20, 1957.

32. *The New York Times,* report on the Assembly of Western European Union (Great Britain, France, West Germany, Italy, The Netherlands, Belgium and Luxemburg represented), October 13, 1957. A poll taken by the French Newspaper *Le Monde* in October 1957 showed the following responses to the question: "The Americans have gained the first leg with the atomic bomb, the Russians have gained the second; in your opinion

Any serious lack of confidence or cooperation by American allies portended difficulty for overall United States
defense plans. Western Europe airbases were an essential part of the Strategic Air Command at this time, and
the Administration planned to place IRBMs in Europe
to bolster American deterrent power until the first generation of long-range missile were operational. Therefore,
the Administration felt that it was essential to maintain
Western European confidence in American military power
and the credibility of the United States promise to protect
Western Europe from Soviet attack.[33]

As the attacks on the Administration increased and
grew in diversity, the government once again rallied its
forces in defense of existing armament programs and long-
range United States nuclear striking power. The Administration spokesman on this occasion was Secretary of State
Dulles:

> . . . I think we have in terms of actual military power, and
> potential military power, for some years to come, a very
> marked superiority over them [Soviet Union], particularly in
> terms of heavy bombers which are now, and for some years
> to come will be, the preferred and most effective means of
> the delivery of missiles.[34]

---

who will win the third?" (referring to the advances being made in military
technology) .

	Russia Favored	United States Favored
French	24%	20%
Belgian	28%	47%
Dutch	20%	56%
West German	17%	62%
United States	18%	61%

The New York Times, October 20, 1957.

33. On March 22, 1957, President Eisenhower met with Prime Minister
Macmillan and it was decided to give Great Britain IRBMs as soon as
they were operational. (Dwight David Eisenhower, *The White House
Years: Waging the Peace* [Garden City, New York: Doubleday & Co., Inc.,
1965], p. 124.) As will be seen below, the initial faltering of confidence in
United States deterrent ability will be one of the many factors that lead
to a fragmentation of the NATO Alliance.

34. *The New York Times,* transcript of news conference by Secretary
of State John Foster Dulles, October 17, 1957.

Two days later the Pentagon defended Administration missile and satellite efforts and stated its confidence that the United States would win the missile race.[35]

The confusing public dialogue over the prospective missile gap continued throughout October 1957 and the debate continued to assume a more partisan military complexion. Militarily, the attacks on the Administration became more specific as the opposing forces in the debate further clarified and solidified their positions. Elements of the United States Air Force and their spokesmen became increasingly critical of the nation's missile posture. A past Air Force research and development expert joined in the castigation of the Administration and specifically blamed Secretary of Defense Wilson and Under Secretary of Defense Donald Quarles for the United States lag behind the Russians in the missile field. He also blamed United States missile deficiencies on interservice rivalry and overemphasis on the balanced budget.[36] At the same time the unofficial spokesman for the Air Force, the *Air Force Association,* stressed the successes of the *Thor* missile and claimed that the American public was being misinformed and misled on United States missile programs.[37] The Army countered by denouncing the Air Force doctrine of air supremacy and called for unity in the missile race.[38]

By early November 1957, the lack of facts and the complexity surrounding the missile race had increased at a rapid rate and no concise, acceptable position of the relative missile development of the United States and the Soviet Union had been established. The political forces

35. *The New York Times,* article by Richard Witkin quoting Vice Admiral John H. Sides of the Pentagon's Weapons Evaluation Group, October 19, 1957.

36. Trevor Gardner, "U.S. Tries Hard to Catch Up," *Life,* Vol. 43 (November 4, 1957), p. 30. (Mr. Gardner was in Charge of Air Force Research and Development until February 8, 1956 when he resigned due to his belief that the missile program was progressing too slowly.)

37. *The New York Times,* November 3, 1957.

38. *The New York Times,* October 27, 1957; *Ibid.,* October 29, 1957.

in the United States were in disagreement, the military controversy continued, and the press varied from one extreme to the other.[39]

At this point in the missile debate, the observations made by a member of *The New York Times* editorial staff appeared to sum up the overall picture presented to the concerned public during the initial phases of the missle gap controversy. James Reston stated that there appeared to be a marked contrast between the public excitement over the Soviet missile successes and the private reactions of officials in Washington who were in a position to know the state of the country's missile and defense programs. However, Mr. Reston contended that it would be some time before the ICBM became operational and until that time the American bomber force would serve as an effective deterrent force to Soviet attack. In addition to the American bombers, the United States would have IRBMs operational in overseas bases before the Soviet ICBM became operational. He stressed the importance of American overseas bases and the need for the United States to maintain the confidence of the NATO allies and stated his belief that the United States had not fully informed its allies and therefore, there was a demonstrable lack of confidence exhibited by America's NATO Allies.[40]

In the fall of 1957, two extremely important events took place simultaneously and had a tremendous impact on the nature of the missile controversy and its future course. Early in November, the Gaither Report was "leaked" to the press and Congress began an intense investigation into United States military preparedness. These two subjects should now be examined.

---

39. Edward L. Katzenback, Jr., "The United States Missile Muddle," *The Reporter*, Vol. 17 (October 3, 1957), p. 12, article stating Russia ahead in the ICBM race; Henry Hazlitt, "The Economic Consequences of the ICBM," (*Newsweek*), Vol. 59 (October 21, 1957), p. 94, called for a balanced United States budget, doubted Russia ahead in ICBM race; "U.S. Taking Lead in Missiles," *U.S. News and World Report*, Vol. 43 (November 11, 1957), p. 44, U.S. is taking the lead from Russia.

40. *The New York Times*, column by James Reston, November 5, 1957.

In early November 1957, a secret event took place within the Executive branch of the government which eventually added considerable impetus to the missile debate. President Eisenhower earlier had appointed a group of distinguished citizens to investigate the future role of civil defense in overall United States defense policy. This committee, later known as the Gaither Committee, began its project within this question, but before its investigation was completed it had looked into every aspect of existing and future United States military posture. The President received the Gaither Committee's classified report and recommendations in October 1957 and in early November the National Security Council was briefed on the report.[41]

Although the Gaither Report remained classified, various persons concerned with the defense field reported "leaks" from informed sources and numerous interviews with the parties concerned during late 1957 and early 1958. From a variety of unclassified sources, the public became aware of the existence of this report and a widely accepted version of its contents emerged over a period of several months.[42]

The Gaither Committee dealt with many major problems of national defense, but its most dramatic impact was on the missile debate. The Committee claimed that due to Soviet missile development the major military danger faced by the United States was the vulnerability of The Strategic Air Command (SAC)* in the event of a surprise attack by the Soviet Union. The Committee's report predicted that by the early 1960s the Russians

---

41. Morton Halperin, "The Gaither Committee and the Policy Process," *World Politics*, Vol. 13 (April 1961), p. 363; this writer is deeply indebted to the work done by Mr. Halperin concerning the Gaither Committee's report; *The New York Times*, news article by John W. Finney, "Gaither Report Divides Leaders," December 21, 1957.

42. *The New York Times*, November 9, 1957; *The New York Times*, November 23, 1957; *The New York Times*, interview with H. Rowan Gaither, December 25, 1957.

*SAC from this point onward will refer to the United States Strategic Air Command.

would have enough operational ICBMs to destroy American strategic retaliatory power.[43] The Gaither Committee concluded by calling for additional military spending for an acceleration of missile programs, the strengthening and dispersal of SAC, and the hardening of missile sites when they became operational.[44]

The Gaither Report did not appear to alter American defense policy substantially, but it did sharply focus public attention on defense problems and intensify the existing missile debate in the United States. Many of the supposed deficiencies sighted in this report were used repeatedly by those concerned with the coming missile gap or by those politically motivated in their attacks on the Eisenhower Administration.[45]

The resistance to the public release or the implementation of the Gaither Committee's suggestions came from almost all elements of the government. President Eisenhower and Secretary of State Dulles did not accept the gloomy status assigned to United States defenses by the report and were unwilling to request the money needed to implement the suggestions made by the Committee. For different reasons, the President and the Secretary of State were supported for the most part by the military establishment and the military's claim that American defenses were much stronger than portrayed by the report. For example, the Air Force would not concede the degree of strategic vulnerability of the Strategic Air Command claimed by the report. Also, resistance to the committee's suggestions came from the military's fear of the possible dominance of civilian expertise in military matters. All of these factors worked to keep the Gaither Report class-

43. Halperin, "The Gaither Committee and the Policy Process," p. 366; *The New York Herald Tribune*, news article by Joseph Alsop, November 25, 1957. This aspect of the Gaither Committee's Report was later substantiated in Mr. Eisenhower's book which listed the contents of the Report. (Eisenhower, *Waging the Peace*, p. 220.)

44. Halperin, "The Gaither Committee," p. 366–368.

45. *Ibid.*, p. 380–381.

ified. Therefore, in spite of considerable pressure on President Eisenhower, the decision was made to keep the contents of the Report "Top Secret."[46]

At this time, the overwhelming assumptions accepted by many members of the conerned public on the Gaither Report were that it indicated serious weaknesses in United States strategic retaliatory power. The "leaked" information on the report was used as substantive evidence of the coming missile gap. Nonetheless, this belief was officially denied by White House spokesmen; and instead they asserted that the Gaither Report did not show United States comparative weaknesses, but "showed just the opposite."[47]

The reporting done on the Gaither Report not only stimulated the public debate on the missile race, but also illustrated that even in the area of classified government documents opposing interpretations arose, based on supposedly authoritative information, and they were presented to the public as factual.[48]

---

46. *Ibid.*, pp. 371–373; *The New York Times,* report on the denial of Lyndon Johnson's request that the report be given to the Senate Preparedness Subcommittee, December 21, 1957.

47. *The New York Times,* "White House says Gaither Report finds U.S. Strong," article by Jay Waltz quoting White House Press Secretary James C. Haggerty, December 29, 1957. (It is not possible to determine if the White House had information not available to other government agencies or to the Gaither Committee, or if the White House was simply attempting to reassure the American public for political reasons.) Later, in his book, President Eisenhower reported that he did not accept the figures of the Gaither Committee and claimed to have access to other, unspecified information. He did mention to Mr. Gaither that the United States had its overseas dispersion of strategic bases which gave it a much more potent (invulnerable) deterrent retaliatory power. (Eisenhower, *Waging the Peace,* p. 221.)

48. The Gaither Report was the most famous of the three studies that were disclosed as having been done during this period (late 1957–early 1958). The other two were the "Rockefeller Report" (*International Security: The Military Aspect*), published as part of The Social Studies Project of the Rockefeller Brothers' Fund Inc. (Garden City, New York: Doubleday & Company, Inc., 1958) and the so-called "Johns Hopkins Report" (classified report submitted to the government sometime before the Gaither Report). The Rockefeller Report was much less pessimistic

At this stage of the missile argument, the abundance and diversity of views available to the public inevitably led to the creation of a great deal of confusion. At times the confusion seemed to exist even within the government itself and among those responsible for making and defining United States defense policy.

On the eve of the Gaither Committee's Report to the National Security Council, President Eisenhower gave the first of two special addresses to the nation on *Science and National Security*. His first address was a calm reassurance to the American people that the nation still had a qualitative and quantitative lead over the Soviet Union in total military strength.[49] Yet a week later, after the Gaither Committee had briefed the National Security Council, the President sounded less reassuring and called for a "critical re-examination" of the American defense position due to recent Soviet technological progress.[50]

---

than the two classified reports and dealt with the missile debate only in general terms. (See *Rockefeller Report*, pp. 15, 55–56, and 62.) However, the secret *John Hopkins Report* of 1957, although it received much less attention than the Gaither Committee's Report, was supposed to have been the most pessimistic of the three concerning United States defenses and was supposed to have been the primary basis for the conclusions of the Gaither Committee ("Johns Hopkins Report," *U.S. News and World Report*, Vol. 44 [January 31, 1958], p. 50, interview with Dr. Ellis A. Johnson, Director of Operations Research Office and Director of the Johns Hopkins Report). Public information surrounding the "Johns Hopkins Report" of 1957 is scarce and therefore it is not possible to determine the accuracy of this statement by Dr. Johnson. As will be seen below, in December 1959 there was another report originating in the Washington Center for Foreign Policy Research, John Hopkins University which was unclassified and highly relevant to the debate at that time (1959). An attempt will be made to avoid confusion in analyzing these two different reports originating either directly or indirectly at Johns Hopkins University, referred to as *Johns Hopkins Report 1959*. Ex-President Eisenhower dealt with the problems surrounding the Gaither Committee's Report in pp. 219–224 *Waging the Peace* and confirmed most of the above. Mr. Eisenhower did report that in the course of the study, Mr. Gaither had become ill and his place was taken by Mr. Robert C. Sprague, Chairman of the Sprague Electric Company.

49. *The New York Times,* text of President Eisenhower's speech, November 8, 1957.

50. *The New York Times,* text of President Eisenhower's speech, November 14, 1957; *Ibid.,* November 23, 1957.

Two days after the President's second speech, his Secretary of Defense was questioned on national security at a press conference and admitted that it was rather obvious that the United States was behind the Soviet Union in the satellite and missile field, but that the United States had managed to close military gaps in the past when challenged and would do so in this case.[51] Several days later, Secretary McElroy appeared to reverse his position in testimony before a Congressional committee when he testified that he was not at all certain from intelligence available to him that the Soviet Union was ahead of the United States in the missile race. Significantly, when questioned about the possibility of a Soviet surprise attack then or several years later, he answered that the United States had an ample deterrent to any attack on America at this time and for several years to come. This position had been stated earlier by the Deputy Secretary of Defense and eventually became the Administration's basic answer to the charges made by its critics.[52]

As the Eisenhower Administration struggled to reassure the public and define the status of United States defenses, Democratic leaders continued their attack on Administration policies. Immediately after President Eisenhower's second speech on national security, the Democratic Advisory Council blamed the Administration for falling behind the Russians in ICBM development.[53] This charge was wholeheartedly supported by the Chairman of the Democratic National Committee.[54]

Individual political figures continued their attacks on

51. *The New York Times,* text of Press Conference by Secretary of Defense Neil H. McElroy, November 16, 1957.

52. U.S. Congress, House, Committee on Appropriations, Sub-committee on Department of Defense Appropriations, *Hearings on the Ballistic Missile Program,* 85th Cong., 1st sess., Vol. 8, pt. 1 (November 20 to November 21, 1957), p. 48; *The New York Times,* statement quoting Donald Quarles, Deputy Secretary of Defense, November 19, 1957.

53. *The New York Times,* text of statement by Democratic Advisory Council of Democratic National Committee, November 17, 1957.

54. *The New York Times,* statement by Paul Butler, December 9, 1957.

the Administration,[55] and at this time individual positions were taken that started a debate destined to become one of the prime campaign issues in the 1960 Presidential elections. Senator John F. Kennedy (Democrat-Massachusetts) stated that the United States was losing the missile race with the Soviet Union due to "complacent miscalculations, penny pinching, budget cut-backs, incredibly confused management, and wasteful rivalries and jealousies." The Massachusetts Senator continued this rather colorful attack on the Eisenhower Adminstration when he stated:

> The people of America are no longer willing to be lulled by paternalistic reassurances, spoon-fed science fiction predictions, or by the pious platitudes of faith and hope.[56]

Later in the year, his future opponent for the presidency in 1960, Vice President Richard Nixon, answered these and other charges when he called upon the people to support the missile program[57] and assured the nation that the United States had not lost the overall military advantage over the Soviet Union that it had enjoyed in the past and would continue to enjoy for some years to come.[58]

By the end of 1957, Mr. Nixon and the entire Administration appeared to be fighting a losing battle in their attempt to convince the American people of the soundness of United States defense posture. The mass media seemed intent on accepting some sort of "missile gap" and with one exception printed articles strongly endorsing the "missile gap" as an existing reality, either at the time or for the immediate future.[59]

---

55. The *New York Times*, statement by Senator Henry Jackson on Soviet lead in ICBM race and Administration negligence, December 9, 1957.

56. *The New York Times*, November 7, 1957.

57. *Ibid.*, December 9, 1957.

58. *Ibid.*, news article by John W. Finney, December 17, 1957.

59. During this period, only *The New Republic* expressed skepticism on the Russian lead: Kurt Stehling, "The Missile Experts," *The New*

Concurrently with the controversy within the mass media, a substantially different and more sophisticated debate took place within the congress of the United States. Although the transcripts of Congressional testimony were available to the press (except for the "deleted" portions), most newspapers and magazines tended to oversimplify the arguments and stayed within the rather narrow area of the missile race rather than delving into the complexity of the whole subject of existing and predicted United States deterrent posture.[60]

In spite of the fact that the Congressional hearings were conducted on a higher level of sophistication than the public debate, naturally, these hearings were not completely free of partisan considerations or preconceived notions. An illustration of how these attitudes handicap objective research can be shown by an investigation into the attitudes of the Chairman of the Senate Armed Services Subcommittee on Preparedness—Lyndon B. Johnson.[61]

Senator Johnson announced that his subcommittee would hold a "searching inquiry" into United States defense posture. Although Senator Johnson said that he wanted a "non-partisan, constructive, and patriotic" hearing to be held, he accepted the following basic hypotheses:

Republic, Vol. 137 (December 23, 1957), p. 7; whereas, other major American mass media accepted some sort of Soviet lead: Stewart Alsop, "How can We Catch Up?", The Saturday Evening Post, Vol. 230 (December 14, 1957), p. 23; "Congress Starts Digging," Business Week (November 30, 1957), p. 27; "Getting Back Into the Missile Race," Business Week (November 16, 1957), p. 204; "How Defense Planners Size Up the Missile Race," U.S. News and World Report, Vol. 43 (November 15, 1957), p. 57; "How Much Time is Left?" Air Force, Vol. 40 (December 1957), p. 56; George C. Price, "Arguing the Case for being Panicky," Life, Vol. 43 (November 18, 1957), p. 125; The New York Times, editorial, November 26, 1957; "Scientists Explain U.S. Technological Lag," Aviation Week, Vol. 67 (December 30, 1957), p. 73.

60. Ibid.

61. Senator Johnson, with Senator Kennedy and Senator Symington, also became a major candidate for the Democratic party nomination for the presidency in 1960.

(1) that the Russians were ahead of the United States in missile development; (2) that the lack of national leadership had caused this weakness; and (3) that the United States had a "record of underestimation of [Soviet] military progress."[62] Just before the hearings began, Senator Johnson compared the existing (1957) United States military position to the period before the attack on Pearl Harbor and stated that the United States had a long way to go to catch up with the Soviet Union in the missile field.[63]

The 1958 *Hearings* before the Preparedness Subcommittee of the Senate Armed Service Committee helped to clarify the basic positions of the different government factions which found themselves in conflict with each other. These factions were found within the military services, the scientific community, and the Administration itself.

Within the military establishment, the basic division of the services that had been observed in the past was emphasized during the missile debate. The Army and the Navy were on one side and the Air Force was on the other. Congress was primarily interested in missile development, but the military establishment was more interested in the larger problem of the nature of a future war and the role each branch of the military services would be called upon to play in this conflict.

In a released, censored version of testimony given before the Preparedness Subcommittee, the spokesmen who represented the Navy did not appear to be concerned with the "missile gap" or even with the possible failure of the United States to deter Soviet nuclear attack. On the contrary, the Chief of Naval Operations appeared to believe that the United States and the Soviet Union were rapidly reaching the point where they could destroy each other;

---

62. *The New York Times,* November 6, 1957; *Ibid.,* November 11, 1957; *Ibid.,* November 23, 1957.
63. *Ibid.,* December 19, 1957.

and therefore the need was not for a more powerful deterrent, but for the capability to fight the most logical type of war in which the United States might become involved—a conventional limited war.[64] Another naval expert contended that the United States was ahead of the Soviet Union in overall military strength and was going to stay ahead.[65]

For the most part, the Army seemed willing to concede a technological lead to the Soviet Union, but the Army placed a great deal more emphasis on the impact of this advantage in fighting a limited war than as a missile threat to United States security.[66] The Army position was later reaffirmed by the Secretary of the Army when he emphasized that the real threat to the United States was a series of limited wars with the Soviet Union that would "nibble away" at the world position of the United States. He continued by stating that the United States and the Soviet Union were at the same stage in the development of long-range missiles.[67]

Throughout these important *Hearings*, most representatives of the Army and the Navy admitted certain deficiencies in United States defense efforts but they did not claim that these deficiencies were in the long-range missile field or the American strategic deterrent. The weaknesses were said to be within existing Army and Navy programs de-

---

64. *The New York Times,* released version of testimony given by Admiral Arleigh A. Burke, January 30, 1958.

65. *Ibid.,* article by Will Lissner quoting former Chairman of the Joint Chiefs of Staff Admiral Arthur W. Radford, January 9, 1958.

66. U.S. Congress, Senate, Armed Services Committee, Preparedness Subcommittee *Hearings,* 85th Cong., 1st and 2nd sess., Vol. 2, pt. 1 (November 25 to December 17, 1957), testimony by General Maxwell D. Taylor, Chief of Staff, United States Army, pp. 479–480; testimony by General James A. Gavin, Chief of Operations and Planning, United States Army, p. 511. General Gavin later resigned from the Army and wrote a book that placed more emphasis on missiles in military strategy. See: Gavin, *War and Peace in the Space Age.*

67. *The New York Times,* article by John D. Morris quoting Secretary of the Army William M. Brucker, January 25, 1958.

signed to meet the more limited challenge of a local conflict. Therefore, the main emphasis of these two services was placed on obtaining funds to prepare for this type of threat.

Although the Army still challenged the Air Force's supremacy in developing certain medium range missiles, it was the Air Force that had the responsibility for the development of long range missiles and for the maintenance of the security of the United States through the deterrent power of the Strategic Air Command. Logically, the most relevant testimony before the Subcommittee came from the Air Force.

General Nathan Twining, the Chairman of the Joint Chiefs of Staff, stated in forceful language his answer to those who believed that the Soviet Union was ahead of the United States in military strength: "This is a dangerous misapprehension. I can state with the fullest confidence that this is not true."[68] When General Twining was questioned concerning future dangers arising from existing bomber production, he reiterated his confidence in SAC and its deterrent strength.[69] The Air Force Chief of Staff, General Thomas D. White, agreed with General Twining on the existing deterrent strength of SAC, but went on to contend that in view of the potential Soviet missile threat the security of the United States could be endangered sometime in 1959 if more long-range bombers were not ordered immediately.[70]

The Air Force testimony was unanimous in denying any immediate Soviet strategic threat against United States security, but most of the Air Force Generals did call for an increase in budgetary allocations for the num-

68. U.S. Congress, Senate, Committee on Armed Services, Preparedness Subcommittee *Hearings*, 85th Cong., 1st and 2nd sess., Vol. 13, pt. 2 (January 1958) , p. 1824.

69. *Ibid.*, pp. 1832–1834.

70. U.S. Congress, Senate, Committee on Armed Services, Preparedness Subcommittee *Hearings*, 85th Cong., 1st and 2nd sess., Vol. 2, pt. 1 (November-December, 1957) , p. 876.

ber of long range bombers. From the public testimony
available, it appeared that the Air Force was much more
concerned about the number of manned bombers needed
to meet the Soviet challenge than it was about Soviet
missile production.[71] The lack of concern about missile
development was evidently tempered by a lack of confidence in this new delivery system and by the apparent
existence of intelligence data known to the military services, but not officially released to the public.[72]

Initially, the American scientific community agreed
unanimously that the United States was behind the Soviet
Union in missile development, but the estimates of the
degree and significance of this lag varied greatly. On the
other hand, one group believed that the United States
was only slightly behind and that this fact was not significant due to the initial unreliability of missiles and the
ability of the United States to catch the Soviet Union before their ICBMs became operational.[73] At the other extreme were such missile experts as Dr. Wernher von

71. *Ibid.*, testimony by General Curtis LeMay, Vice Chairman of Staff,
United States Air Force, pp. 57–58; General Thomas S. Power (SAC
Commander), "SAC and the Ballistic Missile," in Eugene M. Emme, ed.,
The Impact of Airpower, p. 487.

72. At least two reports appeared in the summer of 1957 that indicated
that the United States was monitoring missile tests in the Soviet Union
by the use of radar stations. Thomas R. Phillips (United States Army,
retired), "Air Force Covers Up," *The New Republic*, Vol. 137 (July 29,
1957), p. 5; *The New York Times*, news article by Hanson W. Baldwin,
August 19, 1957. It was also reported in November 1957 that the United
States radar intelligence had followed Russian testing since July 1955.
The New York Times, news article by Jack Raymond quoting Major
General John A. Medaris, Chief of the Army Ballistic Missile Agency,
as having said: "We know every time they shoot a missile, how far it
goes, how fast and how accurately it reached its predetermined target
area," November 24, 1957. U-2 photographs were also available to American intelligence at this time, but the public did not learn of these flights
until 1960. See below.

73. "Can the United States still win the Missile Race?" *U.S. News and
World Report*, Vol. 43 (November 15, 1957), pp. 52–56, interview with
Theodore von Karmen, Senior Missile Advisor to NATO and Dr. Walter
R. Dornberger; *The New York Times*, "U.S. Closing Missile Gap with
Soviets," news article by Richard Witkin, November 18, 1957.

Braun who differed from the Army's position and contended that it would take the United States well over five years to catch up with the Soviet Union in missile development, and this could only be done by large increases in budgetary allocations for missile development.[74]

During this period, one of the major public spokesmen for the Eisenhower Administration was Secretary of Defense Neil H. McElroy. As the military services and the scientific community began to define their positions with regard to the missile race, Secretary McElroy attempted to define the position of the Administration. Earlier in the discussion he had admitted that the United States was obviously behind the Soviet Union in the missile-satellite race. Later, before the Senate Preparedness Subcommittee he admitted that the United States was behind the Soviet Union in satellite development, but upon direct questioning he refused to admit that the United States was behind in missile development. The position of the Eisenhower Administration appeared vague during this early debate over the "missile gap" and this vagueness came out in the testimony of Secretary McElroy when he attempted to answer a direct question on the "missile gap." He stated that he had no positive view on being ahead or behind the Soviet Union in missile development, but that the United States "must accelerate our programs in order to stay ahead, if we are ahead, and to get ahead if we are not ahead."[75] Nevertheless, the Secretary of Defense, on this and other occasions, reassured the Congress and the American people that the basic military position of the United

74. *The New York Times,* November 10, 1957. By October 1958 Dr. von Braun revised his estimates and indicated that the Soviet lead was very small and that the United States SAC could offset any lead the Soviet Union may have in strategic weapons. (*The New Republic,* Henry Brandon interviewing Dr. Wernher von Braun, Vol. 139 [October 20, 1958], p. 10).

75. U.S. Congress, Senate, Committee on Armed Services, Preparedness Subcommittee *Hearings,* 85th Cong., 1st and 2nd sess., Vol. 2, pt. 1 (November-December 1957), p. 199.

States was sound and that Russia did not have military supremacy over the United States in the event of war.[76]

Other Administration spokesmen attempted to convey confidence in United States defenses and to downgrade those "journalistic friends and commentators" who supported the missile gap as "backed by half-information" when in reality the United States had an effective deterrent against Soviet attack and was "neck and neck" with the Soviet Union in the missile race.[77]

By the end of 1957 it was possible to determine, in an approximate fashion, the existing military deterrent force the United States possessed to prevent an attack by the Soviet Union. At this time the missile debate was well under way, but long range missiles were still at the testing stage and were not predicted to be operational until sometime in 1959. Therefore, the significant strategic weapons system at the time was the American long-range bomber force and the ability of this force to deliver nuclear weapons on the Soviet Union. According to Air Force estimates, the United States Strategic Air Command had more than 2500 heavy combat jet aircraft by the end of 1957. These bombers were spread out over 32 bases in the United States and 27 overseas bases.[78] If the Soviet Union contemplated the surprise attack on the United States feared by many persons, they would have the almost impossible task of coordinating a simultaneous bomber strike against American air bases varying in range from less than 500 to more than 5000 miles from the Soviet Union. Even if it was assumed that the Soviet Government could accom-

---

76. *Ibid.*, *The New York Times*, news article by John Morrison, January 9, 1958.

77. U.S. Congress, Senate, Committee on Armed Services, Preparedness Subcommittee *Hearings*, 85th Cong., 1st and 2nd sess., Vol. 2, pt. 1 (November-December 1957), testimony by Donald A. Quarles, Deputy Secretary of Defense, pp. 262–264; *The New York Times*, news article by Richard Witkin quoting William M. Holaday, Director of Guided Missiles, Department of Defense, December 6, 1957.

78. *The New York Times*, article quoting General Thomas S. Power, Commanding General of SAC, September 27, 1957.

plish this difficult task, a second factor created serious
doubt that they could not successfully attack the United
States without receiving an unacceptable retaliatory strike
by United States airpower. At this time, it was reported
that the Strategic Air Command kept at least 12 percent
of its bomber force on airborne alert at all times. If the
report was true, this meant that a minimum of 100 American bombers with a nuclear capability were constantly in
the air ready to strike the Soviet Union if so ordered.[79]
However, later reports negated any existing American airborne alert. Facing this large American bomber force
were approximately 150 to 300 Soviet long-range bombers.
Thus, it would seem highly unlikely that the Soviet Union
would risk a first strike at the United States with such a
limited comparative capability.[80]

---

79. U.S. Congress, Senate, Committee on Armed Services, Preparedness
Subcommittee *Hearings,* 85th Cong., Vol. 2, pt. 1 (November-December
1957), testimony by General Curtis LeMay, Vice Chairman of Staff for
the United States Air Force, p. 908. This testimony by General LeMay
was directly contradicted later in the Senate Preparedness *Joint Hearings,
1959.* Secretary of Defense McElroy stated that the United States had no
"airborne alert" at this time, p. 220. See below; Hanson Baldwin, Military
Editor of *The New York Times* contended that the Soviet Union had
only 200 cities with a population over 50,000 people and that of these
only about 60–100 of them could be considered valuable nuclear targets.
Therefore, it would appear that 300 bombers on a ground alert, even
with a fairly high attrition rate due to Russian active air defense, would
be sufficient to deter a Soviet first strike against the United States.
Hanson W. Baldwin, *The Great Arms Race: A Comparison of United
States and Soviet Power* (New York: Frederick A. Praeger, Publisher,
1958), p. 42).

80. The supposed American intelligence estimates of the number of
Russian long-range bombers for this period vary greatly. One source
reported that there were about 500 Soviet Bison bombers. ("Military
Strengths," unpublished Air Force document for 1958 in mimeographed
form, obtained from Professor of Air Science, Lt. Col. Stephen Bull,
Tufts University, AROTC). At the other extreme were published reports
stating that the Soviet Union had only about 100–150 long-range Bisons
("Arms, McElroy, and the Menace," *Newsweek,* Vol. 53 [February 16,
1959], p. 28). Finally, later reports indicated that as of 1963 the Soviet
Union had only about 200 long range bombers (Bulletin of the Atomic
Scientists), Vol. 19 (February 1963), p. 11. It would therefore appear
that at this time the Soviet Union had between 100 and 200 long-range

It was to this strong deterrent force that President Eisenhower referred when he stated in his State of the Union address in January 1958:

> The most powerful deterrent to war in the world today lies in the retaliatory power of our Strategic Air Command and the aircraft of our Navy.[81]

The President went on to reassure further the American people of the extremely significant fact that this force could survive a surprise attack and retaliate against an aggressor. In an effort to stifle further attack on his Administration's defense policies and to add to this already large deterrent force, the President called for an increase of over one billion dollars in the budgetary allocations for missile research and development and for additional funds for increased dispersal and augmentation of the Strategic Air Command (see Appendix B—Defense appropriations) [82].

The political acrimony between spokesmen for the Republican and Democratic Parties continued in the form of charges and countercharges carried through the mass media. The Republicans continued to claim that if any missile lag existed it was the fault of the slow start in missile development by the Truman Administration.[83]

---

bombers with which it could threaten the United States. The above claimed 500 Russian long-range bombers by the Air Force appeared to represent the "bomber gap" figures that had been rejected by most other sources. See Appendix A. For a detailed analysis of first strike counterforce strategies and credibility see: Brodie, *Strategy in the Missile Age* p. 239; Herman Kahn, *On Thermonuclear War* (2nd Ed.) (Princeton, New Jersey, Princeton University Press, 1961), p. 32; Kissinger, *Nuclear Weapons and Foreign Policy*, p. 104; Thomas W. Milburn, "What Constitutes Effective Deterrence?" *The Journal of Conflict Resolutions*, Vol. 3 (June 2, 1959), p. 140; Glenn H. Snyder, *Deterrence and Defense: Toward a Theory of National Security* (Princeton, New Jersey: Princeton University Press, 1961), p. 55.

81. Paul Zinner, ed., *Documents of American Foreign Relations, 1958* (New York: Council on Foreign Relations, 1959), p. 5.

82. *The New York Times*, January 14, 1958.

83. *The New York Times*, article quoting Republican House Whip,

Vice President Richard Nixon took issue with the Democratic attacks on the Eisenhower Administration's defense policies and contended that the United States was ahead of the Soviet Union in military missile development; and he urged the nation to support the President and his policies.[84]

The most significant challenge to the Administration's position was made when the Senate Armed Services Preparedness Subcommittee released its official conclusions. Senator Lyndon B. Johnson spoke for the Subcommittee and stated flatly that the United States was behind the Soviet Union in ballistic missile development and that the Soviet Union was rapidly closing the gap in manned bombers that the United States had enjoyed in the past. The Subcommittee advocated large increases in all bomber and missile programs.[85]

Simultaneously, the Eisenhower Administration gave the American people a different version of United States defense posture when it assured them that United States air power was superior to that of the Soviet Union and refused to concede that the Soviet Union was appreciably ahead of the United States in long range missile development.[86]

The diversity of statements by concerned officials was again reflected in the periodical literature. Many of the major American periodicals claimed that the United States

Leslie Arends (Rep.-Ill.) in which he blamed the Truman Administration for the missile lag, January 7, 1958; *The New York Times,* January 14, 1958; *The New York Times,* article by White House official Sherman Adams attacking the inadequacy of Democratic Defense policies from Pearl Harbor to missile development.

84. *The New York Times,* January 12, 1958; *Ibid.,* January 21, 1958.

85. *The New York Times,* Text of Chairman Lyndon Johnson's report from the Senate Armed Services Subcommittee on Preparedness *Hearings,* January 24, 1958.

86. *The New York Times,* article quoting Secretary of Defense Neil McElroy, January 25, 1958; U.S. Congress, House, Committee on Appropriations, Subcommittee on Air Force Appropriations, *Hearings,* 85th Cong., 2nd sess., Vol. 13 (January 25, 1958), testimony by Chairman of the Joint Chiefs of Staff, General Nathan Twining, p. 31.

had a "big edge" over any potential enemy for years to
come and that the United States was still ahead of the
Soviet Union in the missile race.[87] Some of the more specialized periodicals contended that the United States was
behind and needed a drastically renewed effort in the
missile field.[88]

Early in February 1958, the Military Editor of *The New
York Times*, Hanson Baldwin, attempted to place the
missile debate in a realistic perspective by a series of articles on "Military Power: How the U. S. Stands." The
articles made it clear that even if the Soviet Union did
have a lead in missile development, it was not a long-
range or necessarily threatening advantage. Mr. Baldwin
went on to discuss the basis of the defense controversy
when he dealt with the overall retaliatory strength of the
United States vis-à-vis the Soviet Union and the impossibility of a successful Soviet surprise attack on the United
States retaliatory power. The series concluded by stating
that the United States was still the most powerful military
nation in the world and that the United States had over-
reacted to Soviet technological progress.[89]

Whatever the reasons and motivation for the missile
debate, at this point there can be no doubt that the controversy greatly stimulated the American effort in missile
development and production. The combination of Democratic accusations and Soviet bravado led to increased
spending for missile development and continued examination and reorganization of the United States strategic
policies and missile effort.[90]

87. "Missiles on the Firing Lines," *U.S. News and World Report*, Vol.
44 (January 31, 1958), p. 32; "Is the United States really in Danger?"
The Bulletin of the Atomic Scientists, Vol. 14 (February 1958), p. 83.
88. "What's New in Red Airpower?" *Air Force Magazine*, Vol. 41 (February 1958), p. 19; R. E. Marshall, "The Nature of the Soviet Challenge,"
The Bulletin of the Atomic Scientists, Vol. 14 (February 1958), p. 83.
89. *The New York Times*, news analysis by Hanson W. Baldwin, February 2, 1958; *Ibid.*, February 4, 1958; *Ibid.*, February 6, 1958; *Ibid.*,
February 7, 1958.
90. *The New York Times*, November 8, 1957; *Ibid.*, column by Arthur
Krock, January 23, 1958.

3

THE INITIAL IMPACT OF THE
MISSILE GAP DEBATE; 1958

WHILE THESE MAJOR CONGRESSIONAL HEARINGS WERE BEING held in late 1957, public attention was directed pointedly to the missile controversy. Once these hearings were completed, the public discussion of national security policy subsided noticeably. It seemed that following the initial Soviet successes in the missile and satellite field, the public debate over United States defense policy fell into the background, only to be aroused twice annually to full force by the yearly Congressional Hearings and by national elections when they were held. Both of these occasions brought forth a profusion of comment and controversy on American security. In spite of this basic characteristic of the missile debate, the conflict continuously simmered within the inner circles of the United States Government and the debate occasionally broke into the open in the mass media.

Although the vast majority of the controversy surrounding American missile posture centered in the United States, the reaction to this debate was not limited to the United States but extended to the other major world powers. As early as October 1957 several of America's NATO allies had expressed their doubts concerning the American missile effort and the ability of the United

States to protect its NATO allies from the Soviet Union.[1] In November 1957 pessimists on both sides of the Atlantic predicted that within a year or two the Soviet Union would have hundreds of IRBMs threatening American overseas SAC bases and the nations that contained them. The period of maximum danger was placed at mid-1959 and it was contended that the United States could not match this Soviet threat until sometime in 1960. To those who accepted this foreboding picture, the solution was to be found in building more bombers and increasing the American ability for "in-air refueling" of existing SAC bombers.[2]

One of the strongest European reactions to the American missile crises was stated by the British journal *The New Statesman*. An editorial in this paper said that the Gaither Report had revealed that irrespective of any efforts which the United States might now make, the Soviet preponderance of advanced weapons had reached the stage where America's national survival depended upon Russian benevolence until at least 1961.[3] Obviously, if the security of the United States depended upon such a proposition, the security of the NATO alliance nations was at least as vulnerable.

However, the role of the Western European nations in the American missile crises was not limited to one of being only observers. Both the United States Army and the Air Force had known that the intermediate range ballistic

---

1. See above. At the outset of this discussion on NATO attitudes, it should be emphasized that the missile gap and the possible decrease in the credibility of the American nuclear deterrent was only one of many factors that led to a weakening of the NATO Alliance. Such significant factors as European economic prosperity, nationalism in Europe (especially French nationalism), and changing assessments of the Soviet threat played an equally important role in the partial fragmentation of the NATO Alliance.

2. *The New York Times*, news article by Richard Witkin, November 8, 1957; Henry Kissinger, "Missiles and the Western Alliance," *Foreign Affairs*, Vol. 36 (April 1958), p. 384.

3. *The New Statesman*, January 4, 1958.

missile (IRBM) would become operational long before the ICBM, and that they would be able to reach the Soviet Union only if they were stationed on European soil. For over two years these two military services had participated in an increasingly bitter debate over which of the services would produce the United States IRBM system. In spite of efforts by Secretary of Defense Wilson to limit the Army's role in the development of this system, the controversy still had not been definitely settled and both services had continued to develop their versions of the IRBM in order to develop the system that would serve as a stopgap measure until the ICBM became operational.[4] Both *Thor* and *Jupiter* were ordered into production by June 1958 and were scheduled to become operational from European bases by December of the same year.[5]

In spite of the progress made by the United States in the development of the IRBM, the reaction of America's European allies to the military situation in 1958 was mixed and extremely complicated. The Suez crisis of 1956 had made many Europeans keenly aware of their almost complete dependence on the United States for military security. The lack of American military and diplomatic support during this emergency and the perceived military insecurity of the alleged "missile gap" period led to sincere doubts among some individuals in Western Europe as to the credibility of the United States' ability to defend this area.[6]

---

4. U.S. Congress, House, Committee on Armed Services, Investigation of National Defense–Missiles, *Hearings*, 85th Cong., 2nd., vol. 4 (January-February 1958), testimony by Secretary of Defense Neil H. McElroy, p. 3980.

5. U.S. Congress, Senate, Committee on Appropriations, Department of Defense *Hearings*, 85th Cong., 2nd sess., vol. 5 (June 1958), testimony by Secretary of Defense Neil H. McElroy, p. 7; *The New York Times*, news article by Hanson Baldwin, stating that IRBM's were to be placed eventually in Italy, Turkey, and Great Britain, August 10, 1958.

6. Henry A. Kissinger, *The Necessity for Choice: Prospects of American Foreign Policy* (Garden City, New York: Doubleday & Company, Inc., 1960), p. 113; General Thomas S. Power (USAF, ret.), *Design for*

With the approach of the "missile gap," many Europeans began to feel that the United States was using Western Europe as an instrument of American military policy by placing United States IRBMs on their soil to compensate for American missile and deterrent deficiencies.[7] Finally, the conviction held by some observers of the increased possibility of accidental nuclear war in which Europe became involved due to the existence of American nuclear forces in Europe increased the doubts in many NATO nations as to the wisdom of complete reliance upon American nuclear strength for their defense.[8]

Premier Khrushchev added to the growing uncertainty in Western Europe by threatening that Europe could be "put out of commission" by Soviet military might. Specifically, he warned Western Germany that in the event of war, it would have "no chance of survival" and that the "very existence" of Great Britain would be threatened.[9]

This crisis in the credibility of United States deterrent posture and willingness to use it in the defense of Western Europe caused a prolonged debate on military strategy

Survival (New York: Coward-McCann, Inc., 1965), p. 132. *New York Times,* press conference by President Charles deGaulle, November 11, 1959.

7. Henry A. Kissinger, "Missiles and the Western Alliance," pp. 384–385. (At this time, Dr. Kissinger denied the possibility of a missile gap developing; however less than two years later he believed that the missile gap from 1961 to 1965 was "unavoidable." [Kissinger, *The Necessity for Choice,* p. 27.]) The whole problem of the eventual partial fragmentation of the NATO Alliance is beyond the scope of this paper. However, the following books deal with this problem for the period under discussion: Klaus Knorr (ed.), *NATO and American Security* (Princeton, New Jersey: Princeton University Press, 1959); Robert Endicott Osgood, *NATO: The Entangling Alliance* (Chicago: University of Chicago Press, 1962).

8. Eugene Rabainowitch, "Accidental War, Missiles and the World Community," *The Bulletin of the Atomic Scientists,* Vol. 14 (June 1958), p. 202.

9. Arnold L. Horelick and Myron Rush, *Strategic Power and Soviet Foreign Policy* (Chicago: The University of Chicago Press, 1966), p. 49, quoting Premier Khrushchev.

within the NATO powers. The prospect of a "missile gap" did not substantially weaken the NATO Alliance at this time, but it did furnish one of later arguments used by the Europeans in demanding their own nuclear force.[10]

As the leaders of Western Europe began to question the future of the military security of the NATO area, another highly relevant question arose that proved to be at least as difficult to answer in the long run. Soviet technological progress in the missile field had partially destroyed or at least weakened the confidence of many western leaders in the ability of the United States to deter a Soviet nuclear attack on areas outside of the United States. The Russian missile breakthrough led to a period of intensified assessment and evaluation of Soviet worldwide goals, and more importantly, the means by which the Soviet Union would attempt to achieve these goals. Or, stated in another manner, the question of Soviet intent assumed an even greater importance in any effort to determine the future course of Russian missile programs and the Soviet's willingness to use this power to pursue their foreign policy goals.[11]

The American Chairman of the Joint Chiefs of Staff, General Nathan Twining, summed up the difficulties faced by the United States decision-makers on this problem and stated early in the "missile gap" controversy the policy he felt the United States should follow:

To predict a possible enemy's intentions is a risky game. I believe we have to build our over-all force with the objective

10. Kissinger, *The Necessity for Choice.* p. 113; Arthur M. Schlesinger, Jr., *A Thousand Days: John F. Kennedy in the White House* (Boston: Houghton Mifflin Company, 1965), p. 850. *New York Times,* press conference by President Charles DeGaulle, November 11, 1959.

11. Of all the questions dealt with in this book, the question of Soviet intent is the most elusive and difficult to examine. Despite this problem, it is essential to discuss the arguments of at least some of the opposing schools of thought on this question.

of being able to meet any contingency with priorities based on enemy capabilities and not on enemy's intentions.[12]

However, this same military expert later qualified his originally straightforward statement and demonstrated the difficulty in distinguishing between the enemy's intent, their capabilities, and the American estimate of the two:

> I believe that it is erroneous to compare what the Soviets *might* have in 1962 with what we feel certain we *will* have at the same date.[13]

Added to the complexity of any attempt to deal with possible Soviet intentions was the problem of separating what Americans believed were Soviet goals and the means the Russians would use to pursue them *versus* what the leaders of the Soviet Union viewed as their own goals and the means available to achieve them.

Throughout this period, the American people showed a profound distrust of the Soviet Union, while at the same time they demonstrated a sincere concern for the maintenance of peace with Russia. The Soviet Union had become the main protagonist of the United States following World War II; the American public coupled this basic distrust of Russia with their fear of another surprise attack similar to the one on Pearl Harbor. The attack on Pearl Harbor had left a strong imprint on American strategic thinking. Therefore, the suspected American vulnerability to Soviet missile attack led to a considerable degree of concern in the United States. Many civilian and military experts began to speak of a possible devastating Soviet surprise attack on the United States retaliatory capability.[14]

---

12. Department of Defense News Release No. 1049–58, statement by General Nathan Twining, October 21, 1958.

13. *The New York Times*, quoting General Twining, January 12, 1959.

14. Stuart Chase, *American Credos* (New York: Harper & Brothers, Publishers, 1962), pp. 51, 190; Eisenhower, *Waging the Peace*, p. 551. President Eisenhower contended that the main reason for the continuation

This fear of a possible surprise attack on the United States by Russian missile forces was the basic premise of those who accepted the missile gap thesis. If there was no danger of a surprise Soviet attack, then the existence of a superior Soviet ICBM force ceased to be a threat to the United States unless American leaders contemplated the initiation of hostilities against the Soviet Union.

The combination of the fear of surprise attack and the belief that the Soviet Union would produce missiles as rapidly as American intelligence estimates indicated caused many individuals in the United States to accept the "missile gap" as almost a certainty for the future.

Throughout this period there was a great deal of confusion in the United States as to the exact nature of the Soviet threat. The debate over Soviet strategic military policy had many facets and several basic interpretations arose in the United States in response to the Russian progress in missile technology. At least three schools of thought originated in 1957-1958 in response to the possibility of a shift in the strategic balance of power. The original three interpretations were: (1) that the Soviet Union was preparing for a surprise nuclear attack on the United States as soon as its missile superiority was developed; (2) that by its very nature the destructiveness of nuclear war had made such an attack prohibitive; and (3) that Soviet military doctrine did not accept the absolute advantage accruing to the aggressor in a surprise attack and therefore Russia did not contemplate this action. Due to the fact that the continued debate concerning Soviet intentions and capabilities played such a major role in the acceptance of the "missile gap" by many Americans, these early interpretations must be dealt with in more detail.

Among the first group were those individuals in the United States who argued that the Soviet Union was not

of the U-2 flights over the Soviet Union until 1960 was to prevent a possible surprise attack on the United States.

militarily preparing in order to deter war, but in reality was planning a surprise attack on the United States as soon as they felt they had gained a definite superiority in nuclear striking power. These persons were disturbed by Soviet technological progress and appeared to believe that a successful nuclear surprise attack was not only feasible, but also the ultimate goal of the Soviet Union. Perhaps the best illustration of this attitude was a statement by General Thomas S. Power shortly after the Soviet ICBM test in 1957:

> The sole purpose of their [Soviet Union] spectacular military build-up is to use it for aggression . . . and they will use it against us when they think they are stronger than we are.[15]

Diametrically opposed to those who contended that the Soviet Union contemplated a surprise attack on the United States were the analysts who believed that the rapid development of thermonuclear weapons and the accompanying delivery systems, even as early as 1958, had made a successful nuclear attack impossible to execute. The difficulties involved in simultaneously finding and destroying the retaliatory power of an enemy were viewed to be so great as to prohibit any major power from attempting this complex task. Therefore, since no nation could be certain of destroying its enemy's nuclear striking force, no nation would attempt a surprise attack.[16]

The third major theme developed during this period

---

15. *The New York Times*, statement by General Power (Commanding Officer, Strategic Air Command) before the Air Force Association, December 17, 1957. This same theme was expanded in Power, *Design for Survival* pp. 43–46. This book was written in 1959, but not published until 1964 due to suppression by the Secretary of Defense.

16. Arthur Lee Burns, "The International Consequences of Expecting Surprise," *World Politics*, Vol. 10 (July 1958), p. 531; Pierre M. Gallois, "Nuclear Aggression and National Suicide," *The Reporter*, Vol. 19 September 18, 1958), p. 24; Morton A. Kaplan, "The Calculus of Nuclear Deterrence," *World Politics*, Vol. 11 (October 1958), p. 36; George W. Rathjens, Jr., "Deterrence and Defense," *The Bulletin of the Atomic Scientists*, Vol. 14 (June 1958), p. 225.

was based upon a detailed analysis of Soviet military doctrine by civilian experts in the United States. This group rejected the probability of a Soviet surprise attack, basing their argument on the belief that the military doctrine of the Soviet Union repudiated this strategy as ineffective and likely to endanger the survival of the Soviet Union itself. It was contended that the Soviet Union believed that World War III would be a protracted struggle like World War II and ultimately would be decided by the sum of the military, economic, and morale potentials of the adversaries.

Furthermore, the Soviet leaders explicitly distinguished between the necessity of a Soviet preemptive strike in response to an imminent American attack on their homeland and the dangers inherent in a preventative surprise attack on the United States. In the case of an imminent attack by the United States, Russia would have no choice but to launch its own delivery vehicles immediately; but the Soviets felt that a preventative attack on the United States would not be to their advantage in the long run.[17]

Based on this assessment of Soviet military strategy, one American analyst contended in 1958 that the Soviet Union had assigned its long-range ballistic missile to the defensive mission of deterring a United States attack on the Soviet Union rather than the offensive role of a first strike weapons system.[18]

Evidently, the leaders of the Soviet Union had decided that general war was not in the national interests of their nation and that they would seek to avoid all-out war while they pursued a policy of peaceful expansion of their influence and power.[19]

---

17. Raymond L. Garthoff, *The Soviet Image of Future War* (Washington, D. C.: Public Affairs Press, 1959), pp. 14, 82. Herbert S. Dinerstein, "The Revolution in Soviet Strategic Thinking," *Foreign Affairs*, Vol. 36 (January 1958), p. 249.

18. Raymond L. Garthoff, "Missiles in Soviet Strategy," *Air Force*, Vol. 41 (July 1958), p. 91. This point of view will be expanded in detail in the conclusion of this study.

19. *Ibid.*, p. 2. Another group of experts has recently contended that

Statements by Russian military and civilian leaders on a number of occasions tended to support this latter point of view. In 1957, in one of the few major public statements on Soviet military strategy, Colonel A. N. Lagouskii indicated his belief that World War III would be a magnified version of World War II. This same expert expressed his belief that no single weapon would prove decisive in a future war and that the Soviet strategy would be to strike the enemy's "main economic base" and not his nuclear striking force (not a first strike, surprise doctrine).[20] Nonetheless, there was increasing evidence that Soviet civilian leadership understood the enormous destructive power of modern weapons and had begun to demonstrate a willingness to pursue a policy of peaceful coexistence with countries of different social systems.[21]

These three interpretations of the Soviet concept of the efficacy of surprise attack (along with variations on the same themes) were the major hypotheses used by those engaged in the "missile gap" controversy. All three originated around 1958 and suffered somewhat from proximity with the events that occurred simultaneously with the analysis.

Later, more evidence became available on the Soviet attitude toward the strategic uses of surprise attack and this evidence tended to confirm the belief that the Soviet Union rejected surprise attack on the United States as a means of pursuing national goals.

with the death of Stalin, the leaders of the Soviet Union began to abandon the Stalinist idea that a surprise attack would be a temporary factor in final victory in a future war. See: Horelick and Rush, *Strategic Power and Soviet Foreign Policy*, p. 25.

20. Oleg Hoiffding, "Strategy and Economics: A Soviet View," *World Politics*, Vol. 11 (January 1959), pp. 317–319. This article is a review of A. N. Lagouskii (Colonel), *Strategiia i Ekonomika* (Moscow: Voennoe Izdatel'stus Ministerstva Oborny Soivza SSR [with the approval "imprimatur" of the Ministry of Defense of the Soviet Union], 1957).

21. N. S. Khrushchev, *World without Arms: World without Wars* (Moscow: Foreign Language Publishing House, 1959), p. 62; N. S. Khrushchev, *New York: Documents on Trip* (New York: Concurrent Press, 1960), p. 39.

There did not appear to be much doubt that by 1955 the
Soviet Union had changed from the old Stalinist policy of
denying the value of surprise attack and had begun to
admit the possible advantages that would accrue to a nation that struck first with nuclear weapons. Simultaneously, Russian strategy continued to deny that surprise
attack would be a *decisive* factor in all-out war.[22] Interestingly, for the most part the Soviet Union approached the
question of surprise attack based on the premise that the
United States would launch such an attack on Russia.[23]
When Soviet leadership did consider the possible military
decisiveness of a first strike on the United States, they
evidently concluded that such an attack would not lead
to a "quick victory" and therefore was not worth the risk
involved.[24]

Throughout the period of the supposed missile gap,
Soviet strategic policy makers, like their American coun-
terparts, did not resolve many of the conflicting military
doctrines proposed for national security. The Soviet debate over whether a future general war would be a short
war decided primarily by nuclear weapons or a protracted
war that used all of the factors of military power was not
settled. Nor had the final choice been made whether to
develop massive missile-nuclear strength at the expense of
a large conventional force.[25]

In 1962, an important book on Soviet military strategy
was published in Russia. This book was written by a num-

22. Raymond L. Garthoff, *Soviet Strategy in the Nuclear Age,* (Revised
edition) (New York: Frederick A. Praeger, 1962), p. 83.

23. Thomas W. Wolfe, *Soviet Strategy at the Crossroads* (Cambridge,
Massachusetts: Harvard University Press, 1964), p. 112. If the Soviet
Union did fear an American surprise attack, then logically the leadership
of the Soviet Union could not have admitted that an American nuclear
attack on Russia would prove decisive—to have done so might have
encouraged just such an attack.

24. Garthoff, *Soviet Strategy,* pp. 86–87.

25. Wolfe, *Soviet Strategy at the Crossroads,* pp. 34, 130. In a slightly
varied form this same argument was conducted in the United States
during this same period.

ber of leading Soviet military theoreticians headed by Marshal Vasily Sokolovsky, Chief of the Russian General Staff from 1953 to 1960. In spite of the interjection of distorted political preconceptions, this book offered some valuable insights into Soviet strategic military thinking. Marshal Sokolovsky's book demonstrated that even by 1962 the conflict between the Russian advocates of nuclear-missile power and the advocates of large conventional forces still had not been resolved. At this time Soviet doctrine envisaged a future war in which strategic nuclear power could be decisive, but in which the initial exchange of nuclear weapons would have to be followed by operations of large numbers of highly mobile troop units.[26] This compromise in Soviet strategic policy was reflected in the fact that during this period the Soviet armed forces were made up of a large conventional force and several hundred long-range nuclear delivery vehicles.

From 1957 to 1962, American policy makers did not rule out the possibility of a surprise attack by the Soviet Union. Indeed, such an American policy could have proved very dangerous for United States security. When the United States did conclude that the Soviet Union would not attempt to destroy American retaliatory power, the decision was based primarily on the recognized American strategic superiority. The fact remains that during the period of the alleged missile gap the Soviet Union did not believe in the efficacy of a surprise attack on the United States and made no attempt to prepare for such an attack.[27]

26. Vasily D. Sokolovsky (editor), *Military Strategy: Soviet Doctrine and Concepts* (New York: Frederick A. Praeger, 1963) (Translated by Mr. Richard Rockingham, Translation Service Branch, Foreign Technological Division, Wright Patterson Air Force Base, Ohio; with minor revisions by Mr. Rockingham), p. 196.
27. This fact was strongly supported by the analysis at the time and by the fact that at no time did the Soviet Union maximize its bomber or missile production capability. This point is dealt with in detail in the conclusions of this paper.

Even though the Soviet Union did not prepare for a nuclear attack on the United States, this did not prevent the Russian leaders from attempting to exploit the American belief in Soviet strategic superiority in ICBMs.[28]

On Aviation Day in July 1955 the Soviet Union mustered what appeared to be an impressive "fly-by" of their new *Bison* heavy long-range bomber. The number of aircraft that flew over the reviewing stand impressed western observers and created the impression that the Soviet Union had embarked upon large scale development and production of heavy bombers.[29] Following this Air Show, United States intelligence estimates began to indicate the possibility of a "bomber gap" by 1957. In actual fact, the Soviet Union decided to limit its production of long-range bombers even though American estimates of Russia's capabilities indicated that the Soviet Union had the ability to produce large numbers of these heavy bombers.[30] Finally, persuasive evidence became available to indicate that the impressive "fly-by" had not been a number of different *Bison* squadrons (10 Aircraft), but had been the *same* squadron flying in circles, passing over the reviewing stand every few minutes.[31]

The apparent willingness of many American civilian and military experts to accept the existence of the "bomber gap" before there was conclusive evidence to indicate a substantial Russian production program was not lost on the leaders of the Soviet Union. They were impressed with the strong tendency in the West to exag-

---

28. This view, although not original with the authors, is the major theme of Rush and Horelick, *Strategic Power and Soviet Foreign Policy.*

29. Allen Dulles, *The Craft of Intelligence* (New York: Harper & Row, Publishers, 1963) , p. 149.

30. Bart Bernstein and Robert Hagan, "Military Value of Missiles in Cuba," *The Bulletin of the Atomic Scientists,* Vol. 19 (February 1963) , p. 11. During this period the Soviet Union built only 20 percent of the heavy bombers that American intelligence estimated its economy could have sustained.

31. Dulles, *The Craft of Intelligence,* p. 149.

gerate the Soviet Union's strategic capabilities and the Western proclivity toward pessimism in their calculations of the estimated strategic military balance.[32]

The failure of the United States to intervene in Hungary in 1956 and the American attitude toward the Suez crisis of the same year further demonstrated to the leaders of the Soviet Union that even with a weak nuclear force—far inferior to that of the United States—the Soviets could use their limited strategic force as a potent instrument in the conduct of their foreign policy.[33]

By 1956-1957 it appeared that the Soviet leaders had begun to formulate their policy based on the premise that the era of thermonuclear weapons created tremendous uncertainty in all military calculations of the strategic balance. By deepening and exploiting an opponent's uncertainty, and by concealing Russia's own lack of certainty, the Soviets hoped to exploit an exaggerated version of their military power. Therefore, some observers have contended that the successful test of the Soviet ICBM in 1957 signalled the start of a systematic effort on the part of the Soviet Union to deceive the United States regarding Russian strategic capabilities and intentions.[34]

The major Soviet spokesman who developed this theme was Premier Khrushchev. On November 13, 1958 he indicated that, "The production of the intercontinental ballistic rockets has been successfully set up."[35] At this time, the United States had not tested successfully its first ICBM, the *Atlas*[36]; this missile was not tested successfully until September 1959.[37]

32. Horelick and Rush, *Strategic Power and Soviet Foreign Policy,* p. 29.
33. *Ibid.,* p. 31.
34. *Ibid.,* pp. 5, 14, 35. Also, see numerous statements by N. S. Khrushchev throughout the period.
35. "Soviet Union reports ICBM's in Production," quoting Premier Khrushchev, *Aviation Week,* Vol. 69 (December 1, 1958), p. 63.
36. *The New York Times,* November 29, 1958. *Atlas* test a success.
37. Power, *Design for Survival,* p. 146.

The following month, Premier Khrushchev met with Senator Hubert Humphrey (Democrat-Minnesota) in an eight hour interview in Moscow and emphasized the superior range of the Russian ICBMs and stated that all of the United States was vulnerable to Soviet rockets. In a public reply to Premier Khrushchev's statement, President Eisenhower stated that the range of the American missiles was "sufficient" and that the American people should keep the problem of Soviet progress in missiles in perspective with the overall military power of the United States.[38]

During 1959, Premier Khrushchev increased his effort to convince the United States of Soviet missile strength. He addressed the 21st Extraordinary Congress of the Communist Party of the Soviet Union and announced: "We have organized serial production of intercontinental ballistic rockets."[39] Later in the year, Premier Khrushchev indicated that Russia was mass producing ICBMs on an "assembly line."[40] And by May of 1959 he implied that the Soviet Union would soon have the quality and quantity of ICBMs needed by the Soviet Union and therefore, Russia could curtail production of rockets in the near future.[41]

The fact remains that the Soviet leaders knew before the end of 1959 that relatively few Russian ICBMs would be operational by 1961. If the decision had been made to produce rockets at maximum capability, it would have taken at least two years to transform a complete and new weapons system like the first generation ICBM into an operational military capability. The Soviet Union decided not to produce large numbers of first generation liquid

38. *The New York Times*, December 11, 1958.
39. Khrushchev, *World without Arms*, p. 71.
40. "News Digest," quoting Premier Khrushchev, *Aviation Week*, (November 23, 1959), p. 35.
41. *Developments in Military Technology and Their Impact on United States Strategy and Foreign Policy, Study #8* (The Johns Hopkins University, Washington, D.C.: Government Printing Office, 1959), quoting a speech by Khrushchev at Kiev, May 11, 1959, p. 110.

fuel missiles.[42] Between 1957 and 1962, the Soviet Union built less than four percent of the ICBMs that American intelligence estimated Russia's economy could have sustained.[43] By the end of 1961 the Soviet Union had an extremely limited ICBM capability, especially when compared with the overall delivery system of the United States. (See Appendix A).

Therefore, it appeared that the Soviet Union attempted to exploit American uncertainty and the American willingness to accept exaggerated Soviet missile claims. Many of the more militant aspects of Soviet foreign policy during this period have been attributed to this elaborate deception by the Soviet Union.[44]

The possibility of a change in the strategic military balance, coupled with an apparently more aggressive Soviet foreign policy, forced the Eisenhower Administration to calculate as closely as possible the condition under which Russia might resort to general war. President Eisenhower arrived at the conclusion that the Soviet Union would not risk all-out war except under the most extreme provocation from the United States. He based this belief on two

---

42. Theodore C. Sorensen, *Kennedy* (New York: Harper and Row, Publishers, 1965), p. 611. Mr. Sorensen indicates that the first generation Soviet missiles were too cumbersome and expensive to be developed and that the Soviets therefore went on to the development of their second generation missiles (just as the United States did; see next chapter). *Joint Hearings, 1960*, testimony of General Bernard Schriever, Commander of the Air Research and Development Command, United States Air Force. In his testimony, General Schriever indicated that the normal lead time for a missile system was 24 to 30 months. (That is, from the time a decision is made to make a missile system operational to the time that it actually becomes operational. This decision is made after the missile has been successfully tested), p. 57. In Rush and Horelick's *Strategic Power and Soviet Foreign Policy* the authors stated that the leaders of the Soviet Union knew before the end of 1959 that relatively few Russian ICBMs would be operational by 1959 due to the time required to transform a new weapons system like the ICBM into an operational military capability; p. 27.

43. Bernstein and Hagan, "Military Value of Missiles in Cuba," p. 11.

44. Horelick and Rush, *Strategic Power and Soviet Foreign Policy*, p. 37.

major assumptions concerning the Russian Communist
Party's attitude toward all-out war: (1) their fear that a
general war might upset the narrow base of popular support of the Communist Party in the Soviet Union, and
(2) their desire to protect the industrial accomplishments
of Russian Communism from destruction.[45]

An obvious corollary to these fundamental assumptions
that was often stated by American civilian and military
leaders was the basic American confidence in the continued existence of a United States nuclear retaliatory
force capable of inflicting damages too great to be toler-
ated by any aggressor that attacked the United States.[46]
While this message was conveyed to a rather limited number of interested persons, various other Government
spokesmen attempted to convey to the American people
the image of an increasingly powerful, secure United
States.[47]

Nonetheless, the critics of the Eisenhower Administration continued their attacks on the American missile program. And on several occasions the Administration admitted that it had doubts as to the future position of the
United States in the missile race. When Senator Stuart

45. Eisenhower, *Waging the Peace*, p. 368.

46. Thomas S. Power, "A Look at SAC's Future," *Air Force*, Vol. 41
(June 1958), p. 123. (General Power was the Commanding Officer of SAC
at this time); Thomas D. White (Chief of Staff, United States Air
Force), "The Air Force and How We are Doing It," *Air Force*, Vol. 41
(August 1958), p. 38; U.S. Congress, Senate, Committee on Appropriations, *Hearings*, Department of Defense Appropriations for 1958, 85th
Cong., 2nd sess., Vol. 5 (June 1958), testimony by General Thomas D.
White, p. 393; U.S. Cong., House, Committee on Armed Services, *Hearings*, Investigation of National Defense, Missiles, testimony by Secretary
of Defense McElroy stating that the United States had the military
capability to make the cost to an aggressor "unbearable," 85th Cong., 1st
sess., Vol. 4 (January–February 1958), p. 3975; *Ibid.*, Testimony by
Admiral Arleigh Burke (Chief of Naval Operations), p. 4561.

47. *The New York Times*, article quoting the Deputy Secretary of
Defense in charge of missile development, William M. Holaday, February
13, 1958; *Ibid.*, article quoting General Bernard Schriever, United States
Air Force Missile Director, March 15, 1958.

Symington challenged Secretary of Defense McElroy on the missile strength of the United States compared to that of the Soviet Union, the Secretary of Defense replied:

> We have no positive evidence they [Russia] are ahead of us in long-range missiles. We are conducting ourselves on the assumption that they are, but our intelligence gives us no positive evidence that they are.[48]

Later, the Secretary of Defense admitted that by 1960 the Soviet Union "should have a rather substantial ICBM capability," but that the United States had no reason for an "inferiority complex" on American weapons systems.[49]

The "missile gap" controversy in the United States tended to focus public attention on alleged American intelligence estimates on comparative military strength. The problems that surrounded the determination of the source and accuracy of the alleged intelligence estimates made public were complex, and at times, impossible to solve due to the strict secrecy maintained by the various agencies and departments of the United States Government. However, throughout the period under consideration public attention was called to the various unofficial intelligence estimates used to support the contentions of the major participants in the controversy.[50]

---

48. *The New York Times*, April 4, 1958.

49. *U.S. News and World Report*, interview with Secretary of Defense McElroy, Vol. 44 (April 25, 1958), p. 69. In this case, Senator Symington appeared to be speaking of a numbers lag and Secretary McElroy appeared to be dealing with American deterrent posture. As will be seen below, many persons played the "numbers game" with comparative missile strength and seemed to ignore the question of whether these figures were significant when applied to the *overall* deterrent posture of the United States. The distinction between these two approaches led to a great deal of confusion during the "missile gap" controversy.

50. The following books appear to be the best sources available on the general problem of United States intelligence collection and operations: Roger Hilsman, *Strategic Intelligence and National Decisions* (New York: The Free Press, 1956); Harry H. Ransom, *Central Intelligence and National Security* (Cambridge: Harvard University Press, 1958); Dulles, *The Craft of Intelligence*; William M. McGovern, *Strategic Intelligence*

In the summer of 1958, the first of many public attempts was made to estimate the future comparative missile strength of the United States and the Soviet Union. (See appendix A.) A leading newspaper columnist, Joseph Alsop, predicted the following future comparative United States-Soviet Union ICBM strength:[51]

	1959	1960	1961	1962	1963
United States	0	30	70	130	130
Soviet Union	100	500	1000	1500	2000

The possibility of a dangerous "missile gap" period was expanded in the mass media and a number of convincing cases were developed that supported the "missile gap" thesis.[52]

Perhaps the best illustration of the confusion that arose from the intelligence community during this period occurred in August 1958. The constant critic of the Eisenhower Administration's missile program, Senator Symington, sent a letter to President Eisenhower on August 29 in which he claimed that the United States lagged unjustifiably behind the Soviet Union in missile development. Senator Symington cited as his authority "his own intelligence sources" and claimed that the full extent of the danger had not been estimated accurately by the Central Intelligence Agency (CIA).[53]

Two days earlier, in a press conference, President Eisenhower had denied that the "gap" existed.[54] Later, in his reply to Senator Symington he indicated that there could

and the Shape of Tomorrow (Chicago: Henry Regnery Co., published in cooperation with Foundation for Foreign Affairs, Inc., 1961); Andrew Tully, The CIA (New York: William Morrow & Co., Inc., 1962).

51. Thomas R. Phillips, "The Growing Missile Gap" (citing J. Alsop for July 1958), The Reporter, Vol. 20 (January 8, 1959), p. 11.

52. Ibid., p. 16; James E. King, Jr., "Arms and Man in the Nuclear Rocket Era," The New Republic, Vol. 139 (September 1, 1958), p. 17; The New York Times, news analysis by Richard Witkin, January 12, 1959.

53. Eisenhower, Waging the Peace, p. 389.

54. The New York Times, news conference by President Eisenhower, August 28, 1958.

never be complete certainty on comparative missile development of the two powers, but if there was any lag in development it was due to the last Democratic Administration.[55]

Based upon recent evidence, it appeared that Senator Symington's "own intelligence sources" were from the Pentagon (probably the Air Force) and were the product of rivalry among the military services; while President Eisenhower relied on the more accurate estimates of the Central Intelligence Agency which had no obvious vested interest in this question.[56]

The Eisenhower-Symington exchange took place publicly and was part of the growing partisan conflict that surrounded the "missile gap" controversy.[57] This controversy had begun in the fall of 1957, was intensified prior to the 1958 congressional elections, and became a full-fledged political issue in the 1960 Presidential campaign.

Early in August 1958, with the congressional elections three months away, the Democrats began to broaden and intensify their attacks on the defense policies of the Republican Administration. The continuous attacks of the past on the Eisenhower missile program by various Democratic politicians were supplemented by a critical Democratic report to the House of Representatives. This report charged the Republicans with causing a three year lag in American missile development and accused the Eisenhower Administration of withholding funds from this program to prevent deficits in the budget.[58] The House Republican Minority Whip, Leslie Arends, imme-

---

55. Eisenhower, *Waging the Peace*, p. 390.
56. *The New York Times*, "The CIA," by a team of correspondents including Tom Wicker, John W. Finney, Max Frankel, E. W. Kentworth, and others, April 29, 1966. (It should be kept in mind that the CIA had been flying U-2 intelligence flights over the Soviet Union since 1956.) *Ibid.*, April 27, 1966.
57. *The New York Times*, Eisenhower news conference, August 28, 1958; *Ibid.*, article quoting Stuart Symington, September 1, 1958.
58. *Ibid.*, news article by C. P. Russell, August 12, 1958.

diately answered this Democratic accusation when he said:
". . . if the United States program does lag, the blame
lies on the tragically confused Truman Administration."
He labeled the charges "Democratic party propaganda"
and accused the Democrats of attempting to drag the successful United States weapons program into the "dangerous arena" of partisan politics.[59]
Later in the month, in the same news conference referred to above, President Eisenhower attempted to answer
his critics when asked about the possibility of a "missile
gap":

> There is still a long ways to go before the airplane, I would
> say, is made completely obsolete. So, while, if there is any
> gap, I am quite certain that our enormous strength in fine
> long-range airplanes is—I say it isn't a "gap"—it is—if the
> rate of development is not rapid as you might see it, just if
> you are talking about money and money won't do it, in my
> opinion, the airplane can take care of that deficiency.*[60]

As the 1958 campaign progressed, *The New York Times*
added its prestigious and relatively nonpartisan voice to
support the belief that the United States was lagging behind the Soviet Union in the missile race and spoke of
the dangers of the "growing stockpile of long-range rockets Moscow is accumulating."[61]

---

59. *The New York Times*, article quoting Minority Whip Leslie Arends,
August 14, 1958.

* At this point the President was "cut-off" by a reporter who stood
up and said: 'Thank you, Mr. President."

60. *The New York Times*, transcript of President Eisenhower's news
conference, August 28, 1958. This quote not only indicates that there
was some confusion on the part of the President, but also tacitly admits
the possibility of a "missile lag," even though this "lag" would not
adversely effect the United States overall deterrent posture. This same
possibility was later admitted by Secretary of Defense McElroy when
he said there was a possibility that the Soviet Union was ahead of the
United States in the development of the ICBM, but not in overall military strength. He also pointed out that the Administration did not
believe any additional funds were needed by the Department of Defense.
Ibid., September 3, 1958.

61. *The New York Times*, editorial, September 1, 1958.

The attackers of the Eisenhower Administration's defense policies were not only Democratic Congressional leaders, but included such Democratic dignitaries as ex-President Harry Truman. As these attacks increased, Vice-President Richard Nixon counterattacked and accused the Democrats of giving a false picture of United States security to America's friends and enemies abroad. Mr. Nixon stated that if there was a missile gap it was created by the Truman Administration and was being closed by President Eisenhower. Mr. Nixon was quick to point out that the Truman Administration had spent 30 times more money supporting the peanut industry than it had spent on missile development.[62]

At the end of the 1958 campaign, President Eisenhower again tacitly admitted that the "missile gap" existed as a legacy of the Truman Administration. But he went on to reassure the American people that, "The so-called missile gap of six years ago is speedily being closed."[63]

The "missile gap" controversy was not a major factor in the elections of 1958. The arguments had not developed fully at this stage and the 1958 Congressional elections were decided primarily by local issues and candidates. However, the limited political debate preceding this election foreshadowed the highly partisan nature that the missile controversy could assume. In 1960, when the presidency of the United States was at stake, these initial indications of strong partisanship in the debate over United States military posture and preparedness were amplified, and the missile controversy became one of the major issues of the Presidential campaign.

By the end of 1958, the Eisenhower Administration appeared to have strengthened the organization of the

---

62. *The New York Times*, news article by W. H. Lawrence, October 2, 1958.

63. *Ibid.*, text of President Eisenhower's speech delivered at a Republican rally in Chicago, October 23, 1958; *Ibid.*, the same theme repeated in a speech in Baltimore, November 1, 1958.

United States agencies responsible for national defense. The President had succeeded in pushing a reorganization of the Defense Department through the Congress. In an attempt to reduce the rivalries and the diverse influence of the military services, substantial alterations were made in the relationship of the Defense Department and the individual military services. An attempt also was made to remove the duplication of effort and waste by bringing research and development in the Defense Department under more centralized control.[64]

The Department of Defense indicated its belief that the strategic military posture of the United States was second to none. It acknowledged that the Soviet Union had the capability to build a substantial number of missiles, but did not believe the Soviets would necessarily use this capacity.[65] There was no evidence that the Soviet Union was producing long-range missiles at this time. In fact, available evidence indicated that the Soviet Union experienced difficulties in the development of their ICBM. Although the exact nature of these problems was not determined, the long interlude in Soviet ICBM testing after the original tests in 1957 indicated that some complications arose.[66]

As 1958 came to an end, a general attitude of optimism appeared to have gained acceptance by many in the United States. There was general, but certainly not unanimous, agreement that the United States held a qualitative and quantitative lead over the Soviet Union in long-range and medium bombers. The United States had a far larger stockpile of nuclear weapons than the Soviet Union and it was predicted that in 1959 the United States would

64. Eisenhower, *Waging the Peace,* pp. 345–353.
65. U.S. Library of Congress, Legislative Reference Service, *United States Defense Policies in 1958* (Washington, D.C.: Government Printing Office, July 10, 1959), p. 8.
66. Baldwin, *The Great Arms Race,* p. 18.

have from 4000 to 5000 delivery vehicles capable of carrying thermonuclear warheads to the Soviet Union.[67]

One of the major United States weekly news periodicals confidently told the American public that the balance of power had shifted to the United States and that America was "strongly ahead" of the Soviet Union in the arms race. The same article characterized Soviet missiles as being unable to reach the United States with operational missiles while American missiles were being "zeroed in" on the Soviet heartland. (This referred to the placing of 60 *Thor* missiles in Great Britain and the construction of three *Atlas* sites in the United States.) [68]

---

67. *Ibid.*, pp. 22, 39.

68. "Superweapons Race: Balance of Power Shifts to the U.S.," *U.S. News and World Report*, Vol. 43 (December 12, 1958), p. 35.

4

THE DEBATE INTENSIFIES: 1959

IN JANUARY 1959, THE CONTROVERSY THAT SURROUNDED THE possibility of a "missile gap" attained its highest degree of public attention thus far in the United States.[1] The debate took place in the mass media, in major Congressional hearings, and within the Eisenhower Administration itself. This period was characterized by a considerable number of confusing, and at times, contradictory reports and statements.

The exact reasons for the strong reemergence of the missile crisis as a major public issue were difficult to determine. By the end of 1958, the Eisenhower Administration appeared to have the situation surrounding the missile controversy well under control. In November 1958, the United States had successfully tested the American *Atlas* ICBM and later in the year the Air Force *Thor* had been sent to Great Britain. Also, all concerned parties admitted that at that time the United States strategic bomber forces were superior to those of the Soviet Union in both long-range and medium-range bombers.[2]

---

1. The coverage of the missile controversy by representatives of the mass media greatly increased in January 1959. The combined stimulus of the Joint Hearings, 1959 and the "leaks" to the news media added substantially to the intensity of the debate. See footnotes on next several pages.

2. Baldwin, *The Great Arms Race*, p. 22; U.S. Congress, Senate, Committee on Armed Services, Preparedness Investigating Subcommittee and Committee on Aeronautical and Space Science, *Joint Hearings,*

From the evidence available, it appeared that one of the events that initiated the intensification of the missile controversy was a "secret background briefing" given by Secretary of Defense McElroy. In this briefing early in 1959, Secretary McElroy supposedly stated that by 1961–1962 the Soviet Union would have a three to one advantage over the United States in numbers of operational ICBMs.[3] Although it was impossible to determine with certainty if Secretary McElroy made this statement, a great deal of evidence accumulated to support this contention. And the fact remained that these figures were attributed to Secretary McElroy for the next several years and were never denied by him.[4]

86th Cong., 1st sess., 1959, testimony by Secretary of Defense McElroy, pp. 38–39. (These hearings will be referred to as the *Joint Hearings*, 1959.)

3. *The New York Times*, February 9, 1961. A "background briefing" is one that is given by a high government official to members of the press or Congress, but is considered an "unofficial briefing." The information given in the briefing is to be used for "background" only and is not intended for public release. As will be seen below, it appears that this type of briefing not only helped to create the "missile gap," but also was used to destroy the "missile gap" myth.

4. "In Missiles: A 3-year Gap Ahead," *Business Week* (December 5, 1959), p. 25; "Letting Down Our Defenses," *The New Republic*, Vol. 140 (July 5, 1959), p. 2; "Arms—McElroy and the Menace," *Newsweek*, Vol. 53 (February 16, 1959), p. 27; "Defense: Atlas at the Gap," *Time*, Vol. 73 (February 23, 1959), p. 22; U.S. Congress, Senate, Committee on Armed Services, Preparedness Investigating Subcommittee and Committee on Aeronautical and Space Science, *Joint Hearings*, 86th Cong., 2nd sess., 1960 (Febuary–March). Under questioning by Senator Symington, the new Secretary of Defense, Mr. Gates, stated that he did not know if Mr. McElroy had made the statement or not. Secretary Gates said that the Department of Defense had a "research group" checking out the statement and they still had not been able to determine if Secretary McElroy made it. Mr. Gates concluded: "It is my personal impression that he must have said it." Secretary Gates said Mr. McElroy's figures were based on Soviet capability and not on known intelligence of what the Soviet Union was doing, pp. 476–478. On December 1, 1959 Secretary of Defense McElroy resigned and was replaced by acting Secretary of Defense Thomas S. Gates, Jr. *The New York Times*, December 2, 1959. Secretary Gates was officially confirmed by the United States Senate at the end of January, 1960. *The New York Times*, January 23, 1960.

Throughout the early months of 1959, the heightened debate was covered extensively by the mass media. One of the most vocal military analysts of the comparative military posture of the major powers wrote in several influential periodicals and contended that the "missile gap" had arrived and that the United States retaliatory forces had reached a point where they could be substantially wiped out by a surprise Soviet attack.[5]

On the other hand, a less pessimistic attitude appeared in *The New York Times*. An attempt was made to portray a balanced analysis of the possibility of a "missile gap."[6] Editorially, this newspaper no longer admitted the existence of a "missile gap" and took the position that the United States had made "remarkable progress" in the missile field, but urged that America exert an all-out effort to assure that the "missile gap" specter never becomes a reality.[7] Mr. Hanson Baldwin, the Military Editor of *The New York Times*, assumed a comparatively optimistic attitude. After it was admitted that the Soviet Union was ahead in rocket thrust, Mr. Baldwin declared that political partisanship and lack of accurate intelligence estimates had blurred the missile controversy. He further contended that the predictions of future missile strength were based upon the missile production *authorized* by the United States versus the American estimates of the *maximum capability* of Soviet missile production, when no one really knew what either would be. Mr. Baldwin's conclusion was that Russia might have a slight lead in ICBMs, but that

5. Thomas R. Phillips (Brigadier General, United States Army, retired), reprint of an article originally published in *The St. Louis Post-Dispatch*, *The New Republic*, Vol. 140 (January 5, 1959), p. 5; Phillips, "The Growing Missile Gap," *The Reporter*, Vol. 20 (January 8, 1959), pp. 10–17; Phillips, "We Can't Buy Time that has been Lost," *The New Republic*, Vol. 140 (January 19, 1959), p. 6.

6. *The New York Times*, "U.S. Raising Missile Goals as Critics foresee Gap," news analysis by Richard Witkin, January 12, 1959.

7. *The New York Times*, editorial, January 16, 1959.

". . . there is no good evidence that any real missile gap need develop."[8]

Meanwhile President Eisenhower promised the American people a "sensible posture of defense," but warned them against "feverish building of vast armaments to meet glibly predicted moments of national peril."[9] The President emphasized the military strength of the United States when the "balanced forces" of the nation were viewed[10] (referring to the powerful deterrent power of SAC), and deplored the "hangdog" attitude of many Americans towards United States missile progress.[11]

Another element that added substantially to the controversy over United States defense posture early in 1959 was the various investigative hearings conducted by the numerous committees of the United States Congress. In the Senate, the most important (although not the only) investigation took place in the combined hearings of the Committee on Armed Services (Preparedness Subcommittee) in conjunction with the Committee on Aeronautical and Space Sciences. In the House, the major hearings occurred before the House Appropriations Committee for 1960 (Subcommittee on National Defense). Although the value of the open testimony given in these hearings was limited because of government secrecy, a close study of this testimony revealed a great deal about the defense policies and military posture of the United States.

The hearings dealt with numerous issues and highly complex problems. However, three major questions appeared consistently throughout the 1959 investigations.

8. *The New York Times*, "Missile Gap Debate blurs Broader Issues," by Hanson W. Baldwin, January 15, 1956. (emphasis added).

9. *The New York Times*, text of President Eisenhower's State of the Union Address, January 10, 1959.

10. *The New York Times*, text of President Eisenhower's news conference, January 29, 1959.

11. *The New York Times*, text of President Eisenhower's news conference, January 29, 1959.

These crucial questions were: (1) What is the present and future deterrent posture of the United States vis-à-vis the Soviet Union? (2) What are the plans and programs for future United States missile and bomber development and production in relation to Soviet programs? And, (3) What are the budgetary considerations relevant to questions number one and two above?

The question of the most immediate importance was whether the Strategic Air Command could fulfill its mission in the event of sudden aggression against the United States by the Soviet Union. In response to this fundamental inquiry, General Thomas S. Power, the Commanding Officer of SAC, stated that American airpower could:

> . . . destroy the warmaking capacity of an aggressor to the point that he would no longer have the will or the capability to wage war. The important thing is that the Strategic Air Command has that capability today. What is more important is the fact that Mr. Khrushchev and the Soviets are well aware of our capability.[12]

To fulfill this mission, it was contended that the United States had a "marked superiority" over the Soviet Union in heavy bombers and a "moderate superiority" in medium bombers. Also, intelligence estimates gave no indication that the Russians were closing this American lead in manned bombers as had been predicted a year earlier (January 1958) in the first series of the Preparedness Subcommittee *Hearings*.[13]

Further testimony indicated that SAC had about 1500 medium-range B-47 bombers and about 500 long-range B-52's and that a "considerable" number of these aircraft

---

12. U.S. Congress, Senate, *Joint Hearings* (January 29 and 30, 1959), pp. 121–122.

13. *Ibid.*, testimony by Secretary of Defense Neil McElroy, pp. 38–39. It should be kept in mind that neither side had operational ICBMs at this time.

were on "ground alert." These strategic bombers were scheduled to be airborne 15 minutes after a warning of possible enemy attack was received. Most military experts believed that this alert system would serve as a strong deterrent to a potential aggressor.[14]

The threat to the Strategic Air Command's overseas bases posed by the Soviets intermediate range ballistic missile was dealt with by the Air Force Chief of Staff, General Thomas D. White. General White stated that at the present time the Russians did not have missiles with sufficient range to threaten these bases and therefore these aircraft would be assured of getting airborne.[15]

Even though the Eisenhower Administration's military and civilian experts were in agreement on the present strong deterrent position of the United States, serious doubts by some military leaders became evident in the estimates given for the future security of this country. The period 1962-1963 was said to be the period of "maximum danger" when the Soviet Union could launch a "relatively large number of missiles in salvo." This new period of "maximum danger" represented a revision from earlier estimates of the time period for the appearance of the supposed "missile gap" from 1960 to 1962-1963.[16]

The American military response advocated for this period of "maximum danger" varied from requests for an "airborne alert" in the fairly near future to emphatic

---

14. U.S. Congress, House, Committee on Appropriations, *Hearing on Fiscal Year 1960 Defense Budget*, 86th Cong., 1st sess., Vol. 10, pt. 2 (February 19, 1959), testimony by SAC Commander General Thomas Power, p. 378. Later it was reported that the United States had about 400 SAC bombers on 15 minute ground alert and that the number was scheduled to go up to 600 in the near future. *The New York Times*, news article by Jack Raymond, March 7, 1959.

15. *Ibid.*, testimony by General Thomas White, Chief of Staff, United States Air Force (February 18, 1959), p. 864.

16. U.S. Congress, House, *Hearings on Fiscal Year 1960*, pt. 5 (April 9, 1959), testimony by Major General Bernard Schriever, Commander of the Air Force's Ballistic Missile Division, p. 724.

appeals for more bombers and missiles.[17] As one prominent Air Force General was quoted as having said concerning bombers and missiles: "I want more and I want it faster."[18]

In the meantime, the most vocal critic of the Eisenhower Administration's missile program, Senator Stuart Symington, called for an immediate airborne alert of SAC bombers and predicted that the Soviet advantage in ICBMs would be four to one within the next several years.[19]

Secretary of Defense McElroy once again became the major spokesman in defending the defense policies of the Eisenhower Administration. He stated on several occasions that United States intelligence estimates did not indicate that the Soviet Union was ahead of the United States in missile development, but he did concede that the Soviet Union could catch and surpass the United States if they used their full missile production capability.[20] Then, in a significant verbal exchange with Senator Symington, the following important policy statement was made:

Secretary McElroy: It is not our intention or policy to try to match missile for missile in the ICBM category of the Russian capability in the next couple of years. Our position, Mr. Symington, is that our diversified capability to deliver the big weapon is what we are going to count on as our ability to deter general war.

Senator Symington: What you are in effect saying is that we are planning in this fashion in spite of our intelligence estimates that the Russians are going to produce a great many more missiles, ICBM's, than we are; is that correct?

Secretary McElroy: We are planning based on an assumption that they have that capability, and if they use that capability—and we are also assuming that they will from the

17. U.S. Congress, House, *Hearings on Fiscal Year 1960*, pt. 1 (February 18, 1959), testimony by Air Force Chief of Staff, General Thomas White, pp. 864–865.

18. *The New York Times*, report on the release of previously censored testimony by General Thomas Power, SAC Commander, before House Appropriations Hearings, April 6, 1959.

19. U.S. Congress, *Joint Hearings, 1959*, p. 220.

20. U.S. Congress, Senate, *Joint Hearings, 1959*, pp. 49, 52, 54.

standpoint of our counter-force—then they will have a year from now, two years from now, a larger number of this particular element in the retaliatory force than the United States will have.[21]

At the same time, at the request of Senator Symington, Secretary McElroy read into the record a statement that Secretary McElroy had made earlier in an executive session before the Senate Armed Services Committee:

> I would like to make a final comment because I think that it should be understood that from the standpoint of the Department of Defense we are assuming, as I think we should assume, that they [the Soviet Union] will have these numbers in being at the times when the national intelligence estimates say they could have it.[22]

Several important aspects of the missile controversy were partially cleared up by this candid testimony by Secretary of Defense McElroy. First, the testimony added credence to the report that the Secretary of Defense earlier had stated that in several years the Soviet Union could have a three to one missile advantage over the United States. Second, the United States government accepted at this time that the Soviet Union would produce missiles according to the capability credited them by United States intelligence estimates. Third, the United States was going to rely on the American "diversified capability to deliver big weapons" (primarily the SAC bomber force) to deter war rather than rely strictly on a missile force. And, finally, the testimony that the United States did not intend to match the Soviet Union "missile for missile" tended to confirm the fact that the United States did not plan production of a large number of first generation liquid fuel missiles, but would wait until second generation solid fuel missiles became operational before large numbers were produced.[23]

---

21. U.S. Congress, Senate, *Joint Hearings, 1959*, p. 46.
22. *Ibid.*, p. 47. (exact numbers were deleted.)
23. At no time did the United States program have more than about

The idea that the second generation of solid fuel missiles would be the most important generation of missiles was not new; it had been articulated a year earlier.[24] The expensive and cumbersome nature of the first generation liquid fuel missile combined with the fact that this generation was primarily a first strike weapon led many observers to conclude that major emphasis should be placed on the development of the solid fuel second generation missile.[25]

Closely connected with this problem of emphasis on first or second generation missile production was the annual debate over the allocation of funds for the various projects of the Department of Defense. This controversy was highlighted by the Congressional investigations on national security and Department of Defense appropriations. With limited resources available, the question of how much was to be spent on the various projects was of the utmost importance.

Earlier in 1958, Congressional pressure had led to a supplemental budgetary request for Fiscal 1958 by President Eisenhower for the dispersal of SAC and the acceleration of the ICBM program.[26] By mid-1958, the Eisenhower Administration increased its original budgetary request for Fiscal 1959 for national defense purposes by $2.75 billion over the original request made six months

---

200 Atlas and Titan liquid fuel missiles scheduled for production, while it planned for the production of over 1600 solid fuel second generation Minutemen and Polaris missiles. (Only 130 liquid fuel missiles actually were produced.) "United States Planned Delivery Systems," *The Bulletin of the Atomic Scientists*, Vol. 19 (April 1963), p. 38. (See also appendix A.)

24. "Next Generation Seen as Missile Race Key," *Aviation Week*, article quoting Air Force Ballistic Missile expert, General Bernard Schriever, Vol. 68 (January 27, 1958), p. 35.

25. Robert C. Albrook, "How Good Are Our Missiles?" *The Reporter*, Vol. 18 (February 18, 1959), p. 23; Albert Wohlstetter, "The Delicate Balance of Terror," *Foreign Affairs*, Vol. 37 (January 1959), p. 226.

26. U.S. Congress, House, Committee on Armed Services, Investigation of National Defense: Missiles, *Hearings*, 85th Cong., 2nd sess., Vol. 4 (January–February 1958), p. 3982.

earlier.[27] By early 1959, Congressional pressure had been responsible partly for the increase of the number of projected first generation ICBM squadrons from 13 to 20 for Fiscal 1960.[28]

The 1959 predictions of a future "missile gap" and the confusion that surrounded the development of a second generation of missiles led many members of Congress to question once again the appropriations set forth in the Administration's budget and the efficacy of the proposed budget figures to guarantee the future security of the United States. The proposed appropriation for missile development for Fiscal 1960 was $245 million less than what had been spent in 1959 and many members of Congress wanted to know why this situation existed when some of them believed that a missile gap was either in existence or imminent.[29]

After some initial confusion over the difference between actual expenditures for a given year as opposed to what had been appropriated, Secretary of Defense McElroy explained that the reduction in appropriations for Fiscal 1960 was due to the fact that at least two more advanced missiles had supplanted the development of the proposed first generation version. The submarine, surface-launched *Regulus* was replaced by the second generation solid fuel *Polaris* (sub-surface launched) and the slow, air-breathing *Snark* was replaced by the progress in the development of the *Atlas* ICBM and eventually by the *Minuteman*. Therefore, the *Regulus* and *Snark* programs no longer required

27. U.S. Congress, House, *Ibid.*, Vol. 5 (June 1958), p. 4; *The New York Times*, July 25, 1958. These funds were to be used primarily for more B-52 long-range bombers and more K-135 jet tankers for in-flight refueling.

28. *The New York Times*, "U.S. Raising Missile Goals as Critics Foresee 'Gap,'" by Richard Witkin, January 12, 1959. There were ten missiles per squadron, thus raising the projected number of first generation missiles from 130 to 200. This number was never produced as second generation missile went into production ahead of schedule. (see Appendix A)

29. U.S. Congress, Senate, *Joint Hearings*, p. 28.

appropriations for 1960.[30] In addition to the removal of missile programs that no longer were needed, Secretary McElroy emphasized that for the immediate future the United States relied on the superior American bomber forces as the deterrent to Soviet aggression.[31]

It was also asked if the Joint Chiefs of Staff concurred with this statement and the Secretary of Defense submitted a unanimously supported statement by the Joint Chiefs on this matter.

The Joint Chiefs of Staff consider that the Fiscal Year 1960 proposed expenditure figure of $40,945 million is adequate to provide for the essential program necessary for the defense of the nation for the period under consideration. They find no serious gap in the key elements of the budget in its present form, but all have reservations with respect to the funding of segments of their respective service programs.[32]

A number of the critics of the Eisenhower Administration's defense policies did not accept the reassurances given by Administration spokesmen. The most vocal critic,

---

30. *Ibid.*, pp. 9–12.
31. *Ibid.*, p. 13.
32. *Ibid.*, p. 21. Statement was signed by every member of the Joint Chiefs of Staff. The specific service reservations are to be found on pp 21–24. None of these reservations dealt with serious strategic shortcomings. However, this basic agreement between United States government civilian and military leaders should not lead the reader to the conclusion that there was no disagreement on military policy within government circles. The Air Force Ballistic Missile Division Commander, Major General Bernard Schriever called for an acceleration of the United States missile effort on numerous occasions. (U.S. Congress, House, Committee on Appropriations, *Hearings* on Fiscal Year 1960 Defense Budget, 86th Cong., 1st sess., Vol. 12 [April 1959]), pp. 709, 724; *The New York Times*, January 30, 1959 (Censored version of General Schriever's testimony before the *Joint Hearings*, 1959). Also, in a released censored version of the testimony from an "executive session" of the *Joint Hearings* reported in *The New York Times*, the SAC Commander General Thomas S. Power called for an increased spending program for first generation missiles, while the Air Force Chief of Staff, General Thomas D. White disagreed and supported the President's spending program. *The New York Times*, March 16, 1959.

once again, was Senator Stuart Symington, and his criticism went beyond the normal dissatisfaction expressed by many critics of the Eisenhower Administration. Senator Symington stated that he had been briefed by the Central Intelligence Agency four times in the past year on the projected comparative missile strength of the United States and the Soviet Union. He declared that although he disagreed with the CIA's estimates based on "other information I had," the estimates had been the same all four times. Then, Senator Symington charged Secretary of Defense McElroy with "downgrading" these figures in recent testimony before the House Armed Services Committee.[33] Senator Symington, in response to the reassurances of American security given by the Secretary of Defense, publicly charged that:

> The Secretary's statements are apparently based on a recent downward revision in intelligence estimates of Soviet ICBM capability for the next three or four years.[34]

Several days later, Senator Symington was quoted as having charged the Eisenhower Administration with an attempt to lull the American people into a "state of complacency not justified by the facts."[35] Senator Symington made this final prediction:

> Now I want to make this prediction to you: In three years the Russians will prove to us that they have 3,000 ICBM's. Let that be on the record.[36]

---

33. U.S. Congress, Senate, *Joint Hearings,* pp. 25–27. At this point in the testimony, Secretary of Defense McElroy stated that these charges would have to be answered in "executive session" and the subject was dropped, p. 27.

34. *The New York Times,* quoting Senator Symington, January 24, 1959.

35. Ford Eastman, "Senate Unit to View Space Status," *Aviation Week,* Vol. 70 (February 2, 1959), p. 32.

36. *The New York Times,* released version of censored testimony of Senator Stuart Symington, *Joint Hearings,* 1959, March 16, 1959.

Secretary of Defense McElroy denied that the Administration had "tailored" intelligence estimates of Soviet missile strength to meet economies in the budget. He stated that American intelligence estimates were based on the best intelligence information available for the period through the year 1962. Mr. McElroy assured the American public that the diversified delivery system of the United States placed this country in a position not only to fight a general war, but also to win it; and therefore the Soviet Union was deterred from initiating such a war. The Secretary of Defense concluded that the United States was in that position for the period through 1962.[37]

The charges of military inadequacy made against the Eisenhower Administration were serious enough to induce President Eisenhower to address the nation in response to the continued furor over defense policies. The President stated that the accusation "that our defenses are presently or will some time in the future be inadequate to meet the Communist challenge" was "simply not true" and was "without foundation."[38]

Throughout the *Joint Hearings,* Senator Symington wanted to hear testimony from the Director of the Central Intelligence Agency, Allen Dulles, and question him about the "downgraded" intelligence estimates. When Mr. Dulles finally testified, it was in "executive session." The testimony was never released to the American public. In a later speech on the military-economic challenge of the Soviet Union, Mr. Dulles did not deal with the question of revised intelligence estimates, but limited himself to statements on American military superiority at the present time and the assurance that "they [the Soviet Union] are well aware of our deterrent force."[39]

---

37. *The New York Times,* article quoting Secretary of Defense McElroy, March 4, 1959.

38. *The New York Times,* text of Radio-Television address to the nation, March 17, 1959.

39. *The New York Times,* text of speech by Dr. Allen Dulles, "The Military-Economic Challenge of the Soviet Union," April 9, 1959.

The highly controversial nature of the questions and testimony before the Congressional hearings led to an intensification of interest in the missile controversy in the United States and a corresponding increase in the coverage of the debate in the mass media. The information available to the public presented the extremes on both sides of the argument and offered evidence to support almost any point of view. However, most periodic literature of the period gave strong credence to the certainty of the alleged "missile gap" of the future.[40]

One of the major exceptions to this acceptance of the overwhelming belief in the coming "missile gap" was found in *The Nation*. This periodical, which consistently negated the prediction of a "missile gap," expressed its editorial position under the title "The Missile Bogey" and stated that Senator Symington was using the alleged "missile gap" to carry him to the presidency.[41]

Once the Congressional hearings were concluded, a number of periodicals attempted an in-depth analysis of the testimony concerned with present and future United States defense posture. Several of these articles made a strong, logical case for the projected "missile gap" and raised highly relevant questions that evidently had not

40. For estimates of future comparative missile strength during this period, see Appendix A. Early in 1959, the following periodicals either printed editorials or "signed articles" that strengthened the belief in the predictions of the future "missile gap." "Arms—McElroy and the Menace," *Newsweek*, Vol. 53 (February 13, 1959), p. 27; "Big Fuss about Missiles—These are the Facts," *U.S. News and World Report*, Vol. 46 (February 6, 1959), p. 33; "Debate over Missiles," *Commonweal*, Vol. 69 (February 20, 1959), p. 532; "McElroy and Missiles," *The New Republic*, Vol. 140 (February 9, 1959), p. 5; "Missile Gap—How Perilous?" *Newsweek*, Vol. 53 (February 9, 1959), p. 23; Thomas R. Phillips, "Mr. McElroy's Maginot Line," *The Reporter*, Vol. 20 (February 19, 1959), p. 25; Richard H. Rovere, "Letter from Washington," *The New Yorker*, Vol. 34 (February 14, 1959), p. 104; "Soviets Study Military Aspects of Space," *Aviation Week*, Vol. 70 (March 9, 1959), p. 313. With this wide cross-section of periodical literature supporting the future existence of the "missile gap" it came as no surprise that this question should become a major political issue in the 1960 presidential election.

41. "The Missile Bogey," *The Nation*, Vol. 188 (February 18, 1959), p. 129.

been answered satisfactorily by the Eisenhower Administration.[42]

In the American press, the question of American military security was engulfed in confusion and contradiction. Many Americans believed that they were "faced with an implacably hostile power" that wanted to destroy the United States at the earliest possible opportunity.[43] Although the spokesmen for the Eisenhower Administration constantly attempted to reassure the American public of United States military strength, American insecurity was heightened simultaneously by statements made by United States military and political leaders. Premier Khrushchev also added to this basic insecurity by boasting of the progress in Soviet missile technology and production.[44]

At this stage of the missile debate, what might be called a "credibility gap" appeared to develop in the United States. Many observers seriously doubted the reliability (and in some cases the sincerity) of the reported national intelligence estimates presented to the American public by the Eisenhower Administration. There were numerous attacks on the past inability of the United States intelligence community to produce accurate estimates on such recent events as the Russian development of the Atomic and Hydrogen bombs, the Chinese intervention in Korea, the appearance of the Mig-15 fighter; the most recent example was the *surprise* shown by the American public due

---

42. Stewart Alsop, "Our Gamble with Destiny," *The Saturday Evening Post*, Vol. 231 (May 16, 1959), p. 23; Charles J. V. Murphy, "The Embattled Mr. McElroy," *Fortune*, Vol. 59 (April 1959), p. 148; James R. Shipley (Chief of Time-Life Correspondents), "Life and Death Debate over the Missile Program," *Life*, Vol. 46 (March 9, 1959), p. 116.

43. Alsop, "Our Gamble with Destiny," p. 113.

44. *The New York Times*, "Khrushchev Says Soviet Rocket Success Shifts World Balance to Soviets," January 28, 1959; *The New York Times*, article quoting Premier Khrushchev saying that the Soviet Union had ICBMs in "serial production," February 11, 1959.

to the successful Soviet development of the ICBM and the Sputnik earth satellite.[45]

The apparent downgrading of intelligence estimates of predicted Soviet missile production also added an element of uncertainty concerning the Eisenhower Administration's ability to estimate Soviet capabilities accurately and precisely. The many critics who accepted this point of view believed that the United States had consistently minimized Soviet achievements, while American accomplishments had been described in overly optimistic terms.[46]

There was no question that the United States intelligence community had erred in the past in underestimating the capabilities and intent of the Communist nations. But on occasion the error had been to overestimate Soviet capabilities and intentions (the prediction of the "bomber gap" being the best example). Several periodicals pointed this out and concluded that it was possible that the United States might be overestimating Soviet intentions again. The point also was made that only the man at the head of the Executive Branch of the government had access to all of the intelligence estimates and therefore President Eisenhower's estimates probably were the most accurate available.[47]

The whole question of a possible "missile gap" revolved around these various supposed intelligence estimates and the meaning attached to their interpretations. The basic question throughout the whole debate was: Did the projected Soviet ICBM strength indicate the possibility that the United States retaliatory force could be destroyed and therefore prevented from retaliating effectively? Obvious-

---

45. "Arms—McElroy and the Menace," p. 28; "Debate over Missiles," p. 532.

46. *Ibid.*, p. 532.

47. Shipley, "Life and Death Debate over Missile Program," p. 119; "The Missile Bogey," p. 129.

ly, this was a complex question and the answer, if it was to be found, involved several important factors. Most observers accepted the fundamental hostility of the Soviet Union toward the United States and formulated their opinions and analysis based on this premise. With the acceptance of this basic premise, the most important considerations in connection with future United States military security were: (1) the projections of the quantity and capability of future Soviet missile programs, and, (2) the strength and vulnerability of United States retaliatory power in relation to this prospective Soviet nuclear striking force.

The American people were inundated by projected figures of future Soviet missile strength (see appendix A). These figures came from a variety of sources and the claim was made in most cases that they came from some unidentified "official source." Any attempted projection of Soviet missile programs early in 1959 was difficult at best, even for the official intelligence community of the United States Government. When differing supposed projections were relayed to the American people, confusion was the logical result. The supposed "downgrading" of the official intelligence estimates by Secretary of Defense McElroy only added to the existing confusion.

From the figures printed publicly, it appeared that the following projections of comparative missile strength represented in a rough form the original figures accepted by those in the United States who believed in the alleged "missile gap."[48]

---

48. Phillips, "The Growing Missile Gap," p. 11 (Mr. Phillips's figures for 1959, 1960, and 1961 were higher than the above figures); *The New York Times*, "U.S. Raising Goals as Critics Foresee Gap," news analysis by Richard Witkin, January 12, 1959; Joseph Alsop, "After Ike, the Deluge," *Washington Post and Times Herald* (reprinted in the Johns Hopkins Report, 1959), October 7, 1959. One interested critic contended that by 1962 the Soviet Union would have 3000 ICBMs. (*The New York Times*, article quoting Senator Stuart Symington, March 16, 1959.)

	United States ICBMs	Soviet Union ICBMs
1960	30	100
1961	70	500
1962	130	1000
1963	130	1500
1964	130	2000

Following the supposed "downgrading" of intelligence estimates by Secretary of Defense McElroy, a new set of figures began to appear as the "official" estimates. Although these new estimates varied slightly depending upon the source, they looked something like this:[49]

	United States ICBMs	Soviet Union ICBMs
1959	10	10
1960	30	100
1961	80–100	100–300
1962	100–300	500

At the time there was no way to verify either set of projected missile figures. The Government did not release its official estimates for security reasons. Therefore, the public had to rely on more general Administration statements on national security or accept the estimates of the mass media (or combine the two). The Eisenhower Administration continued to reassure the American public of United States military security through the period under consideration and some representatives of the mass media continued to offer so-called intelligence projections that challenged the Administration's contention that America was secure militarily.

In spite of the various predictions for the future, most observers agreed that for the present, (1959), the military

49. Shipley, "Life and Death Debate over Missile Program," p. 119; Charles J. V. Murphy, "The Embattled Mr. McElroy," *Fortune,* Vol. 59 (April 1959), p. 242; Alsop, "Our Gamble with Destiny," pp. 116–117. It should be kept in mind that these are composite figures and that there are some variations in the exact figures given by the above sources. For a comprehensive listing of the missile projections given to the American people during this period, see Appendix A.

security of the United States was assured. The consensus
was that the Strategic Air Command still was invulnerable
to a destructive Soviet surprise attack. Even some of the
strongest critics of the Eisenhower Administration's defense policies admitted that SAC had about 1800 long-
and medium-range nuclear armed bombers stationed
within range of the Soviet Union.[50] The Soviet Union was
credited with having only 150 long-range bombers capable
of reaching the United States.[51] Since, for the time being,
neither side had an operational ICBM, this American force
was viewed as a sufficient deterrent in relation to the limited Soviet strategic capability.[52]

The speculation on American Strategic security not only
centered on projected numbers of long-range delivery
vehicles, but also on the varying degrees of vulnerability of
the various American retaliatory systems to attack by
Russian bombers and missiles. The problem of the projected Russian delivery system in relation to the vulnerability of American retaliatory power in the face of this
threat became one of the most important and difficult
questions of the "missile gap" period. To complicate the
problem even more, intangible questions on such factors
as Russian intent continued to be raised and discussed in
the context of the overall defense problem.

At this time the Strategic Air Command had about 44
major air bases, 29 of them overseas. Since the Soviet long-
range bomber force was viewed as a limited threat due to
its small size (150 bombers) and the long warning time

---

50. Alsop, "Our Gamble with Destiny," p. 115. Later, the question
of ground and airborne alerts and warning times will assume a great
deal more importance than was attached to them at this time. (see
below)

51. *The New York Times*, news article by Hanson W. Baldwin,
March 25, 1959. At this time, reports were uncertain as to the capability
of the Soviet Air Force for in-flight refueling of medium-range bombers.
However, these bombers were given the capability of making a "one-way"
mission against the United States.

52. *Ibid.*

it would offer if used in an attack on SAC, the most important speculation was concerned with the number of ICBMs it would take to effectively neutralize the American SAC bomber force. The estimates of this number varied. The semi-official *Johns Hopkins Report* of December 1959 contended that it would take four to six Soviet ICBMs to destroy an uncovered and unconcealed SAC airfield.[53] Other sources quoted figures as low as two ICBMs per SAC base in order to destroy its effectiveness.[54] These figures dealt only with the destruction of the Strategic Air Command and did not deal with such questions as the difficulty of timing a suprise attack or dealing with the various other United States deterrent forces in existence at that time (e.g. Naval carrier aircraft, IRBMs in England and Turkey and fighter/bombers in Europe) .

Also considered was the encouraging distinction between the vulnerability of the SAC bases and the almost invulnerable nature of a dispersed, hardened missile system. It was contended that it would require a tremendous Russian ICBM salvo to be certain of destroying even the 110 Titan liquid fuel missiles scheduled to be operational early in 1961. The needed ICBM ratio then went up to as many as 30 to 40 Russian missiles per Titan launching site. Thus, a single hardened Titan missile squadron (10 missiles, dispersed) would increase the size of the attack force fiftyfold over that required for the destruction of the

---

53. Washington Center of Foreign Policy Studies, The Johns Hopkins University, *Developments in Military Technology and their Impact on United States Strategy and Foreign Policy, Study #8* (Washington, D.C.: U.S. Government Printing Office, December 9, 1959) , p. 58. (Hereafter referred to as the *Johns Hopkins Report, 1959.*) This study was prepared at the request of the Committee on Foreign Relations, United States Senate by the Washington Center of Foreign Policy Research, The Johns Hopkins University. The Director of the study was Arnold Wolfers with Mr. James E. King, Jr., and Mr. Paul H. Nitze assisting. Miss Ellen Guild and Mr. William Burden, Jr., Research Assistants of the Center also assisted in the preparation of the study.

54. Shipley, "Life and Death Debate over Missile Program," p. 119.

existing SAC bases. Once all of the projected Titans were operational, it would take a Russian missile salvo of 1500 missiles to destroy them.[55]

This encouraging view of long-run American security did not answer the problems of the immediate future of the deterrent posture of the United States in view of Soviet missile progress. Two new elements of national defense gained added attention when the problem was viewed in this context—the early warning and alert system of SAC against enemy attack, and the development of a more diversified force in the form of a submarine launched missile capable of striking the Soviet Union. The former was essential to prevent SAC from being destroyed on the ground and the latter was believed to be an almost invulnerable retaliatory system.

The question of ground or airborne alert systems was shrouded in secrecy and produced many conflicting reports. As seen above in 1957 the "airborne alert" had been declared an existing reality that guarenteed American retaliation in the event of a surprise attack. In testimony before the Senate Preparedness Subcommittee, the Vice Chairman of Staff for the United States Air Force had contended that the United States had 12 percent of the Strategic Air Command on "airborne alert."[56] Early in 1959, it was reported that the United States had between four and six percent of the Strategic Air Command on "airborne alert" (around 100 bombers).[57] If an "airborne alert" did exist at the start of 1959, and this appeared doubtful, it apparently was stopped by Secretary of De-

---

55. *The Johns Hopkins Report, 1959*, p. 58. For the sake of perspective on the missile gap question, it should be pointed out that these Titan missiles were programmed to be operational before the period of supposed "maximum danger" in 1962–1963.

56. U.S. Congress, Senate, Committee on Armed Services, Preparedness Subcommittee *Hearing*, 85th Cong., Vol. 2, pt. 1 (November-December 1957), testimony by General Curtis LeMay, p. 908.

57. Richard H. Rovere, "Letter from Washington," *The New Yorker*, Vol. 34 (February 14, 1959), p. 108.

fense McElroy in January of that year.[58] When Secretary
McElroy testified before the *Joint Hearings* in January of
that year, he stated unequivocally that the United States
did not "have an airborne alert."[59]

Evidently it was believed that the several hundred SAC
bombers on 15 minute "ground alert" were sufficient to
deter a surprise Soviet attack. The dispersal of these bases
and their various ranges from the Soviet Union led to the
conviction that the coordination of a successful Russian attack on all of these bases simultaneously was next to impossible. However, it was pointed out that as the number
of Russian ICBMs increased, the establishment of a better
American warning system against missile attack became
essential. This need was to be met by the construction of
the Air Force Ballistic Missile Early Warning System
(BMEWS).[60]

For several years United States Navy spokesmen had
been warning the nation of the possible missile threat
from Soviet submarines and had called for increased
appropriations for the American antisubmarine warfare
capability and the development of submarine launched
missiles. By the summer of 1959, it was generally admitted
that the Soviet Union had successfully launched a ballistic
missile from a surfaced submarine. It was predicted that
within several years, (by 1961), the Soviet Union would
have operational ballistic missiles that could be submarine
launched.[61]

In this particular field of missile development, it appeared that the United States was ahead of the Soviet
Union. The Navy's *Polaris* missile had been under develop-

---

58. *The New York Times*, January 31, 1959.

59. *Joint Hearings*, 1959, p. 38. In an Airborne Alert a certain number
of long-range bombers would be kept constantly in the air, ready to
retaliate in the case of an enemy attack.

60. *The Johns Hopkins Report*, 1959, p. 54.

61. *The New York Times*, news analysis by Hanson W. Baldwin,
June 23, 1959; *The New York Times*, article quoting Admiral Arleigh
A. Burke, Chief of Naval Operations, August 18, 1959.

ment for several years and was ahead of its original operational schedule. The initial version of this missile could be fired at a range of about 1500 miles from a submerged submarine. The United States Navy planned on having one *Polaris* submarine with 16 missiles operational by the fall of 1960, four more submarines by July 1961, and at least four more by the end of 1963.[62]

The Navy's *Polaris* missile system promised to strengthen substantially the United States deterrent position when it became operational. The dispersal and concealment inherent in this system were ideal characteristics for the invulnerable retaliatory force desired by the United States. In spite of the potential effectiveness of this weapons system, the Navy's *Polaris* program (along with various Army programs) became embroiled in the strong competition with the Air Force for defense budget funds.

This continued rivalry among the American military services helped to sustain the almost constant debate over United States defense policies. There were many aspects to this controversy, but the foundation for the conflict was the struggle for allocations of the available resources. The Eisenhower Administration had established $40 billion a year as a guideline for national defense expenditures. This guideline made the military services competitors for a fixed number of dollars available for national defense spending.[63] From 1955 to 1959, the individual services had received the following percentages of the defense budget: 46 percent for the Air Force, 28 percent for the Navy and Marine Corps, and 23 percent for the Army.[64] The increased costs of the missile and nuclear age placed a great deal of pressure on all three military services to obtain a larger percentage of the defense appropriation. The relatively fixed nature of the defense budget accentuated the interservice struggle for funds and was one of the

62. *The Johns Hopkins Report, 1959*, p. 56.
63. Taylor, *The Uncertain Trumpet*, p. 105.
64. *Ibid.*, pp. 65–66. (See Appendix B.)

prime causes of the service rivalry which undermined national confidence in America's military programs.[65]

The struggle by the various services for additional funds was conducted, as in past years, in accordance with their concepts of the nature of a future war and the forces needed to deal with this threat. Therefore, the debate dealt mainly with the military doctrine accepted by the services and the weapons systems they believed were needed to fulfill the requirements of this doctrinaire approach (see Chapter I).

The exact terminology on military doctrine used by the military services varied throughout the period under discussion. The Air Force continued to take the position that a massive nuclear deterrent was the best means for maintaining world peace (variations on the so-called doctrine of "massive retaliation"), while the Army and the Navy contended that the United States needed a more flexible capability that could be used in response to a variety of types of aggression.[66]

This difference of doctrine was reflected in the statements made by the spokesmen for the military services. The Chief of Naval Operations, Admiral Arleigh A. Burke, stated unequivocally that the United States "has the ability right now, in being, to destroy the Soviet Union several times over." Admiral Burke further contended that the United States would remain ahead of the Soviet Union in strategic retaliatory power.[67] Later, Admiral Burke stated that the United States had too much retaliatory power and that more money should be put into the development of a limited war capability.[68] At the same time, the United States Chairman of the Joint Chiefs of

65. *Ibid.*, p. 105.

66. Taylor, *The Uncertain Trumpet*, p. 58.

67. *The New York Times*, text of speech by Admiral Burke to the Charleston, South Carolina Chamber of Commerce, February 21, 1959.

68. *The New York Times*, text of released, secret testimony given before the House Appropriations subcommittee on Defense Spending, March 31, 1959.

Staff, Maxwell Taylor, said substantially the same thing and declared that the United States had an "excess number of strategic weapons" in its atomic retaliatory force.[69]

While the Army and Navy requested a more flexible military capability in response to various types of possible aggression, some Air Force spokesmen indicated that the "surface" defense budget could be cut by as much as 50 percent without endangering the military security of the United States.[70] The Air Force continued to emphasize the importance of strategic bombing; Air Force leaders admitted that "our margin of deterrence" was adequate at the time, but stated that it was deteriorating and that more B-52's, B-58's and Atlas missiles were needed and needed quickly.[71]

On a more specific level, where there was some agreement on the need to fulfill a given mission, the interservice conflict tended to center on the controversy between the Army's desire to have sole responsibility for continental defense against bomber attack and the Air Force's equally vehement demand for this role. The conflict over the development of the Army's *Nike-Hercules* anti-aircraft surface to air missile versus the Air Force's *Bomarc* replaced the older *Jupiter-Thor* controversy.[72] The Air Force was also in conflict with the Navy over the development of the Navy's *Polaris* missile system and overall role of the Navy in providing part of the strategic deterrent power of the United States.[73]

As the military services of the United States conducted their continuous struggle for appropriations, substantial

---

69. *Ibid.* Later there appeared to be some contradictions in General Taylor's position. In his book, *The Uncertain Trumpet*, he had admitted (p. 131) that the "missile gap" existed.

70. Brigadier General Bonner Fellers, "Where We Stand," *Air Force*, Vol. 42 (March 1959), p. 48.

71. *The New York Times*, news article quoting General Thomas S. Power, Commanding Officer, Strategic Air Command, April 6, 1959.

72. *The New York Times*, June 12, 1959.

73. *The New York Times*, April 17, 1959.

evidence accumulated to indicate that the Soviet Union had run into difficulty in its missile development program. Between August 1957 and April 1958 the Soviet Union had tested six ICBMs; but by March 1959—eleven months later— the Soviets had test fired only one additional ICBM. Secretary of Defense McElroy stated that the Russians had fallen short of producing a "gap" and complained of "widespread misconceptions" as to whether the United States was losing the missile race.[74] In the view of continued difficulties of the Soviet missile program, the Secretary of Defense stated that the United States and the Soviet Union would have operational ICBMs at about the same time.[75]

One of the military men who had been characterized as a critic of the Eisenhower Administration missile program made several statements that added further credence to the belief that the Soviet Union had not progressed as rapidly as originally predicted. This critic, General Bernard Schriever, contended that there was no question that the United States and the Soviet Union were in the same state of missile development.[76]

A recognized foreign missile and aircraft expert, Asher Lee, agreed with this analysis and contended that the missile race was "nip and tuck" at this stage and that the Soviets were running into difficulty in their missile program due to the need to switch to second generation solid

74. "Missiles: Ours and Russias," *Newsweek*, Vol. 54 (July 13, 1959), p. 52; *The New York Times*, news article by Hanson W. Baldwin, March 25, 1959.

75. *The New York Times*, June 28, 1959. At the time, it was not possible to determine if the Soviet Union had run into difficulty with its missile program or if it had decided not to mass produce the unsophisticated first generation missiles and to move on to the second generation. This question is dealt with in detail in the conclusions of this paper.

76. *The New York Times*, quoting Air Force Ballistic Missile Chief, General Bernard Schriever, July 30, 1959; *Ibid.*, October 7, 1959; "The Pushbutton Comes of Age," *Newsweek*, Vol. 52 (December 1, 1959), quoting General Schriever, p. 19.

fuel missiles. This observer stated that the Russians might gain an unimportant, temporary lead in ICBMs, but that no "missile gap" would develop if the United States continued its existing missile programs. Mr. Lee believed that even with a minor Soviet lead in first generation ICBMs, this force would not threaten the retaliatory forces of the United States due to its limited number and restricted accuracy.[77]

The United States also had difficulties with its missile programs during 1959. In June of that year, the Secretary of Defense admitted that the last five American *Atlas* tests had failed and that the date when the *Atlas* was scheduled to become operational was delayed.[78]

In spite of these difficulties in missile development by both of the major military powers, on September 2, 1959, the United States government declared the Atlas ICBM operational and the first Atlas squadron of 10 missiles was turned over to the Strategic Air Command. The American government conceded that the Soviet Union had a similar ICBM capability operational. By the end of the month both sides had approximately 10 operational ICBMs and the age of the intercontinental ballistic missile became a reality.[79]

The advent of the missile age, even the relatively unsophisticated operational first generation missiles, raised serious questions for United States policy makers and created an element of instability in the deterrent situation during these early years of missile development.[80] So long as the operational missiles on both sides appeared to be firststrike weapons, each side remained uncertain as to its potential enemy's intent and capabilities.

77. "The Soviet Air and Rocket Forces," *U.S. News and World Report*, Vol. 47 (July 20, 1959) , pp. 46–48. (An interview conducted with British missile expert Asher Lee.)

78. *The New York Times*, July 27, 1959.

79. *The New York Times*, September 2, 1959; "The U.S. is about Even with Soviet Russia in Military Missiles," *U.S. News and World Report*, Vol. 47 (September 28, 1959) , p. 63.

80. *The Johns Hopkins Report, 1959*, p. 108.

The closed nature of the Soviet society and the difficulties involved in obtaining complete and valid intelligence on Soviet missile sites created a substantial amount of uncertainty in United States government circles, even among the major spokesmen of the Eisenhower Administration.[81] Immediately after his resignation as Secretary of Defense, Mr. McElroy made the following statement in response to a question of the degree of American military risk involved in projected Soviet and American missile programs:

I don't say there will be [a risk], but there can be. If Russia builds what it could, and we build what we intend, they will have more missile capability for the period 1961, 1962, and maybe 1963 than we will have.[82]

This statement was heralded as the Administration's confirmation of the risk of the "missile gap." However, Mr. McElroy clearly stated at the same time that the United States was prepared for either a nuclear or non-atomic war.[83]

Throughout 1959, President Eisenhower had been under severe attack by his defense critics for not removing the $40 billion guideline he had placed on defense spending. The critics contended that the nuclear age required an increase in appropriations and criticized President Eisenhower for his failure to increase the defense budget. Once again, the President attempted to reassure the American people of the basic deterrent strength of the United States. In response to critics who demanded an increase in

81. U.S. Congress, House, Committee on Appropriations, *Hearings* on Fiscal Year 1960 Defense Budget, 86th Cong., 1st sess., Vol. 9 (February 17, 1959), testimony by General Thomas D. White, Air Force Chief of Staff, speaking of the difficulties in obtaining accurate information on enemy missile sites, p. 840.
82. "Big Cut in U.S. Defense Spending," *U.S. News and World Report*, Vol. 47 (December 14, 1959), p. 45. (On December 1, 1959 Secretary of Defense McElroy resigned and was replaced by Thomas S. Gates, Jr., *The New York Times*, December 2, 1959.
83. *Ibid.*

defense spending, he responded with a statement that later became politically controversial as well as relatively famous when he said: "Be not the first by which the new is tried, nor yet the last to lay the old aside."[84]

As 1959 came to an end, *The Johns Hopkins Report* attempted to sum up the overall deterrent posture of the United States and presented a relatively well-balanced analysis of the existing situation derived from unclassified sources. It reported that the advent of the missile age had made the manned bomber forces of a nation highly vulnerable to a surprise attack by the side that first achieved a comprehensive missile capability. The *Report* claimed that the Soviet Union would be the first to achieve this capability and that even an acceleration of the United States missile program could not prevent this if the Soviet Union decided to employ its full capability in missile production. However, the *Report's* summary ended on a fairly optimistic note.[85] After it admitted the possibility that the estimates of Soviet missile production could turn out to be as exaggerated as those estimates made three years earlier about Russian bomber production, the *Report* concluded that the unprecedented level of destruction an aggressor must expect to suffer in a thermonuclear exchange was still the principal stabilizing factor in the strategic equation and was "likely to remain so for the decade ahead."[86]

---

84. *The New York Times*, text of President Eisenhower's news conference, December 3, 1959. Later in the controversy, this attitude was criticized by Senator John Kennedy in his effort to defeat his Republican opponent for the presidency in 1960.

85. *The Johns Hopkins Report, 1959*, p. 57.

86. *Ibid.*, p. 8.

5

POLITICAL PARTISANSHIP AND THE AMERICAN INTELLIGENCE COMMUNITY: 1960

THE YEAR 1960 WAS A PRESIDENTIAL ELECTION YEAR IN THE United States. Even after eight years of the publicly popular Eisenhower Administration, Democratic Party leaders still felt they had a good chance to win the presidency. President Eisenhower was barred by law from seeking a third term and the American public did not have the affection for his heir apparent, Vice-President Richard M. Nixon, that they had for President Eisenhower. Thus, there was no dearth of candidates for the Democratic nomination for the presidency. Before the Democratic convention finished its business in the summer of 1960, at least five men had been seriously considered for the Democratic nomination. Of these five, three played important roles in the development of the "missile gap" thesis in the United States. These three potential Democratic candidates were: Senator Stuart Symington, Senator John F. Kennedy, and the Senate Majority Leader Lyndon B. Johnson. The two remaining candidates—Senator Hubert H. Humphrey and Adlai Stevenson—did not participate to any great degree in the defense debate that persisted in the United States throughout the campaign.

The controversy over the possibility of a "missile gap" and the accompanying charges that the Eisenhower Ad-

ministration had failed to maintain a secure United States
defense posture and American military prestige abroad
became one of the major issues of the 1960 Presidential
campaign. However, this was only one of several major
issues in this campaign and its importance should be
studied with this in mind in order to avoid a serious
distortion of the overall issues in the presidential campaign of 1960.

Well before the 1960 campaign began, the Democratic
critics of the defense policies of the Eisenhower Administration had objected to the manner in which the President
ran the defense efforts of the United States (see above).
As early as January 1959, Senator Kennedy announced his
dissatisfaction with the military policy of the Eisenhower
Administration and expressed his disagreement with the
intelligence estimates on Soviet ICBM strength.[1] Later in
the same year he indicated his continued dissatisfaction
with the United States as the second strongest military
power in the world, and went on to call the upcoming
election in November 1960 the most important election
in the history of the United States.[2]

Throughout 1959 the criticism from Senator Symington, Senator Johnson, and the Democratic Advisory Committee was continuous and sharp.[3]

Early in 1960 as the Democratic presidential hopefuls
began to develop their campaign strategies and issues for
the election, the mass media continued to provide oppor-
tunities for public expression of those who claimed a

---

1. *The New York Times*, January 17, 1959.
2. *Ibid.*, September 28, 1959.
3. *The New York Times*, March 11, 1959; *Ibid.*, September 28, 1959;
Ibid., October 18, 1959. (All of these articles quoted Senator Symington
as attacking the defense policies of the Eisenhower Administration);
The New York Times, October 12, 1959 (Associated Press article that
quoted Senator Johnson as critical of American defense policy); *Ibid.*,
article quoting the Democratic Advisory Committee when it called for
a "crash program" to bridge the "missile gap," June 17, 1959.

missile gap existed.[4] The estimates of Russian ICBM strength presented in these news sources varied from a three to one advantage to a Russian lead of six to one over the United States in ICBMs.[5] One major newspaper columnist devoted a series of five articles in *The New York Herald Tribune* expounding the "missile gap" theme and appeared to have added substantially to the belief in the missile crises facing the United States.[6] Added to the increased alarm in the mass media were the voices of several prominent civilian experts on national defense and United States foreign policy. A number of these observers published lengthy works that accepted the "missile gap" as a reality for the immediate future.[7]

While the proponents of the "missile gap" thesis continued to develop their case for the existence of a Russian missile advantage in the future, President Eisenhower began to lay the foundation for his defense of United States military security policies and his budget for fiscal 1961. Under the title of "Pentagon Study to Minimize Fear over Missile Gap," *The New York Times* indicated that the President had ordered a Pentagon study to answer his critics and prepare for the upcoming attacks resulting from the annual Congressional investigations into United States defense posture.[8]

---

4. "The Age of Damocles," *The New Republic* (editorial), Vol. 142 (January 18, 1960), p. 4.

5. Frank Gibney, "The Missile Mess," *Harper's Magazine,* Vol. 220 (January 1960), p. 38.

6. *The New York Herald Tribune,* series of articles by Joseph Alsop, beginning January 24, 1960.

7. Kissinger, *The Necessity for Choice.* (This work was originally published in 1960 and accepted the "missile gap" as "unavoidable" for the period 1961–1965 as one of its basic premises), p. 27; John W. Spanier, *American Foreign Policy since World War II* (revised edition) (New York: Frederick A. Praeger, 1962). (The first edition of this book was published in 1960 and accepted the missile gap at the time for 1961–1962 and interestingly, when the revised edition came out in 1962, it still accepted the missile gap as an existing reality), p. 169.

8. *The New York Times,* news article by Jack Raymond, "Pentagon Study to Minimize Fear of Missile Gap," January 11, 1960.

President Eisenhower then went on to assure the American people of United States military strength and his belief in the concept of a "balanced forces" military approach to deter Soviet attack. After citing United States progress in missile development (the *Atlas* was operational), the President assured the American public that the United States, with 2100 strategic bombers, was in a secure military position vis-à-vis the Soviet Union.[9]

In addition to this reassurance, President Eisenhower's Budget Message for Fiscal 1961 called for an increase in the number of operational B-52 bomber wings from 11 to 14—an increase in the number of B-52s from 495 to 630.[10]

At the same time that the President attempted to encourage the American public about their military security, an event occurred that seriously damaged the confidence of many Americans in the defense posture of the United States. The Commanding Officer of the Strategic Air Command, General Thomas S. Power, in a speech before the Economic Club of New York, claimed that the 100 American nuclear launching installations virtually could be destroyed by a limited number of Soviet missiles. General Power stated:

> ... it would take an average of three missiles in their current state of development, to give an aggressor a mathematical probability of 95 percent that he can destroy one given soft target some 5,000 miles away. This means that, with only

9. *The New York Times*, text of President Eisenhower's news conference, January 14, 1960; *Ibid.*, January 17, 1960. (This 2100 strategic bombers gave the United States three times as many long-range bombers as the Soviet Union and twice as many medium-range bombers.

10. *The New York Times*, text of President Eisenhower's Fiscal 1961 Budget Message, January 19, 1960. (There were 45 B-52 long-range bombers per wing at this time. The basic appropriations for the military services was to remain approximately the same as it had been since 1955. Of the $40.9 billion to be spent for national defense, the Air Force got $18.6 billion, the Navy $11.6 billion, and the Army $9.3 billion. The Fiscal 1961 budget called for only 50 million dollars more in spending for national defense than the Fiscal 1960 Budget.) *Ibid.*

some 300 ballistic missiles, the Soviets could virtually wipe out our entire nuclear strike capability within a span of thirty minutes.[11]

General Power went on to state that this threat was further heightened by the fact that only half of these Soviet missiles would have to be ICBMs while the remainder could be IRBMs. General Power concluded his foreboding statement when he declared that in view of the fact that Premier Khrushchev claimed that the Soviet Union was producing 250 missiles a year in one factory,[12] the Soviet Union could accumulate the number of missiles needed to destroy SAC before the United States had developed an adequate warning system against missile attack.[13] This speech aroused a tremendous amount of controversy and doubt in the United States and became one of the major elements of controversy discussed in the United States Senate *Joint Hearings, 1960*.[14]

---

11. U.S. Congress, Senate, Committee on Armed Services, Preparedness Investigating Subcommittee in conjunction with the Committee on Aeronautical and Space Sciences, *Joint Hearings*, Missiles Space and other major defense matters, text of General Power's speech before the Economic Club of New York, January 19, 1960, 86th Cong., 2nd sess. (February 2, 3, 4, 8, 9, and March 16, 1960), p. 4 (hereafter referred to as the *Joint Hearings, 1960*). The figures used by General Power in this speech came from an Air Force study done by Dr. Rodney Smith, Chief of Operations Analysis, Headquarters, The Strategic Air Command. Before General Power gave his speech before the Economic Club on January 19, the speech had been submitted to the Pentagon "for clearness as to correctness, policy, and security" approximately one month before the speech was given. General Power claimed that the speech had been approved by the Air Staff, by the Department of Defense, by the Joint Chiefs of Staff and by the State Department. *Joint Hearings, 1960*, p. 13. (This problem will be dealt with in the conclusions of this paper.) Secretary of Defense Gates rejected General Power's analysis as "unrealistic" and "oversimplified." *Joint Hearings, 1960*, p. 14.

12. "News Digest," *Aviation Week*, quoting Premier Khrushchev (November 23, 1959), p. 35.

13. *Ibid.*, pp. 4–5. General Power went on to call for an airborne alert for SAC. This subject will be dealt with below.

14. *The New York Times*, January 20, 1959; *The New York Herald Tribune*, series of five articles on the "missile gap" by Joseph Alsop, beginning January 24, 1960; *The New York Times*, January 29, 1960.

At least one author claimed that General Power's speech signaled the beginning of the "missile gap" and that instantaneously "agitation about the 'missile gap' swept the country."[15] However, the missile controversy had been in existence for several years before this speech and it was too complex and diversified a question to be attributed to any one event or any one man.

Immediately after General Power's speech, another element of uncertainty entered the missile gap controversy. There was already a great deal of confusion surrounding United States intelligence estimates of Soviet missile programs. In testimony before the House Appropriations Subcommittee on Defense Appropriations for Fiscal 1961, the Secretary of Defense, Thomas Gates, increased this uncertainty. In presenting the Eisenhower Administration's new intelligence projections on future Soviet missile strength, Mr. Gates stated:

> Heretofore we have been giving you intelligence figures that dealt with the theoretical Soviet capability. This is the first time that we have an intelligence estimate that says, "This is what the Soviet Union probably will do." Therefore, the great divergence, based on figures that have been testified to in years past, narrow because we talk about a different set of comparisons—ones that we based on Soviet capabilities. This present one is an intelligence estimate on what we believe he [the Soviet Union] probably will do, not what he is capable of doing.[16]

Secretary Gates implied that the predicted three to one Soviet advantage was based on what the Soviet Union *could* produce and not what they *would* produce. He went on to say that the current intelligence estimates did not

15. Fred J. Cook, *The Warfare State* (New York: The Macmillan Company, 1962), pp. 11–12.

16. U.S. Congress, House, Committee on Appropriations, *Hearings Department of Defense Appropriations for 1961*, testimony by Secretary of Defense Thomas Gates, 86th Cong., 2nd sess., pt. 1 (January 1960), p. 23. Testimony referred to above applies to previous "secret" Congressional testimony.

indicate that the Soviet's superiority in ICBMs would be as great as previously predicted.[17] The Secretary of Defense did admit that the Soviet Union would have "moderately more" ICBMs than the United States in the future, but that there was no "deterrent gap."[18]

The Secretary of the Air Force, Dudley C. Sharp, publicly stated essentially the same position as the Secretary of Defense and declared on nationwide television that the predicted three to one "missile gap" would be "considerably smaller" than earlier projections indicated.[19]

Secretary Gates received immediate support from President Eisenhower on the new estimates. The President, in an effort to reduce the criticism of his defense policies, reminded the nation of the earlier fictitious "bomber gap" and the accompanying demands from Congress for more money to fill this supposed gap.[20]

The recently revised intelligence estimates and the new intelligence formula for arriving at them came under immediate attack by key Democratic political figures. Senator Lyndon Johnson declared that the new intelligence formula was "incredibly dangerous" and stated that "the missile gap cannot be eliminated by the mere stroke of a pen."[21] Senator Johnson was joined by his colleague on the Senate Armed Service Committee, Senator Symington. Senator Symington charged the Administration with issuing "misinformation" about the missile gap and claimed that the Eisenhower Administration had changed "the ground rules for evaluating the facts."[22] Senator Syming-

---

17. Ibid., pp. 23–24. The New York Times, [emphasis added] January 20, 1960.

18. The New Yok Times, quoting Mr. Gates, February 1, 1960.

19. Joint Hearings, 1960, reprint of the transcript of Secretary Sharp's interview on Columbia Broadcasting System, "Face the Nation," January 24, 1960, p. 475.

20. The New York Times, text of President Eisenhower's press conference, January 27, 1960.

21. The New York Times, quoting Senator Johnson, January 24, 1960.

22. Ford Eastman, "Gates Defends New Intelligence Concept," Aviation Week, Vol. 72 (February 1, 1960), p. 31.

ton declared vehemently that "the intelligence books have been juggled so the budget books may be balanced."[23]

Throughout this period (late January 1960) the two opposing groups on either side of the missile gap controversy continued to solidify their basic arguments and positions. Most of those involved in the debate at the government level already had such strong commitments that objectivity on their part was open to doubt. A nongovernment expert who was not immediately involved in the controversy attempted to analyze the missile debate. Mr. Hanson W. Baldwin, Military Editor of *The New York Times*, basically supported the position of Secretary Gates and accused the Democrats of trying to make a campaign issue out of supposed United States defense deficiencies. Mr. Baldwin denied that the new estimates were based on Russian "intent" rather than "capability." He contended that they were based upon the fact that the United States knew more about the Soviet production of missiles than American intelligence had known a year earlier. Mr. Baldwin stated that the Soviet Union had only two long-range missile sites and that both of these were testing sites. He concluded his argument when he stated that there was no "deterrent gap" and there were serious doubts about the existence of the "missile gap."[24]

At the end of January 1960 the annual Senate Preparedness *Hearings* began (now the *Joint Hearings, 1960*). These hearings dealt with a multitude of problems concerned with United States national defense policy, but two major issues emerged and the question of the missile gap crystallized around these. The first problem was concerned with United States intelligence estimates on future Soviet missile production and the second dealt with the

23. *The New York Times,* quoting Senator Symington, January 28, 1960.

24. *The New York Times,* news article by Hanson W. Baldwin, January 22, 1960; *Ibid.,* January 23, 1960. Mr. Baldwin identified the two Soviet testing sites as one at Kapustin Yar near Stalingrad (Volgagrad) and one near Tyura Tam near the Aral Sea.

vulnerability of the American strategic retaliatory power when compared to the Soviet first-strike nuclear capability. These two problems were closely related, but for the sake of clarity, they will be dealt with separately at first.

The open sessions of the *Joint Hearings, 1960* began early in February 1960 and were concluded March 16, 1960. Before the hearings were completed an already confused situation became almost chaotic. The testimony before the committee became so confused that at one point the Chairman, Senator Johnson, had to suspend the public hearings temporarily in an attempt to clarify the situation in closed session.[25] Within the Government of the United States there appeared to be at least two sets of intelligence figures on future Soviet missile strength (see below). Some military and political leaders accepted the pessimistic estimates and the other leaders accepted the estimates that showed a more favorable future United States deterrent posture. Outside of the government, attitudes appearing in the mass media reflected the chaos that arose out of the *Joint Hearings, 1960* and those individuals who played partisan politics with national defense policy had more than enough so-called official material to substantiate their cases (or at least enough confusion with the government circles to add substantially to their position's credibility).[26]

The first witness who testified before the Committee was the Director of the Central Intelligence Agency, Mr. Allen Dulles. According to a released, censored version of Mr. Dulles's testimony, he told members of the Joint Committee that the Soviet Union would have an "enormous advantage in missile striking power" over the United

---

25. *The New York Times*, news article by Jack Raymond, February 11, 1960; *Joint Hearings, 1960*, see testimony by General Nathan Twining, Chairman of the Joint Chiefs of Staff, pp. 402–435 (especially pp. 402–412). These hearings were held February 2, 3, 4, 8, and 9, 1960 and then suspended until Secretary of Defense Gates attempted to clarify the situation in the final public hearing on March 16, 1960.

26. These conclusions on this period are intended as an introduction to this confusing series of events and will be cited with references below.

States in the years to come. Specifically, he reportedly testified that the Russians would have a "quantitative and qualitative lead in intercontinental ballistic missiles" in the years to come.[27] Due to the fact that a transcript of Mr. Dulles's testimony was never released, it was impossible to determine with certainty if he actually made these statements. However, later testimony and discussion in the *Joint Hearings, 1960* tended to substantiate the fact that a version of these statements was made by Mr. Dulles.[28]

After Mr. Dulles testified before the Joint Committee, numerous other witnesses testified in open session. From the evidence available, there appeared to be "several" intelligence estimates in circulation among those responsible for the conduct of United States defense policy.[29]

From the statements made at this time there appeared to be at least two sets of intelligence figures originating from two sources presented to the Joint Committee—one from the Central Intelligence Agency presented by Mr. Dulles and one from the Joint Chiefs of Staff presented primarily by General Twining.[30]

---

27. *The New York Times,* "Democrats say CIA Missiles Date Justifies Concern," January 30, 1960.

28. *Joint Hearings, 1960,* pp. 402–412. Several days before Mr. Dulles testified in closed session before the Joint Committee, Secretary of Defense Gates told a closed session of the House Appropriation Committee just the opposite with regard to the future of United States defense posture, See above, Ford Eastman, *Aviation Week,* p. 31.

29. *Joint Hearings, 1960,* testimony by Major General J. J. Walsh, Headquarters, Chief of Intelligence, U.S. Air Force, General Walsh stated that there were "several" intelligence estimates, p. 114; *Ibid.,* testimony by General Nathan Twining, Chairman, The Joint Chiefs of Staff, pp. 402–412.

30. *Ibid.* The possibility also existed that there was a third estimate originating from the United States Air Force. Testimony by an Air Force spokesman indicated that the National Intelligence Estimates was not accepted by this branch of the service of the military. *Ibid.,* pp. 115–116. The National Intelligence Estimate was produced by the National Intelligence Board which consisted of the Director of the Central Intelligence Agency as Chairman, and representatives of the Air Force, Navy, Army, the Atomic Energy Commission, The Federal Bureau of

The last person to testify before the Joint Committee was adjourned for a month was the Chairman of the Joint Chiefs of Staff, General Nathan Twining. It was his testimony which forcefully indicated the possibility that there was more than one basic intelligence estimate circulating within the government. It immediately became evident that General Twining had not seen all of the charts from the National Intelligence Estimate or that he was using different figures than those presented by Mr. Dulles. From this point on, the *Joint Hearings, 1960*[31] deteriorated to the point of being incomprehensible on this question, even to those directly involved.

While the Joint Committee's public hearings were adjourned, the Director of the CIA, Mr. Dulles, was recalled to testify in closed session in an attempt to clarify the situation.[32] However, it was later reported that Mr. Dulles's second appearance before the Joint Committee had failed to clear up the confusion surrounding the various sets of intelligence figures.[33]

Several days later, Secretary of Defense Gates attempted to end the confusion and claimed that no information had been withheld from General Twining or the Department of Defense by the Central Intelligence Agency. He further contended that the confusion arose from old 1958 estimates and how they had been made. Secretary Gates concluded:

What General Twining had not seen was the revised form

Investigation, the State Department and the National Security Agency. *The New York Times*, February 11, 1960. From the testimony given at the *Joint Hearings, 1960*, it was not possible to tell whether General Twining or Mr. Dulles gave the National Intelligence Estimates (or if either one of them did).

31. *Ibid.*, pp. 402–412. This session, held on February 9, 1960, was the last open session of the Committee held in February. When it reconvened on March 19 in open session, it heard testimony from Secretary of Defense Gates and then adjourned for the year (see below).

32. *The New York Times*, February 10, 1960.

33. *The New York Times*, February 25, 1960.

in which the 1958 information was presented to the Committee. It represented no change in any intelligence estimates and no one could seriously believe that it did.[34]

The exact situation in early 1960 was impossible to determine due to the highly classified nature of the material involved. However, certain basic questions on this matter were answered partially by later testimony and evidence that became available at a later date. The Chief of Naval Operations, Admiral Arleigh Burke, told the *Joint Hearings, 1960* that the new United States intelligence estimates were based on Soviet missile production rather than the maximum capability of the Soviet Union to produce missiles. Admiral Burke contended that American intelligence estimates were revised because the American intelligence community had more accurate data on existing Soviet missile programs. Admiral Burke concluded: "It was obvious Russia wasn't exercising her maximum capability."[35] When Admiral Burke was challenged by Senator Symington on the higher figures given by Mr. Dulles to the Committee in closed session, he replied that the subject was too sensitive to be discussed in open session; and he restated his belief that the new estimates were not based on "intent" but on Russian programs and therefore were more realistic estimates.[36]

The final public testimony before the *Joint Hearings, 1960* was given March 16 by the Secretary of Defense, Thomas Gates, in an effort to clear up the apparent chaos that surrounded the missile controversy. Secretary Gates began his testimony with a strong assertion of United States deterrent power and stated that "any surprise attack upon the United States would result in unacceptable

---

34. *The New York Times*, "Pentagon Forms a 'Truth Squad' to Rebut Critics," news article by Jack Raymond, February 28, 1960.

35. *Joint Hearings, 1960* testimony by the Chief of Naval Operations, pp. 293–294.

36. *Ibid.*, pp. 294–295. It was not possible to discover which set of figures was being used by Admiral Burke.

destruction to the attacker." The Secretary of Defense then attempted to answer the critics of the government on the confusion surrounding present intelligence estimates. Mr. Gates stated that last year the National Intelligence Estimate on the number of Soviet ICBMs was calculated to cover either one of two possibilities. The first was based on the premise that the Soviet Union would pursue an "orderly" ICBM production program. The second assumed that the Soviet Union would pursue a highly accelerated or "crash" program. During the past year the United States had obtained additional information on the Soviet missile program and this information indicated that the Soviet Union was not engaged in a "crash" program to build first generation ICBMs. The new estimates, therefore, were based on an "orderly" Soviet Union missile production program.[37] When the Secretary of Defense was questioned on the alleged fact that General Twining had not seen all of the intelligence figures available, Mr. Gates stated that General Twining had seen all of the important intelligence information and that the information he had not seen "was not an essential element of intelligence."[38]

37. *Joint Hearings, 1960,* testimony by Secretary of Defense Thomas Gates (March 16, 1960), pp. 441–442.

38. *Ibid.,* p. 442. This testimony did a great deal to help clarify the situation, although it did not succeed completely. It appeared that until the Eisenhower Administration had ruled out the possibility of a "crash" program of Soviet missile production, there were two sets of intelligence figures–one for a "crash" program and one for an "orderly" program. Once this was done, there was only one set of figures for future Soviet missile strength and the evidence indicates that this was the set used by General Twining. Later, Allen Dulles confirmed this fact and wrote that the Soviet Union chose to rely on a more "orderly" building program of ICBMs, relying on the next generation of improved ICBMs to provide the Soviet Union with its basic ICBM capability. (Dulles, *The Craft of Intelligence,* p. 165.) The exact situation that caused the confusion on intelligence estimates early in 1960 still had not been clarified completely in 1966. The most authoritative statement made on the situation came from Mr. Eisenhower several years after he left office when he wrote: "By January of 1960 new intelligence reports narrowed to almost negligibility the extent of the Soviet lead in long-range and sea-launched missiles; this lead would soon disappear."

Finally, Secretary of Defense Gates stated that President Eisenhower and the Joint Chiefs of Staff substantially agreed that the United States deterrent force was sufficient to destroy any aggressor, even after a surprise first strike on the United States with nuclear weapons.[39]

The question of the strategic vulnerability of United States retaliatory power was debated concurrently with the uncertainty over American intelligence figures on future Soviet missile strength. These two questions were closely related and confusion on one of them inevitably led to confusion and misunderstanding on the other. Earlier in 1960, the discussion of American strategic vulnerability had been intensified by General Power's speech of January 19, 1960 (see above) and the *Joint Hearings, 1960* explored this subject in some detail. The combination of General Power's contention that 300 Russian missiles could destroy the Strategic Air Command and the high degree of uncertainty as to how many missiles the Soviet Union was in the process of producing added substantially to the complexity and importance of the missile gap controversy.[40]

Some of the key military and civilian personnel in the United States government once again disagreed on the basic requirements for future United States security.

The SAC Commander, General Power, believed that for the moment the Strategic Air Command was "the most powerful military force in the history of the world" and was a powerful deterrent to Soviet aggression.[41] However, he declared that he was not satisfied with the progress

---

Eisenhower, *Waging the Peace,* p. 390.) The conclusions of this paper will deal in detail with some of the questions raised by the confusion that surrounded this period of American intelligence efforts as reported in public sources.

39. *Joint Hearings, 1960,* pp. 479–480.

40. It is worth noting at this time that Secretary of Defense Gates rejected General Power's analysis as "unrealistic" and "oversimplified." *Joint Hearings, 1960,* p. 14.

41. *Joint Hearings, 1960,* p. 23.

being made by the United States to protect this force from destruction in the future. In order to accomplish this task, General Power called for an immediate large-scale airborne alert, the production of more long-range bombers, and the development of funds for the new B-70 strategic bomber.[42] To institute even the airborne alert envisioned by General Power, the cost was estimated at $700 million for the first year and an additional one billion dollars for each additional year.[43] Nonetheless, Lieutenant General Bernard Schriever supported General Power's call for an airborne alert, though he showed no enthusiasm for General Power's other suggestions.[44]

Among those opposing the airborne alert were not only officers of the Army and Navy, but also spokesmen for the United States Air Force. The Air Force Chief of Staff, General Thomas White, stated that the United States did not need an immediate airborne alert, but should make the preparations necessary should one ever be needed.[45] The Chairman of the Joint Chiefs of Staff, General Twining (a career Air Force Officer), stated his case in even stronger language and contended that an airborne alert "would be wasted."[46]

Closely connected with the alleged need for an airborne alert was the question of how much warning time the Strategic Air Command would receive in the event of a surprise attack by the Soviet Union. In General Power's opinion the existing 15 minute ground alert offered sufficient warning time against a surprise bomber attack, but

42. *Ibid.*, p. 21, 36. General Power did admit by implication, under intense questioning, that the Soviet Union had only one ICBM base operational at the time. *Ibid.*, pp. 25, 49.
43. *Ibid.*, testimony by the United States Air Force Chief of Staff, General Thomas D. White, p. 152.
44. *Ibid.*, testimony by General Bernard Schriever, Commander, Air Research and Development Command, United States Air Force, p. 75.
45. *Ibid.*, p. 124.
46. *Ibid.*, p. 386. General Twining did indicate that the new budget provided for a "very limited airborne alert" for the next year, although it would be nothing like the size requested by General Power. *Ibid.*, p. 385.

was not sufficient in the event of a Soviet missile attack.[47] Therefore, General Power called for an improved early warning system against a missile attack on the United States. On this point, there was fundamental agreement by both military and civilian leaders. General Schriever pointed out that the SAMOS reconnaissance satellite and MIDAS early warning satellite systems were receiving the highest priority.[48] Also, the Ballistic Missile Early Warning system was scheduled to go partly into effect later in 1960.[49]

The strongest defense of the United States existing and future deterrent posture that was made during the *Joint Hearings, 1960,* came from the Chief of Naval Operations, Admiral Arleigh Burke. In the midst of what appeared to be an incredibly complex and confusing situation, Admiral Burke bluntly challenged General Power's thesis that 300 Russian missiles could destroy the United States retaliatory forces. Admiral Burke pointed out the significant fact that since it was extremely difficult at this stage of missile development to get one missile to fire at a specific time, it was impossible to launch a salvo of 300 missiles that would arrive at designated targets at the same time (even if the Soviet Union had 300 missiles).[50] Admiral Burke stated in the most forceful terms possible the present and future deterrent posture of the United States:

---

47. *Ibid.,* p. 4.

48. *Ibid.,* p. 60.

49. *Ibid.,* p. 80. It should also be kept in mind that the U–2 had been flying intelligence missions over the Soviet Union since at least 1956 and United States radar stations had been monitoring Soviet missile tests since the same date (see above).

50. *Ibid.,* p. 315. The difficulties of launching a large number of missiles in salvo referred to by Admiral Burke existed in 1960. However, the advent of numerous more sophisticated second generation missiles would reduce these difficulties considerably in the future. Admiral Burke also pointed out that the United States Navy had over 200 attack aircraft on carriers capable of carrying nuclear weapons and by the end of 1960 the Navy would have two submarines capable of launching 16 Polaris missiles each, and that neither of these elements were considered in General Power's estimates. *Ibid.,* p. 320.

We have the ability now, right now, to destroy any enemy that wants to attack us or does attack us, regardless of what it [the enemy] does, or when it does, or how it does it or anything else.[51]

Logically, the confusion and contradiction that arose within the *Joint Hearings, 1960* were reflected by the press in its reporting to the American public. Early in February, a *New York Times* editorial declared that the division among the military had caused "bewilderment in Congress and the country." This newspaper attempted to pinpoint the reasons for this confusion and listed interservice rivalry, confusion within the intelligence community, and personal rivalry within the military as the prime causes. In spite of the admitted confusion and lack of certainty on the United States deterrent posture, the editorial indicated that the Soviet Union would have a clear lead over the United States in ICBMs in the future and gave the following figures on future United States-Soviet missile strength to support this contention:[52]

	United States ICBMs	Soviet Union ICBMs
Feb. 1960	3	10
June 1960	18	38
June 1961	40–50	140–200
1963	200	500

51. *Ibid.*, p. 313. Although the question of interservice rivalry has not been dealt with specifically at this time, the conflict continued throughout the *Joint Hearings, 1961*. See testimony by Admiral Burke, pp. 314–316 on his belief that a limited war was more likely than general all–out war for the next five years and the need for military forces to fight this war; also, testimony by General Lyman L. Lemnitzer, Army Chief of Staff, p. 268; testimony by retired General Maxwell D. Taylor, pp. 186, 221 and the Air Force testimony throughout most of the hearings.

52. *The New York Times*, editorial, February 7, 1960. At the same time, *Time* magazine printed figures that were substantially the same ("The Coming Missile Gap," *Time*, Vol. 75 February 8, 1960), p. 18. It is worth noting that these figures represented a substantial downward revision from 1959 of the public estimates of the comparative future missile strength of the two powers that were presented to the public a year earlier (see Appendix A).

The popular periodical press intensified its coverage of the defense debate and gave the outward appearance of having penetrated the existing confusion and found the correct answer to the question on the future of American national security. Representatives of both the so-called "liberal" and "conservative" periodical press expressed the belief that the alleged future "missile gap" was a reality and accused President Eisenhower of taking a "desperate gamble" with the future of United States military security.[53] Another periodical accused the President of a "complacency gap" and called for more funds for national defense.[54]

The apparent lack of decisiveness and the contradictions within government circles immediately stimulated a lively political verbal exchange between the Republican supporters of the Administration's defense policies and critical Democrats, including the three potential Democratic presidential candidates for 1960. In an effort to preempt the Democratic attacks on the Administration's defense policies, the Republican National Committee attacked Senator Symington and his past role as the Secretary of the Air Force under President Truman. Simultaneously Sen-

---

53. "Dollars and Defense," *Commonweal*, Vol. 71 (February 5, 1960), p. 514. The only major periodical (except for *The Nation*) to negate the missile gap during this period was *U.S. News and World Report;* see: "It's Russia's Turn to Worry About the Missile Gap," Vol. 48 (February 22, 1960), p. 45; and "The Truth about Missiles," Vol. 48 (February 29, 1960), p. 42.

54. "TRB from Washington," *The New Republic,* Vol. 142 (February 15, 1960), p. 2. This same periodical attacked the Administration earlier in the month in an editorial entitled: "Defense Facts and Fancy," Vol. 142 (February 1, 1960), p. 3; *Life* magazine also ran an editorial that attacked the Eisenhower Administration's budget and predicted a future "missile gap" ("Needed: A Mightier Sword," *Life,* Vol. 48 (February 18, 1960), p. 32; *The Reporter* ran an article by Thomas R. Philipps that was highly critical of the Administration and its missile programs. (Thomas R. Philipps, "The Great Guessing Game," *The Reporter,* Vol. 22, February 28, 1960), p. 26; and the semiofficial Air Force magazine printed an article critical of the existing national defense programs. Claude Witze, "Can the Airborn Alert Prevent a Space Age Pearl Harbor," *AIR FORCE,* Vol. 42 (March 11, 1960), p. 33.

ator Everett Dirksen (Senate Minority Leader, Republican-Illinois) accused the Democrats of leaking national security information from the *Joint Hearings* and Senator Leverett Saltonstall (Republican-Massachusetts) used the adequacy of the "mixed forces" concept of the Administration to forestall criticism.[55]

On the Democratic side, Senator Johnson characterized the conflicting statements before the Joint Committee as "baffling" and contended that Russian ability to launch ICBMs was "increasing instead of decreasing" as some Administration spokesmen had contended.[56] The most vehement critic of the Eisenhower Administration's military policies, Senator Stuart Symington, accused the President of misleading the American people and stated: "Above all, they [the American people] are entitled not to be misled by false information."[57]

President Eisenhower's initial reaction to the missile controversy in early February 1960 was one of amazement "about all of this business of catching up."[58] But as the criticism of his Administration increased, the President became angry and called the charges that he had misled the American people "despicable."[59] Two days later the President addressed the nation in an attempt to clear up any misunderstanding that might exist and assured the American people that the United States had forged an "indestructible force of incalculable power."[60]

55. *The New York Times*, quoting the Republican National Committee's publication *Battle Line*, February 11, 1960; *Ibid.*, quoting Senator Dirksen, February 10, 1960; *Ibid.*, quoting Senator Saltonstall, February 20, 1960.

56. *The New York Times*, February 7, 1960; *Ibid.*, February 15, 1960.

57. *The New York Times*, February 20, 1960.

58. *The New York Times*, text of news conference by President Eisenhower, February 7, 1960.

59. *Ibid.*, text of President Eisenhower's news conference, February 18, 1960; *Ibid.*, "Angry President Denies Misled U.S. on Defense," news article by Jack Raymond, February 18, 1960.

60. *The New York Times*, text of speech by President Eisenhower to the Nation, February 22, 1960. Later, President Eisenhower, in *Waging the Peace* charged that the "missile gap" crisis was a "useless piece of

Senator Dirksen continued the Republican counter-attack on the Democratic critics of the Administration and accused them of giving the American nation a distorted picture of United States defense posture and of "assisting the Communist propagandists" by their charges of inadequacy in American national defense programs.[61]

But the Democratic critics were not silenced by these Republican verbal forays. Senator Johnson continued to challenge the Administration's defense programs and to question whether the United States was moving fast enough to meet the growing power of the Soviet Union,[62] while at the same time Senator Symington predicted that Soviet ICBM strength would be from 20 to 50 percent higher in 1960-1962 than had been predicted a year earlier.[63]

Throughout the period of the *Joint Hearings, 1960,* there was a constant flow of partisan debate in the United States over the alleged missile gap. But once these hearings were completed in March of that year the political leaders of both parties appeared to lose interest in the controversy and little was said on the missile question until the 1960 presidential campaign got into full swing later in the summer.

Secretary Gates' testimony on March 16 before the Joint Committee was an attempt to reassure the American people of the existence of a strong American deterrent. The following month the Pentagon released a document intended to re-enforce the government's claim. The Penta-

---

demagoguery" and that it disappeared a month after his successor took office (see below) . (Eisenhower, *Waging the Peace,* p. 390.)

61. *The New York Times,* February 24, 1960.
62. *The New York Times,* February 23, 1960; *Ibid.,* February 24, 1960.
63. *The New York Times,* February 23, 1960. If the figures apparently accepted by Senator Symington in 1959 are used to calculate this predicted estimate by Senator Symington, by 1962 the Soviet Union would have between 1500 and 2500 ICBMs compared to 100—130 ICBMs for the United States during the same period. (See Appendix A and the unrevised 1959 figures.)

gon paper declared that the United States had an over-whelming military superiority over the Soviet Union and once again stated the official government position in its belief that Russia had not embarked upon a "crash" ICBM building program.[64]

In May of 1960 an event occurred that proved very relevant to the missile controversy. The Soviet Union shot down the United States high flying U-2 reconnaissance aircraft that had been flying intelligence missions over the Soviet Union for about four years. The immediate impact of this event was the break-up of the Paris Summit Conference between Premier Khrushchev and President Eisenhower and an increase in East-West tensions. However, beneath the surface acrimony and diplomatic maneuvers was a question of great significance to the missile gap debate. This question involved the accuracy of the photographs taken by the U-2 and the extent to which these photographs revealed accurate intelligence on Soviet missile production and deployment. At the time, President Eisenhower defended the U-2 flights because: "These flights have given us information of great importance to the nation's security. In fact, their success has been nothing short of remarkable."[65] Later an important official in the Kennedy Administration admitted that the U-2 flights had shown that Khrushchev was bluffing and the Russians

64. *The New York Times*, "U.S. says Bombers Provide Big Edge," news article by Jack Raymond, April 10, 1960. It was not clear why the debate died down so quickly. It was possible that the public was satisfied by the strong Administration statements of American security. But it appeared more likely that once the Congressional Hearings were over, the critics lost their major source of information (and misinformation) and their major access to the mass media.

65. *U.S. Department of State Bulletin*, speech by President Eisenhower, June 6, 1960. Several years later, the CIA official in charge of the U-2 program, Raymond Bissel, Jr., stated that "the detail of the photos was so sharp that one could almost read the tail-markings of bombers photographed from a height of 14 miles." (Charles J. V. Murphy, quoting Raymond Bissel, Jr. in "Khrushchev's Paper Bear," *Fortune*, Vol. 70 (December 1964), p. 227.)

were not producing the first generation ICBM in quantity.[66]

Although the downing of the U-2 caused the Eisenhower Administration a great deal of embarrassment and led to an increase in the tensions of the "cold war," it did strengthen the credibility of the Administration's intelligence estimates and increased the acceptance of their validity in the eyes of some of the American public.[67]

To the Soviet Union, the U-2 flights posed a different question. Although the rest of the world hadn't known about the U-2 flights, the leaders of the Soviet Union had known beforehand that the U-2 was flying unmolested over their territory. The problem for Premier Khrushchev was to convince the world of two facts: (1) that the U-2 flights indicated no weakness in the air defenses of the Soviet Union, and (2) that the U-2 had not compromised the secrecy of the supposedly large Soviet missile program. As evidence of the effectiveness of Soviet air defenses, Premier Khrushchev cited the fact that the U-2, which flew even higher than American bombers, had been shot down by these defenses.[68] During May and June of 1960 Premier Khrushchev constantly made statements to the effect that the Soviet Union had "undoubted superiority" over the United States in the modern means of nuclear weapons delivery.[69] Premier Khrushchev also emphasized that the U-2 had photographed only the missile testing

---

66. Theodore C. Sorensen, *Kennedy* p. 611. Mr. Sorenson also indicated that Senator Kennedy had not been given access to the U-2 evidence during the campaign and saw only evidence to indicate a "dangerous situation" militarily for the United States in the year to come. *Ibid.*, p. 612. This problem is dealt with in the conclusions of this paper.

67. Thomes W. Wolfe, *Soviet Strategy at the Crossroads*, p. 32. The author was a member of the Rand Corp. at the time.

68. *Pravda, May 29, 1960. The Current Digest of the Soviet Press,* Vol. 12, No. 22, p. 5.

69. *Pravda,* reprint of a speech by Premier Khrushchev in Vienna, July 8, 1960. *The Current Digest of the Soviet Press,* Vol. 12, No. 27, p. 9.

areas of the Soviet Union and not the "military-strategic rocket bases" of the Soviet Union.[70]

As the excitement over the U-2 affair began to subside, the Republicans and Democrats moved toward their nominating conventions to pick the man they hoped would be the next President of the United States. The conventions were held in July 1960; compared to the excitement over the missile gap the previous winter, the controversy during the early summer was rather quiet and restrained.

Within the Republican party, Nelson Rockefeller, a remote possibility for the Republican nomination, stated that the Russian missiles were superior to those of the United States and warned that SAC was vulnerable to Soviet attack.[71] As it became evident that Richard Nixon was going to be the Republican presidential nominee, the Republicans solidified behind his candidacy and supported the record of the Eisenhower Administration. In accepting the nomination, Mr. Nixon assured the nation that the United States was the strongest military power in the world and would never settle for second best.[72]

The Democrats had a much more closely contested struggle for the Presidential nomination, but the outcome seemed to be based more on personalities and organization than on the issues involved. During the preconvention period Senator Kennedy made several passing references to the "missile gap" and called for stepped-up "development and production of the ultimate missile that can close the gap."[73] But once he obtained the nomination,

70. *Pravda, June 22, 1960, The Current Digest of the Soviet Press,* Vol. 12, No. 25, p. 7.

71. *The New York Times,* text of Nelson Rockefeller's statement on the problems facing the Republican Party in 1960, June 9, 1960.

72. *Ibid.,* text of Richard M. Nixon's acceptance speech to the Republican National Convention, July 29, 1960.

73. *U.S. News and World Report,* partial text of speech by Senator Kennedy before the United States Senate on June 14, 1960, Vol. 148 (June 27, 1960) , p. 64; Senator John F. Kennedy, "Disarmament Can Be Won," *The Bulletin of the Atomic Scientists,* Vol. 16 (June 1960) , p. 218; *The New York Times,* June 15, 1960.

he made no immediate reference in his acceptance speech to the missile crisis but spoke vaguely of the threat from abroad and the challenge of the advancements in technology.[74]

Both party platforms dealt with national defense problems in very general terms and gave no indication of the previous intensity of the national concern over defense policy shown by party leaders.[75]

Interest in the missile controversy appeared to decline during the remainder of the summer. During this period *The New York Times* found very little to report on the missile controversy and the few periodicals that did print articles on the subject once again presented both the pessimistic and optimistic view of the future of United States deterrent posture.[76] Militarily, during this period, the United States successfully tested its *Polaris* missile (*Polaris* A-1—Range 1150 miles) from a submerged submarine and it was indicated that this highly effective deterrent weapons system would become operational the fall of 1960.[77] Later in the summer, the Director of the Navy's *Polaris* system stated that the United States was $2\frac{1}{2}$ to 3

74. *The New York Times,* text of John F. Kennedy's acceptance speech to the Democratic National Convention, July 16, 1960.

75. "Platforms," *The New Republic,* texts of the defense sections of the Republican and Democratic platforms, Vol. 143 (August 8, 1960), pp. 10-11.

76. Of the periodicals that did cover the question, the following article in *Commonweal* was a good example that added credence to the existing belief in the missile gap: "The Pentagon in Politics," *Commonweal,* Vol. 71 (June 22, 1960), article accused the Pentagon of helping the Republicans gloss over the Soviet missile threat, pp. 457–458; while the *Reader's Digest* published a couple of articles that tended to downgrade the Soviet missile threat: Roscoe Drummond, "Our Strength in Being," *Reader's Digest,* Vol. 77 (July 1960), p. 38; Dr. Lee A. DuBridge (President, California Institute of Technology), "Let's Stop Being Defeatist about Defense," *Reader's Digest,* Vol. 77 (July 1960), p. 37; and the following article in *Business Week* added to the growing confidence in the American deterrent posture: "ICBM Speed-up Brings U.S. Gain in Missile Race," *Business Week* (July 2, 1960), p. 8.

77. *The New York Times,* news article by Hanson W. Baldwin, July 21, 1960.

years ahead of the Soviet Union in submarine launched missiles. But, on the whole, the summer remained a quiet one in the field of the debate on national defense policy.[78]

In late August of 1960, the presidential campaign got well under way when Senator Kennedy charged that the United States had lost its military security and declared that "the balance of power is slowly shifting to the Soviet-Red China bloc."[79] This speech signalled the beginning of an intense attack by the Democratic presidential nominee on the defense policies of the Eisenhower Administration that continued until the end of the campaign.[80]

After reassuring the American public of United States military strength, the Republican nominee, Richard Nixon, chose to attack the Democrats and Senator Kennedy rather than substantially answer the criticsm of the Eisenhower Administration. He charged the Democrats with a "past performance as wide as the dangerous missile gap which they handed over to President Eisenhower."[81] In reference to Senator Kennedy's charges, Mr. Nixon called for a halt to the talk of United States weakness and accused the Democratic nominee of being the "spokesman of national disparagement."[82]

---

78. *The New York Times,* August 8, 1960.

79. *The New York Times,* August 27, 1960.

80. *The New York Times,* September 8, 1960; *Ibid.,* September 13, 1960; *Ibid.,* Senator Kennedy called for a crash missile program to close the "missile gap," September 15, 1960. A member of the Kennedy campaign staff claimed that the intelligence information from the U-2 flights was withheld from the Senator and that all the evidence made available to Senator Kennedy indicated that the United States faced a "dangerous situation" in the future. Sorensen, *Kennedy,* p. 612 (see above). Another member of the Kennedy Administration wrote in 1964 that: "It was with honest surprise and relief that in 1961 he [President Kennedy] found the situation much less dangerous than the best evidence available to the Senate the year before." The question of whether Senator Kennedy had complete access to intelligence information before the election will be dealt with in the conclusions. This same charge was made by Senator Symington, *The New York Times,* "Missile Gap Secrecy Charged to GOP," February 10, 1961.

81. *The New York Times,* September 30, 1960.

82. *The New York Times,* September 21, 1960; *Ibid.,* September 22, 1960.

Up to this point in the campaign, both candidates dealt with the missile controversy in general terms and the issue did not appear to have been defined nor did the candidates appear to have clarified the exact questions involved. In October, Senator Kennedy apparently decided that rather than fight the debate strictly on the question of American military weakness and insecurity, he would define the problem as the continued decline of American prestige abroad and in the minds of the American people. Senator Kennedy stated in the simplest language possible that United States "power and prestige in the last eight years has declined."[83] This charge was followed immediately by a clash between Senator Kennedy and Vice-President Nixon in the fourth of their nationwide television debates.[84]

President Eisenhower responded immediately to the charges that the United States had lost prestige under his Administration. He called such charges a "debasement of the truth" and accused the Democrats of "frantically merchandising doubt and fear" and characterized the dominant wing of the Democratic Party as "those of little faith."[85] Mr. Nixon added that United States prestige was at an "all time high."[86]

The issue surrounding United States missile efforts had been joined, not on the overall adequacy of United States defenses, but on the question of the prestige of the United

83. *The New York Times,* October 16, 1960.

84. *Ibid.,* October 22, 1960; four days later Senator Kennedy reemphasized his charge that United States prestige had declined during the Eisenhower Administration; *Ibid.,* October 26, 1960. In spite of this apparent shift of emphasis by Senator Kennedy to the question of United States prestige (and the shift of emphasis in this paper), Senator Kennedy continued to attack what he believed were the inadequacies of the Eisenhower Administration's defense policies. See: *The New York Times,* October 24, 1960.

85. *The New York Times,* text of a speech given by President Eisenhower in Chicago, October 23, 1960.

86. *Ibid.,* October 21, 1959.

States, and ironically, American prestige abroad rather than as viewed at home. One British newspaper pointed out at the time that this was an "absurd" issue on which to fight an election in the United States. Nonetheless this became one of the key issues pursued by Senator Kennedy during the closing weeks of the campaign.[87]

However, the question of American prestige was not limited to the strictly military implications of the missile race. Very early in the missile controversy, Premier Khrushchev had attempted to tie Soviet rocket and ICBM development with the rather spectacular Russian space achievements. He stated that the Russian satellite was a product of the fact that the Soviets had developed the ICBM rocket necessary to launch it into orbit and indicated that progress in one field meant progress in the other.[88] *The New York Times* admitted that the two could not be separated and that Russian space accomplishments did indicate a highly developed ICBM capability.[89]

Early in the presidential campaign of 1960, Senator Kennedy took the same position and tied the commendable past record of Russian space achievements to the progress made by the Soviet Union in the alleged development of a large scale missile delivery system.[90] The addition of the "space race" into the presidential campaign served to increase the complexity of an already confusing situation.

Immediately following Senator Kennedy's first major charge of the decline of American prestige abroad, Senator William Fulbright (Democrat-Arkansas) was quoted as saying that United States Information Agency* polls on foreign opinion were being withheld from the public by

87. "United States Prestige Abroad: What the Polls Show," *U.S. News and World Report*, reprint of the full text of an editorial in the *London Daily Telegraph* of October 28, 1960, Vol. 49 (November 7, 1960), p. 62.
88. *Pravda*, October 11, 1957, *The Current Digest of the Soviet Press*.
89. *The New York Times*, October 7, 1958.
90. *Ibid*, August 27, 1960.
* Hereafter referred to as USIA.

the White House for partisan reasons. The Arkansas Democrat accused Vice-President Nixon of "deceiving the American people" by saying that United States prestige was at an all time high.[91]

Several days later, the charges made by Senator Fulbright were at least partially substantiated. *The New York Times* managed to obtain the complete text of a USIA poll taken in June 1960. This report was classified as "Secret" by the White House and no explanation was offered on how this newspaper had obtained such a sensitive document. The poll itself was a comprehensive document that dealt with many aspects of public opinion in Great Britain and France and the opinions expressed in these nations on a comparison of the United States and the Soviet Union. Of primary interest were the sections of the document on the European view of the comparative United States-Soviet military strength and space achievements. In both of these categories, the poll showed that in Great Britain and France the Russians were given a substantial lead over the United States. This was especially true in the category of space achievements—as of May 1960, 81 percent of the people of Great Britain indicated their belief that the Soviets were ahead, while 74 percent of the people in France indicated the same belief. Militarily, the percentages of belief in Soviet superiority were not as high, but nonetheless the poll indicated that a plurality of those polled who expressed an opinion in both Britain and France believed that the Soviet Union was superior militarily to the United States.[92]

In a different USIA poll taken in 1960 and not released until after the election, substantially the same belief on comparative military strength was shown for West Germany and Norway, with only the Italians indicating a

91. *The New York Times*, October 21, 1960.
92. *The New York Times*, complete text of USIA poll taken in June 1960 in Britain and France, October 27, 1960. (The exact figures of the poll can be found in Appendix C Polls. See Poll #1.)

plurality belief in United States military superiority over the Soviet Union.[93]

There did not appear to be any doubt that a plurality of people in Western European nations felt that United States prestige had dropped in 1960. In addition to the "secret" USIA polls, this belief was confirmed by a World Gallup Poll taken in November 1960.[94]

It was impossible to determine the exact effect of the public release of the USIA poll by *The New York Times* several weeks before the American people cast their ballots in the 1960 presidential election. However, the evidence in the USIA poll certainly substantiated Senator Kennedy's claim that United States prestige abroad (at least in Europe) had dropped under the Republican Eisenhower Administration. Polls taken by the American Institute of Public Opinion (Gallup) in the United States during October 1960 indicated that if the American people had voted early in October, the vote would have been very close to 50 percent for each candidate. However, a poll taken at the end of the month, after the "prestige" issue had arisen, gave Senator Kennedy a 53 to 47 percent lead over Vice-President Nixon.[95]

This shift of attitude among a small but significant per-

---

93. Horelick and Rush, *Strategic Power and Soviet Foreign Policy*, Intelligence, "Free World Views of U.S.-U.S.S.R. Power Balance," (R–54–60), August 29, 1960 (Chicago: The University of Chicago Press, 1965), p. 64. See: Poll #2 in Appendix C.

94. Hazel Gaudet Erskine (article editor), "Report from the Polls," *Public Opinion Quarterly*, reprint of World Gallup Poll (November 1960, Vol. 25 [Spring 1961], p. 133. See Poll #3, Appendix C. In the same periodical, an earlier World Gallup Poll (March 21, 1958) indicated that in every major capital in Western Europe, more people thought that United States prestige had gone down in 1957 and early 1958 than thought American prestige had risen. Thus, the loss of American prestige in Western Europe appeared to have begun in 1957, probably with the Soviet successful ICBM test and the Sputnik earth satellite. *Ibid.*, Vol. 25 (Summer, 1961), p. 136.

95. *Ibid.*, polls taken by the American Institute of Public Opinion from early August 1960 to November 7, 1960, p. 129. (The text of the polls can be found in Appendix C, Poll #4).

centage of the American electorate probably was caused by a multitude of factors, but it seemed that the "prestige" issue was one of its causes. In 1956, more Americans had indicated their belief that the Republican Party could do the best job of increasing the prestige of the United States throughout the world. By 1960, this attitude had been reversed and more people looked to the Democratic Party to increase American world wide prestige.[96]

Concurrently and closely related to the political debate in the United States over American prestige abroad, a more esoteric and probably more important problem was subjected to careful and thoughtful analysis. The rapid technological advancement in nuclear weapons and their delivery vehicles caused many interested individuals within the NATO alliance to question the meaning of these changes when applied to the concept of Western defense and deterrence and specifically, the role of the United States in the defense of Western Europe through its power to deter a Soviet attack on this area.

On several occasions in the past, the United States government had felt it necessary to publicly assure its NATO allies of American "nuclear superiority" over the Soviet Union and of the ability of the United States deterrent force to prevent a Russian attack on Western Europe.[97]

By September 1960 a number of civilian analysts on both sides of the Atlantic attempted to answer some of the basic questions raised by the advent of the operational ICBM and the alleged Soviet lead in this field. A respected British spokesman stated unequivocally that:

. . . confidence in the ability of the United States to guaran-

---

96. *Ibid.*, American Institute of Public Opinion, poll taken July 27, 1960, p. 132. (See Poll #5, Appendix C.)

97. *The New York Times*, "U.S. Informs NATO it Leads Russians in Nuclear Arms," quoting Secretary of Defense Gates before the Industrial Council of NATO, December 15, 1959; *Ibid.*, quoting acting Secretary of State Herter at a closed meeting of the NATO Council, April 3, 1959.

tee the security of Western Europe is decreasing as Russia becomes a formidable nuclear power.[98]

An equally respected French military analyst stated substantially the same thing and implied that the Soviet ICBM superiority cast very serious doubts on the capability and willingness of the United States to defend Western Europe.[99]

The doubts of the credibility of the United States ability and willingness to defend Western Europe were not limited to the allies of the United States but also began to appear in works done by American analysts of military policy. The same theme sounded by European writers appeared in an analysis of the problems by an American writer:

> The recent growth of Soviet military strength, especially in missiles, makes it uncertain, if not improbable, that the United States would in the future protect its allies from nuclear blackmail or invasion by making a credible threat of massive destruction against the Soviet Union.[100]

During the same year (1960), several books were published by well-known authors who took the same basic approach to the difficulties created for the NATO Alliance by the alleged increase in Soviet strategic military strength.[101]

98. Alastair Buchan, "The Future of Western Deterrent Power, III, A View from the United Kingdom," *The Bulletin of the Atomic Scientists,* Vol. 16 (September 1960), p. 227.

99. Raymond Aron, "The Future of Western Deterrent Power, I, A View from France," *The Bulletin of the Atomic Scientists,* Vol. 16 (September 1960), pp. 266–267.

100. Klaus Knorr, "The Future of Western Deterrent Power, II, A View from the United States," *The Bulletin of the Atomic Scientists,* Vol. 16 (September 1960), p. 271.

101. Henry A. Kissinger, *The Necessity for Choice,* especially pp. 41–42; Liddell Hart, *Deterrent or Defense* (New York: Frederick A. Praeger, 1960), especially pp. 91–92, 135, 140. For a detailed analysis of the military problems of the NATO Alliance, see: Snyder, *Deterrent and Defense.*

The difficulties and confusion for United States and European security that had been created by the alleged "missile gap" were passed on to the newly elected President of the United States, John F. Kennedy.

---

especially Chapter III. The problems created within the NATO Alliance by the supposed "missile gap" will be dealt with in more detail in the conclusions of this paper.

6

THE MISSILE GAP MYTH
DESTROYED: 1961

FOLLOWING JOHN F. KENNEDY'S ELECTION TO THE PRES-
idency in November 1960, the missile controversy once
again disappeared from the public view. The periodical
literature and newspapers found very little to say about
the subject during the final months of 1960, and the
political figures involved appeared content to leave the
question alone for the time being. Hanson Baldwin calm-
ly assessed the situation in December 1960 and found no
reason for the United States to be disturbed over its defense posture.[1] American military leaders were silent on
major defense policies.

With the arrival of 1961 came a renewed interest in the
missile debate and the controversy began again in earnest.
President-elect Kennedy renewed his charges of inadequacies in United States missile programs. He stated that the
United States missile and space programs lagged behind
the Soviet Union and called for a "crash" program to develop a sophisticated and secure missile deterrent system.[2]

The political-military differences between the President-elect and the out-going President of the United States

1. *The New York Times*, news analysis by Hanson W. Baldwin (Military Editor) , December 11, 1960.
2. "What Kind of Defense?" *The New Republic*, text of Mr. Kennedy's
response to an American Legion question: "What must we do to regain
our Strength?", Vol. 144 (January 9, 1961) , p. 6; *The New York Times*,
January 12, 1961.

continued to the very end of the Eisenhower Administration. In President Eisenhower's farewell address, along with his now famous warning of the dangers of the "military-industrial complex," Mr. Eisenhower assured the American people of the powerful deterrent posture of the United States military forces. Then, President Eisenhower attempted, officially, for the last time to dispel what he believed was a myth of the "missile gap":

> The bomber gap of several years ago was always a fiction and the "missile gap" shows every sign of being the same.[3]

Later in the month, the head of the Air Force's Research and Development Command, General Bernard Schriever, supported the President's statement and claimed that the Soviet Union was not strong enough to attempt a surprise attack on the United States. General Schreiver refused to concede that Russia was ahead of the United States in missile development and went on to claim that in reality the United States was ahead of the Soviet Union in missile development.[4]

When President Kennedy came into office, opinion on defense policy remained split on the "missile gap" controversy. Henry Kissinger's book, *The Necessity for Choice,* recently had been published and several periodicals supported his acceptance of the missile gap thesis. (See above.) An article in *The New Yorker* advocated the idea that the "missile gap" was "unavoidable" and would in all

---

3. *The New York Times,* text of President Eisenhower's farewell address to the nation, January 13, 1961.

4. "1960—Best Year We've had in the Missile Business," *U.S. News and World Report,* interview with General Bernard Schriever, Chief of Air Force Research and Development Command, Vol. 50 (January 23, 1961), pp. 69–70. In the past General Schriever had claimed that the missile race was either "nip and tuck" (*The New York Times,* January 8, 1958) or that the missile race was even between the United States and the Soviet Union ("The Pushbutton Comes of Age," quoting General Bernard Schriever, p. 20. In 1960, General Schriever admitted that there was a "numbers gap," but denied that meant that there was a "missile gap." (*Joint Hearings, 1960,* p. 75).

probability "never be closed."[5] One periodical, unfriendly to the Eisenhower Administration, quoted parts of Mr. Kissinger's book in an article entitled: "The High Price of Ike" and blamed President Eisenhower for the development of the "missile gap" that "would last for the next several years."[6] A more specialized periodical, *Missiles and Rockets,* stated that the Soviet Union had a three to one advantage over the United States in ICBMs and questioned whether the United States had enough bombers to prevent a "deterrent gap."[7]

On the other side of the debate, at least one major periodical contended that the world balance in missiles was shifting to the United States and listed an impressive chart of the alleged military strengths of the existing and projected missile and bomber postures of the two major powers to support its contention that there was no missile gap.[8]

During the same month, (January 1961), the House Republican Policy Committee attempted to answer the Democratic charges on the "missile gap" and submitted a set of figures on comparative United States-Soviet Union military strengths that later appeared to be the official Pentagon figures for January 1961. This estimate of the existing comparative strategic strength showed the following:[9]

5. Richard H. Rovere, "Letter from Washington," *The New Yorker,* Vol. 36 (January 21, 1961), p. 116. (Quoting Mr. Kissinger).

6. "The High Price of Ike" (by TRB from Washington), *The New Republic,* Vol. 144 (January 30, 1961), p. 2.

7. James Baar (Editor of Military Affairs), "Latest Report says Missile Gap Continues," *Missiles and Rockets,* Vol. 8 (February 13, 1961), p. 14.

8. "Is the World Balance in Missiles Shifting to the U.S.?" *U.S. News and World Report,* Vol. 59 (January 23, 1961), pp. 65-66. See Appendix A, January 23, 1961.

9. *The New York Times,* reprint of the figures submitted by the House Republican Policy Committee on January 25, 1961, February 9, 1961. In *The New York Times* of April 16, 1964 roughly these same figures were used by the Pentagon as their estimate as of January 1961; see *The New York Times,* April 16, 1964. These figures ignored the various American IRBMs, medium-range bombers, and carrier based aircraft—all capable

United States	Soviet Union
16 Atlas ICBMs	35 T-3 ICBMs (8000 Miles)
32 Polaris Missiles	none comparable
600 long-range bombers	200 long-range bombers

After President Kennedy's inauguration in late January 1961, the new President questioned the adequacy of United States defenses and stated: "We are moving into a period of uncertain risk." President Kennedy did not believe that the United States had a consistent, coherent military strategy. He instructed the new Secretary of Defense, Robert S. McNamara, to conduct a special study of the entire defense strategy and weapons systems of the United States and to make recommendations to the White House by the end of February. Meanwhile, President Kennedy had ordered an increase in the airlift capacity of the Army, a step-up in the Polaris missile system, and an acceleration of the entire missile effort of the United States.[10]

Almost immediately after President Kennedy announced the establishment of a committee to study United States defenses, an event occurred which presaged the end of the belief in the existence of the "missile gap." This event, in itself, did not end the debate, but it laid the foundation upon which the missile gap myth was eventually destroyed. Early in February 1961 strong evidence indicated that Secretary of Defense McNamara had stated in a "background briefing" to the press that there was "no missile gap." The briefing reportedly was given the sixth of February, and the following day the front page

---

of hitting a Soviet target. The Russians had no capability in any of these three categories that could reach the United States. Also, Appendix A indicates that 1961 saw a profusion of estimated missile strengths, yet none of these figures for this year indicate a "missile gap" favoring the Soviet Union, with the possible exception of very early 1961 estimates.

10. *The New York Times*, text of President Kennedy's first State of the Union Message, January 31, 1961. At this time, President Kennedy also attacked wasteful duplication and the interservice rivalry within the military services.

of *The New York Times* carried a lead article entitled: "Kennedy Defense Study Finds No Evidence of 'Missile Gap.' "[11]

The White House reacted immediately and denied the alleged report by Secretary McNamara that there was "no missile gap" and stated that this report was "absolutely wrong."[12] The next day, in a press conference President Kennedy was asked to clear up the record on the reported "background briefing" by McNamara. President Kennedy avoided answering the question and simply stated that he had not received the defense report from his study commission on United States defense policy and that "it would be premature to reach a judgment as to whether there is a gap or not a gap."[13] Then, in response to a question about the wisdom of background briefings to the press by high Administration officials, the President stated: "Well, they are hazardous in many cases—[laughter] and I think our Mr. McNamara might agree with that now."[14]

---

11. *The New York Times*, news article by Jack Raymond, "Kennedy Study Finds No Evidence of 'Missile Gap,' " February 7. 1961; *Ibid.*, statement repeated, February 9, 1961; Several years later, President Eisenhower wrote that after his successor assumed office "word conveniently leaked out of the Pentagon that the 'missile gap' had been closed." Eisenhower, *Waging the Peace*, p. 390. Also, in Mr. Schlesinger's book, *A Thousand Days*, Mr. Schlesinger claimed that Mr. McNamara had "disowned" the "missile gap" in February 1961; p. 499 (his italics). From the evidence available, it appeared that Mr. McNamara had "slipped in this "background briefing" and also that the United States government once again found itself with several intelligence estimates on comparative strategic military strength. (See below.)

12. *The New York Times*, February 8, 1961.

13. Harold W. Chase and Allen L. Lerman, eds.. *Kennedy and the Press: The New Conferences*, texts of all President Kennedy's news conferences (New York: Thomas Y. Crowell Company, 1965) , pp. 19–20.

14. *Ibid.*, p. 20. Later in the month, Secretary McNamara denied he had said there was "no missile gap" *(The New York Times*, "Missile Gap Report Denied by McNamara," February 17, 1961; and in April 1961 Secretary McNamara claimed that a "missile gap" existed. (U.S. Congress, House, Committee on Appropriations, *Hearings on Department of Defense Appropriations for 1962*, 87th Cong., 1st sess., Part 3 [April 1961]) , p. 60. These events will be discussed below.

Once again, the apparent confusion within the government signalled the beginning of increased partisanship on the issue of American defense policies, only this time the Democrats were on the defensive. The Republican National Committee demanded an apology from President Kennedy to Mr. Eisenhower for the "grand deception" perpetuated during the 1960 presidential campaign.[15] One Republican spokesman sarcastically praised President Kennedy for ending the "missile gap" in "just 18 days."[16] Other Republicans joined the attack and later President Eisenhower wrote: "The nonexistent missile gap had been suddenly closed by unabashed partisan politics."[17]

The counterattack against the Republican accusations came from Senator Symington, and came in an interesting form. Senator Symington accused the Eisenhower Administration of failing to inform Mr. Kennedy of the essential intelligence information during the past campaign. He contended that if this had been done, then the President would be in a better position to inform the American people about the "missile gap." At the time, it was not certain if Senator Symington meant to imply that there was no "missile gap" or that Senator Kennedy had not been informed of the missile gap during the campaign. From statements that had been made in the past, particularly by President Eisenhower, it appeared that Senator Symington strongly implied that the missile gap did not exist; however it was doubtful that this was what he meant

15. *The New York Times,* quoting the Republican National Committee's publication *Battle Line,* February 9, 1961.

16. Baar, "Latest Report Says Missile Gap Continues," quoting Representative Thomas M. Pelly (Rep.-Wash.) , p. 14. Although the vast majority of the periodical literature of this period accepted the report on Mr. McNamara's "background briefing," evidently *Missiles and Rockets* did not and claimed that Russia had a three to one lead over the United States in ICBMs. *Ibid.*

17. *The New York Times,* February 11, 1961; Eisenhower, *Waging the Peace,* p. 390.

to say.[18] Other leading Democrats were content to state that there was still a "missile gap" but that it was not "serious." [19]

In spite of the fact that Secretary of Defense McNamara later denied that he had made a statement negating the existence of a "missile gap,"[20] three major mass circulation national periodicals commented on his February "background briefing" in articles highly critical of President Kennedy and the role he had played in the development of the missile gap thesis.[21] One of these periodicals went so far as to declare that if there was a missile gap, the gap favored the United States and not the Soviet Union and then listed supposed official intelligence figures to support its case.[22] Even the periodical that allegedly served as the unofficial spokesman of the United States Air Force reported the statement Secretary McNamara reportedly made on the missile gap.[23]

It also was reported that former President Eisenhower "was particularly gratified" by Secretary McNamara's statement that there was no missile gap and Mr. Eisenhower pointed out that this was in complete agreement with his own findings while in office.[24]

Throughout February and March 1961, the press corps

18. *The New York Times,* "Missile Gap Secrecy Charged to GOP," quoting Senator Stuart Symington, February 10, 1961.
19. *Ibid.,* quoting Representative George H. Mahon (Democrat-Texas, Chairman of the House Appropriations Subcommittee on Defense Appropriations) , February 12, 1961.
20. *The New York Times,* "Missile Gap Report Denied by McNamara," February 17, 1961.
21. "Defense: The Missile Gap Flap," *Time,* Vol. 77 (February 17, 1961) , p. 12; "The Ammo was Political," *Newsweek,* Vol. 57 (February 20, 1961) , p. 24; "The Truth about the Missile Gap," *U.S. News and World Report,* Vol. 50 (February 27, 1961) , p. 41.
22. "The Truth About the Missile Gap," p. 41. See Appendix A, February 27, 1961 for the weapons chart listed.
23. Claude Witze, "Airpower and the News," *Air Force,* Vol. 44 (March 1961) , p. 39.
24. *The New York Times,* Senator Karl Mundt (Republican-South Dakota) quoting Mr. Eisenhower, February 27, 1961.

in Washington continued to pressure President Kennedy for a definitive answer on the "missile gap" question, and each time the President replied that he was waiting for the completion of the defense study he had ordered the Department of Defense to undertake. On March 1, 1961 President Kennedy said that the study would be completed in several weeks and at that time he would make his recommendations to Congress. On March 8, the President stated that the study would be completed in several days and then he would indicate "what I believe to be the relative defense position of the United States."[25] But for some reason, from March 8 until early October 1961, the Washington press corps discontinued its questions on the missile gap and the issue was ignored in Presidential news conferences.[26]

At the height of the missile debate in February 1961, one qualified observer made an obvious, but nonetheless necessary observation on the limitations placed on the President in his attempt to deal with the critics of his Administration. In a letter to the editor of *The New York Times*, Mr. Harry Howe Ransom pointed out that the President could never admit that a "missile gap" existed, if such were the case. This admission might be taken by the Soviet Union as an invitation to assume a more aggressive foreign policy. [27]

25. *The New York Times*, text of President Kennedy's news conference, March 2, 1961, *Ibid.*, March 9, 1961.

26. Chase and Lerman, eds., *Kennedy and the Press*, pp. 45–117. From March 8, 1961 to October 11, 1961 the President held a total of 11 news conferences and the missile gap question was not raised in one of them; when a major question on national defense was raised on October 11 it dealt with the military credibility of the United States' ability to deter aggression during the Berlin crises rather than directly with the missile gap. *Ibid.*, p. 119.

27. *The New York Times*, "Letters to the Editor," by Harry Howe Ransom (author of *Central Intelligence and National Security*), February 19, 1961. This might be a partial explanation of why the press ceased pressuring the President on the missile gap issue if it could be assumed that the request had been made by the President to give him time to straighten out the United States intelligence picture. However, there is no evidence to indicate that such a request was made.

However, President Kennedy's reluctance to speak out on the "missile gap" was based on factors other than the question of the supposed future attitude of the Soviet Union (although this was obviously a consideration). When President Kennedy assumed office he was faced with at least two and probably three diffierent intelligence estimates of Soviet missile strength. The first public report of the various estimates in 1961 came in February when it was reported that the Air Force estimated that the Soviet Union had 150 operational ICBMs while the National Intelligence Estimate gave a considerably lower figure.[28]

In March 1961 *The New York Times* reported, based on a "qualified source," that "secret" testimony before a Congressional investigating committee had indicated a distinct diffierence between the Air Force estimates of Soviet ICBMs and the Navy estimate. The Air Force reportedly contended that the Soviet Union had 200 ICBMs operational, while the Navy believed they had only 50 ICBMs in operation.[29]

The weight of available evidence indicated that there were at least two estimates of Soviet missile strength early in 1961. If this was the case, President Kennedy's lack of willingness to discuss the missile gap issue became more

---

28. *The New York Times*, news article by Hanson W. Baldwin, February 12, 1961. Mr. Baldwin contended that the Soviet Union still only had two launching pads (see above). One member of the Kennedy Administration later claimed that the President faced three estimates–the Air Force claimed 600–800 Soviet ballistic missiles (he did not designate ICBM or IRBM), the Central Intelligence Agency claimed 450 missiles, and the Navy claimed 200. From the size of these projected numbers, it would appear that they included both ICBMs and IRBMs. (See: Schlesinger, *A Thousand Days*, pp. 499–500). Theodore Sorensen also reported that President Kennedy faced "several estimates when he came to office" (see: Sorensen, *Kennedy*, p. 612).

29. *The New York Times*, news article by Jack Raymond based on "a qualified source" on the testimony of General Lyman L. Lemnitzer, Chairman, Joint Chiefs of Staff, secret testimony before the House Armed Services Committee, March 1, 1961. It appeared as though a higher percentage of the defense hearings in 1961 were held in "closed session" in order to avoid the confusion that had resulted from the "open sessions" held early in 1960.

comprehensible. Faced with this confusion, the President did not make a comprehensive and non-evasive statement on the comparative military strength of the United States and the Soviet Union until he thought the confusion had been straightened out, and this did not occur until November 1961.[30] (See below.)

The question of "why" there were several intelligence estimates during this period was a difficult one. The National Intelligence Board (see above) had the primary responsibility for producing National Intelligence Estimates. The chairman of this Board was the Director of the Central Intelligence Agency, and the Board included representatives of the military services. However, nothing prevented the individual intelligence units of the Armed Services from producing their own intelligence estimates, even if those estimates were not the same as the one produced by the National Intelligence Board. This fact had been admitted publicly in early 1960 by an Air Force spokesman,[31] and the evidence throughout the "missile gap" period indicated the strong possibility that these differing service estimates were "leaked" to a variety of public sources.[32]

One of the major reasons for the variety of intelligence estimates appeared to be the continued conflict of interservice rivalry within the military establishment of the United States and the fact that two opposing doctrines had arisen within the military services on the exact mission of nuclear weapons and what their accompanying delivery vehicles should perform.[33]

---

30. There was also a report, although not substantiated by other evidence, that "new intelligence methods" were developed in the winter of 1960–1961 (see: Schlesinger, *A Thousand Days*, p. 317). Appendix A for the period of early 1961 demonstrates the diversity of estimates available at the time.

31. *Joint Hearings, 1960*, p. 114. (See above.)

32. See Appendix A.

33. An excellent analysis on the question of interservice rivalry can be found in: Samuel P. Huntington, "Interservice Competition and the Political Role of the Armed Services," *American Political Science Review*, Vol. 55 (March 1961), pp. 40–52.

The question of interservice rivalry was an old one. Following World War II and the separation of the Air Force from the Army, the military services were engaged in a struggle they believed was vital to their continued existence. All three major services were involved in a debate that centered fundamentally over the question of the nature of a future war. Logically, the Air Force believed that air power would be the decisive factor in a showdown with the Soviet Union, while the Army and Navy declared their belief in the limited value of the use of air power and contended that any future war eventually would be won by ground and naval forces.[34]

Following the Korean "police action," the rivalry between the services assumed a different nature. No longer did the military services feel that their existence was threatened, and the debate over the nature of a future war assumed a competitive posture rather than one that would exclude any one service from playing a vital role in a future conflict. In theory, the new doctrine gave the Air Force the deterrent mission while the Army and Navy were fundamentally concerned with the possibility of limited war.[35] In practice this theory did not work as planned; several examples illustrated this point very well. The question of which service would develop the intermediate range ballistic missile was debated for over three years before the Air Force finally gained control over IRBM development (Air Force *Thor* versus Army *Jupiter*). This same type of interservice conflict occurred on the question of providing the continental defense system for the United States (Army's *Nike* series versus Air Force's *Bomarc*). And, finally, the Navy and Air Force came into conflict on whether the Air Force should have control over the entire United States weapons systems which constituted the American deterrent force (primari-

---

34. *Ibid.*, pp. 49–50. This question has been dealt with in greater detail in Chapter I of this paper. A similar debate occurred in the Soviet Union.

35. *Ibid.*

ly the Air Force's attempt to gain control over the Navy's *Polaris* missile system) .[36]

As these questions as to which service should develop and control a given weapons system were solved, an equally difficult and more subjective problem grew in importance. This issue, in essence, raised two problems. First, how much nuclear power was needed by a deterrent system to prevent a Soviet attack? No one questioned the need for a deterrent system, only its exact make-up in numbers and types of delivery vehicles. And, secondly, the likelihood of a limited war involving the United States and the forces needed to meet this challenge had to be determined. Viewed from the point of view of the military services, these two problems and the solutions to them were vitally important. With a limited amount of defense appropriations available, the decision to produce a large number of strategic nuclear weapons would obviously cut into the funds for the development of a limited war capability. Or, if the decision were made to place heavy emphasis on preparations for a limited war, the funds available for a large strategic deterrent force were reduced.

These two problems were defined in terms of the military doctrines of the Armed Services and in the defense policy jargon of the day were known as a Counterforce capability (Air Force) versus a Minimum Deterrent (Army-Navy) (see Chapter 1). The counterforce doctrine pursued by the Air Force called for a large number of nuclear delivery vehicles primarily designed to strike the nuclear delivery systems of the Soviet Union. The minimum deterrent doctrine of the Army-Navy called for a smaller nuclear weapons system designed to deter a Soviet attack by threatening to strike at Russian cities. With the money saved on the limited strategic weapons system of the minimum deterrent, the capability to meet limited

---

36. See above.

Communist aggression could be developed and therefore this type of aggression could also be deterred.[37]

This doctrinaire difference of opinion on American deterrent policy between the military services was recognized by many members of the Congress and by the newly elected President of the United States. The difficulty was that in early 1961 President Kennedy and his advisors were just beginning to formulate the new Administration's defense policy and the members of Congress were in strong disagreement over which defense philosophy to accept; therefore they appropriated some funds aimed at fulfilling the needs of both, but did not satisfy either the Air Force or the Army-Navy school of thought.[38]

In view of the past confusion within the United States intelligence community and the extreme uncertainty that surrounded Soviet intentions and capabilities, it came as no surprise that the intelligence estimates of the various military services tended to produce intelligence figures that confirmed their own doctrinaire view of the existing military situation. Early in the missile controversy the difficulties in determining the exact locations of operational Soviet ICBM sites had been admitted by a high Air Force official.[39] Later evidence indicated that the United

37. General Lymen L. Lemnitzer (Chairman, Joint Chiefs of Staff), "Forward Strategy Re-appraised," (reprint of an address by General Lemnitzer to the Association of the United States Army on August 8, 1960), *Survival* (published by The Institute of Strategic Studies, London) Vol. 3 (January-February 1961), p. 22; John F. Loosebrock, "Minimum Deterrence is a Phony," *Survival*, Vol. 3 (March-April 1961), p. 75; Maxwell Taylor (United States Army, ret.), "Security will not Wait," *Foreign Affairs*, Vol. 39 (January 1961), p. 174.

38. Ralph E. Lapp, "Nuclear Weapons Systems," *Bulletin of the Atomic Scientists*, Vol. 17 (March 1961), p. 102.

39. U.S. Congress, House, Appropriations Committee, *Hearings on Fiscal Year 1960*, Defense Budget (testimony by General Thomas D. White, U.S. Air Force Chief of Staff), 85th Cong., 1st sess., Vol. 9 (February 17, 1959), p. 840. Also see *Johns Hopkins Study. 1959*, p. 51. At a later date, there was an unsubstantiated report that the United States U-2 could determine the locations of most Soviet ICBM operational

States constantly revised American intelligence estimates on Soviet missile programs as additional information became available.[40] Inevitably, a number of sets of intelligence figures became available and a certain element of subjectivity entered into the selection of the set claimed to be the "official" intelligence estimate of a given service.[41]

As the controversy continued, President Kennedy found himself in the same position as his predecessor. The President, and the members of his Administration, felt constrained to reassure constantly the Congress and the American public of the basic military security of the United States. President Kennedy repeated almost word for word the statement made by Secretary of Defense McElroy in 1959 when the President declared that the United States was not going to compare military strength with the Soviet Union "missile for missile," but would rely on America's total retaliatory power which would remain after a first strike by the Soviet Union.[42] The Chairman of the Joint Chiefs of Staff reportedly assured a Congressional committee in closed session that the United States was "militarily the most powerful nation on earth."[43]

---

sites. It was claimed that due to the cumbersome, heavy nature of the early ICBM, the Russians had to string them out in a line next to the Trans-Siberian railroad and therefore they could be easily photographed by the U-2 flights. See Charles J. V. Murphy, "Khrushchev's Paper Bear," *Fortune,* Vol. 70 (December 1964) , pp. 58–59. (See Conclusion.)

40. Dulles, *The Craft of Intelligence,* pp. 162–163.

41. During this same period, the Soviet Union added credence to the Air Force's claim of large numbers of Soviet ICBMs. Along with the various statements by Premier Khrushchev, Russian Defense Minister Malinovsky was quoted as having said that the Soviet missiles were "superior" to any others in the world and called Russia's missiles "the world's most powerful missiles." *The New York Times,* May 2, 1961.

42. *The New York Times,* March 27, 1961 (President Kennedy appeared to be relying on the "mixed force" concept of the Eisenhower Administration) .

43. *Ibid.,* news article by Jack Raymond, quoting General Lymen L. Lemnitzer before a secret session of the House Armed Services Committee, May 13, 1961.

However, the political implications of the "missile gap" controversy and the role played by Mr. Kennedy in its development remained a very real concern to the President and his Administration. Under intense questioning by Congressional investigators on the "missile gap," Secretary of Defense McNamara reversed his reported earlier stand and claimed that there was "evidence to indicate that a missile gap may exist up to and through 1964." But Secretary McNamara immediately qualified his statement and indicated that United States missile inventory at the end of fiscal 1963, or at the end of calendar 1963, could exceed that of the Soviet Union and that the "missile gap" was "small."[44]

By the end of March 1961 President Kennedy's study on United States defense policies had progressed far enough for the President to submit his suggested changes in the Eisenhower Defense Budget for Fiscal 1962. The most interesting aspect of these proposals was the indication that the President appeared to be at least as disturbed about the ability of the United States to fight a limited war as he was about the supposed development of the "missile gap." His proposals dealt mainly with modernization of the Army, an increased airlift capability for troops, the expansion of guerilla warfare units, and an increase in tactical air support units. The Administration did demonstrate concern over the vulnerability of the United States nuclear retaliatory forces. However, the changes recommended by the new President were a matter of a shift of emphasis and acceleration of existing programs, rather than a complete overhaul of American defenses.[45] The new budget did not change the number of

44. U.S. Congress, House, Committee on Appropriations, *Hearings* on Department of Defense Appropriations for 1962, 87th Cong., 1st sess., p. 3 (April 1961), pp. 60–61. (Mr. McNamara also stated that there was not a "deterrent gap.")

45. Later, President Kennedy claimed that of $9 billion in additional defense funds spent since he came to office, (only) one-third of these funds had gone for nuclear striking power and the remainder had been

United States strategic missiles programmed for 1965. It did provide for the speed-up of the *Polaris* and *Minuteman* systems and provided for a SAC airborne alert with one-eighth of the aircraft of the Strategic Air Command on airborne alert at all times. However, the President was accused of being as "niggardly" as Mr. Eisenhower when it came to appropriations for additional bombers when he did not raise the number of B-52's and B-58's to be produced and actually reduced the development funds for the B-70 long-range bomber.[46]

By the summer of 1961, the budget for Fiscal 1962 had been approved by Congress and the debate over the "missile gap" returned to its annual summer limbo. In spite of the intensity of the missile issue earlier in 1961, after May of that year every public projection of existing and future Soviet missile strength indicated at least American parity with the Soviet Union in deliverable missile warheads and many projections predicted a United States lead over the Soviet Union in this field. In the number of bombers that could deliver nuclear weapons on the enemy's territory, the United States had a large superiority.[47]

Early in the fall of 1961, a series of events began that culminated in the effective destruction of the missile gap myth. One of the earliest and most prominent columnists who perpetuated the missile gap thesis reported in Septem-

---

used to increase the "flexibility" of the United States response to limited military aggression. See: Stewart Alsop, "Kennedy's Grand Strategy" (an interview with President John F. Kennedy), *The Saturday Evening Post*, Vol. 235 (March 31, 1962), p. 14.

46. *The New York Times*, March 29, 1961; *Ibid.*, May 4, 1961; *Ibid.*, May 12, 1961; *Ibid.*, June 24, 1961; James Baar (Editor of Military Affairs), "Will Time Run out for Kennedy's Buildup of U.S. ICBM's," *Missiles and Rockets*, Vol. 18 (June 19, 1961), p. 12. (This latter periodical was very critical of President Kennedy's readjustments in United States defense planning.)

47. See Appendix A. Throughout the missile gap period the United States bomber superiority over the Soviet Union was never challenged and one source estimated this superiority in 1961 as being 35 to one. (See Appendix A and "Is the U.S. Ahead in the Arms Race?" *U.S. News and World Report*, Vol. 51 (September 18, 1961), p. 44.

ber that American intelligence estimates had been recalculated and United States estimates of Soviet ICBMs were "drastically reduced" from 200 to well under 50 operational ICBMs.[48] Several periodicals that had supported the belief in the missile gap in the past reversed themselves and one magazine that had staunchly perpetuated the missile gap illusion even claimed that the September Soviet test of a "super" thermonuclear bomb had been a demonstration of Russian military weakness and a Russian effort to hide this weakness.[49] At the same time, other periodicals claimed that the United States was far ahead of the Soviet Union in strategic weapons and began to shift the debate to the question of the ability of the United States to fight a limited war in response to less than all-out aggression.[50] One major dissent (though not unexpected) from the growing confidence in United States deterrent posture came from the Air Force's unofficial periodical *Air Force and Space Digest* (formerly *Air Force Magazine*). Under an article entitled: "How Far is the Red Air Force Ahead?" this periodical claimed that the Soviet Union was ahead of the United States in the field of bomber development and called for corrective measures in the form of more money so that the Air Force could correct this deficiency in United States defenses.[51]

48. *The Washington Post,* news article by Joseph Alsop, September 25, 1961.

49. "The Imbalance of Terror" (editorial), *The New Republic,* Vol. 145 (September 18, 1961), p. 1; "Ballistic Missile Program Moves Forward," *Aviation Week,* Vol. 75 (September 25, 1961), p. 123. The next month *The New Republic* printed an article that strongly implied United States strategic superiority over the Soviet Union. See: Morton Halperin, "The Military Problem—Choosing Our Weapons," *The New Republic,* Vol. 145 (October 2, 1961), p. 34.

50. "Is the U.S. Ahead in the Arms Race," p. 44 (see Appendix A for figures on comparative missile strength): T. N. Dupuy, "Can America Fight a Limited War?" (reprinted from *Orbis,* Spring 1961), *Survival,* Vol. 3 (September-October 1961), p. 220.

51. J. S. Butz, Jr. (Technical Editor), "How Far is the Red Air Force Ahead?" *Air Force and Space Digest* (formerly *Air Force* magazine), (September 1961), p. 52.

It was impossible to determine the exact date when the missile gap myth was destroyed. Aside from the unwillingness of the Kennedy Administration to verify a myth that President Kennedy had helped to create, there was a natural inertia within the United States to the change of an accepted idea; nevertheless many segments of the popular media expressed the opinion in January 1961 that there was no missile gap (see Appendix A). After the report of Secretary McNamara's "background briefing" of February 6, the Administration either denied the accuracy of the report, or ignored the missile gap question whenever it was allowed to do so. In the fall of 1961, for a number of reasons, the Administration spoke in greater detail about the deterrent posture of the United States in relation to the Soviet Union. Once the Kennedy Administration publicly dealt in detail with United States deterrent posture, the "missile gap" disappeared as a major public issue in the United States.[52]

During 1961, President Kennedy was confronted by the confusion within the American intelligence community on the various estimates of Soviet existing and projected ICBM strength. In an attempt to reduce the conflicting estimates produced by interservice rivalry within the American military establishment, the President approved the creation of the Defense Intelligence Agency on October 1, 1961. Under this new agency, all of the military services strategic intelligence estimates were combined under the control of the Secretary of Defense in an effort to reduce the number of estimates produced by the Pentagon.[53]

52. As will be seen below, the partisan accusation continued and a brief attempt was made by the Republicans in the 1964 election to raise a "new" missile gap charge against the Democratic Administration of Lyndon B. Johnson. (See Conclusions.)

53. *The New York Times*, "The C.I.A.," series of articles by a team of correspondents–Tom Wicker, John W. Finney, Max Frankel, E. W. Kentworthy, and others, April 29, 1966; Harry Howe Ransom, *Can American Democracy Survive Cold War* (Garden City, New York: Doubleday & Company, Inc., 1963), p. 142.

At a press conference on October 11, 1961, President Kennedy was asked for the first time since March 15 about the adequacy and credibility of United States nuclear strength. In his response, the President did not deal with the question of comparative United States-Soviet strategic power, but emphasized the growing nuclear power of the United States brought about by the acceleration of the American missile program since he came to office. President Kennedy also assured the press that the United States had the military power to meet its overseas commitments.[54]

Apparently the first public, unequivocal Administration statement on comparative United States-Soviet nuclear strength was made several days later by a high official in the Department of Defense. Under-Secretary of Defense Roswell Gilpatric stated that the United States had a second strike capability which was at least as extensive as what the Soviet Union could deliver by striking first. In other words, the United States would have a larger nuclear delivery system left after a surprise attack by the Soviet Union on the United States than the nuclear force employed by the Russians in their first strike.[55] This strong Administration statement could be interpreted in no other way than as a negation of the existence of a "missile gap" as of October 1961.

By early November 1961 the weight of evidence available to President Kennedy was clearly against the earlier high Air Force estimates of Soviet ICBM strength and showed that a comparison of United States-Soviet military strength gave the United States a secure deterrent force for some years to come. On November 8, 1961 the President was once again asked about his 1960 campaign charges of American military inadequacy. This time the President attempted to answer these charges. He stated that many members of the Eisenhower Administration, including President Eisenhower, had admitted that the United States

---

54. Chase and Lerman, *Kennedy and the Press,* news conference, October 8, 1961.
55. *The New York Times,* quoting Mr. Gilpatric, October 22, 1961.

lagged behind the Soviet Union in missile development and that "statements that I made represented the best of my information based on public statements by those in a position to know in the late years of the 1950's." He went on to claim that "based on our present assessments and our intelligence, we . . . would not trade places with anyone in the world." President Kennedy concluded that the military power of the United States was "second to none."[56] Evidently the members of the Washington press corps were finally satisfied with the adequacy of the United States missile programs because the question of the "missile gap" was never asked again in a Kennedy press conference.[57]

Several days later Secretary of Defense McNamara appeared to certify Russia's strategic military inferiority and stated: "I believe we have nuclear power several times that of the Soviet Union."[58]

It seemed that by November 1961 the "missile gap" controversy finally had been settled and the Kennedy Administration had enough faith in the increasing missile strength of the United States to attempt a cutback in long-range bomber production and development. Secretary McNamara already had reduced the development funds

56. Chase and Lerman, *Kennedy and the Press,* text of news conference by President Kennedy, November 8, 1961, p. 125.

57. *Ibid.,* pp. 140–522 (the last news conference by President Kennedy was held on November 14, 1963).

58. "Was there ever a 'Missile Gap'—Or Just an Intelligence Gap?" *Newsweek,* quoting the Secretary of Defense in an interview, Vol. 58 (November 13, 1961), p. 23. In February 1962, Secretary of Defense stated: "Today not even the most boastful Russian rocket rattler asserts that the Soviet Union has the nuclear power to destroy the United States, see *News Release,* No. 239–62, United States Department of Defense, Office of Public Affairs, February 17, 1962. Later in 1962 Secretary McNamara told an interviewer that he was "absolutely confident" that the "missile gap" was a "myth" and had been ended; see: Stewart Alsop, "McNamara Thinks about the Unthinkable," interview with Secretary of Defense Robert McNamara, *The Saturday Evening Post,* Vol. 236 (December 1, 1962), p. 18.

for the B-70 bomber and he began to remove funds from long-range bomber production programs. He also refused to spend $525 million of unrequested funds for the production of a new wing of 45 B-52s and immediately ran into conflict with Congressional advocates of manned-bomber strength.[59]

Throughout 1961, the reporting in the mass media had demonstrated an increased belief in the growing strategic power of the United States in relation to the Soviet Union. By the time President Kennedy and Secretary of Defense McNamara made their statements in November, the majority of the popular press already reflected the repudiation of the missile gap. Immediately following the Kennedy-McNamara statements, *The New York Times* appeared to bury the end of the missile gap. In successive articles with such titles as: "U.S. Missile lead claimed in Study" and "Missile Gap in Reverse," it was stated that even the Air Force accepted new intelligence figures on Soviet ICBMs and that "the once predicted [missile] gap did not develop." To support the contention that the "missile gap" had not developed, *The New York Times* printed the following figures from a "recent intelligence study" on the comparative operational missiles of the United States

---

59. *The New York Times*, Senator Henry Jackson (Democrat-Washington) attacked Secretary McNamara's cutback in the number of manned-bombers. (Boeing Aircraft headquarters was located in Senator Jackson's home state of Washington,) November 6, 1961; *Ibid.*, January 23, 1962. It was later reported that President Kennedy began to believe in November 1961 that the United States planned increases in strategic deterrent power exceeded what he believed was needed for national defense, but he did not care to challenge Congress with reductions in both the manned-bomber and missile programs. Therefore he backed Secretary McNamara in challenging the Joint Chiefs of Staff and the "vociferous B-70 lobby in Congress" but went along with multiplying the *Polaris* and *Minuteman* systems. See Schlesinger, *A Thousand Days*, p. 500. This allegation by Mr. Schlesinger is a little hard to believe in view of the fact that there was a great increase in American missile production throughout his Administration and no indication of a willingness to cut down the number of projected missiles by even a small number.

and the Soviet Union capable of reaching the enemy's territory:[60]

United States	Soviet Union
48 *Atlas*	50 T-3 ICBMs (range
80 *Polaris*	8,000 miles)
60 *Thor*	
45 *Jupiter*	

On November 26, 1961 the Military Editor of *The New York Times*, Hanson W. Baldwin, reaffirmed the position that he had held throughout the debate and stated:

> Indeed, the "missile gap"—its birth, growth, and early death —had an Alice-in-Wonderland quality about it, which could flourish only in a democracy.[61]

Mr. Baldwin blamed the existence of the "missile gap" on interservice rivalry (primarily high Air Force intelligence estimates of Soviet ICBM strength), the political partisanship of "several Senators," "a columnist," and the confusion within the Republican Administration in the late 1950s. He concluded by stating his belief in United States missile superiority over the Soviet Union and his belief that the United States would have a two to one lead over the Soviet Union in medium and long-range bombers for some time to come.[62]

The following day, *The New York Times* ran its final editorial on the missile gap:

> The "missile gap" like the "bomber gap" before it is now

---

60. *The New York Times*, "U.S. Missile Lead Claimed in Study," news article by Jack Raymond, November 19, 1961; *Ibid.*, "Missile Gap in Reverse," November 20, 1961. These reports indicated that the Air Force accepted the new estimates, but the Strategic Air Command still did not accept them.

61. *The New York Times*, "New Figures Close 'missile gap,'" news article by Hanson W. Baldwin, November 26, 1961.

62. *Ibid.*

being consigned to the limbo of synthetic issues, where it has always belonged.[63]

Although this statement may have been true, this was rather strong editorial language for a newspaper which had at times been nebulous in its approach to the question of the "missile gap" and at least once in the presidential campaign of 1960 had printed, editorially, figures that supported the belief in the missile gap.[64]

After November 1961 the missile gap was removed effectively from the American scene. Occasionally statements would be made denying its existence, but the debate stopped. Obviously, the debate over defense policy did not cease with the end of the "missile gap," but continued over such issues as the development of the B-70 bomber, the efficacy of missiles versus bombers, the Army's *Nike* air defense system, the *Skybolt* air-to-surface missile, and many other aspects of the problems of national defense.

The question of a "missile gap" was raised several times at a later date, but for different reasons and in a different context than had been the case in the earlier debate. These problems will be dealt with in the following chapter, Conclusions.

63. *The New York Times*, "The Missile Gap" (editorial), November 27, 1961.
64. *The New York Times*, February 7, 1961 (see Appendix A).

7

CONCLUSIONS

THE INTRICACIES INVOLVED IN THE CREATION OF THE "MISSILE gap" and its exact impact on United States foreign and domestic policy proved to be a complex problem to analyze. Yet in spite of the multitude of factors involved and the secrecy that surrounded the controversy, an analysis of the phenomenon of the missile gap led this writer to numerous observations and conclusions on this interesting and significant development in post World War II United States defense policies.

Once the "missile gap myth" had been destroyed, it became possible to attempt to answer some of the fundamental questions raised by this controversial period in the history of United States defense policy. The alleged missile gap raised critical questions for the concerned observer and the policy maker on the weaknesses of the formulation of military policy and the concurrent problem of educating, and not propagandizing, the interested public on these difficult questions.

For the purpose of clarity, these conclusions are divided into three parts:

1. Soviet Strategy, American Intelligence, and the Missile Gap.
2. Budgetary, Partisan, and Military effects of the Missile Gap.
3. The Impact of the Missile Gap Abroad.

Soviet Strategy, American Intelligence, and the Missile Gap

During the 1950s and early 1960s, the major problem faced by the various persons responsible for maintaining United States security (and their critics) was the determination of how much power an American retaliatory system should possess in order to fulfill its mission of preventing a Soviet attack on the United States. The essential corollary to this problem was the question of how much destruction the leaders of the Soviet Union might risk in order to destroy the United States. Both of these questions were based on the assumption of aggressive Soviet intent and were highly subjective in nature. Therefore, the essence of the debate over the exact make-up of United States deterrent forces centered on two questions to which there were no absolute answers—only various estimates based on the subjective approach taken by the analyst involved. The subjective nature of these questions and the answers given to them determined the basic assumption of whether or not a missile gap was imminent. Thus, there was a high degree of fundamental uncertainty inherent in the missile gap controversy due to the disagreement on basic assumptions among the parties concerned. This was especially true during the early stages of the missile debate before "hard" intelligence information became available, but it remained true throughout the controversy.

Well before the intercontinental ballistic missile became a reality, the psychological foundation for the acceptance of the belief in Soviet strategic superiority had been laid. The surprise attack by the Japanese on Pearl Harbor had a definite impact on American strategic thinking. Logically, American policy makers and military leaders were determined that such a catastrophe would never occur again. Combined with this determination was the belief by many Americans that the Soviet Union would attempt a surprise attack on the United States as soon as Russia thought it had the nuclear power to undertake such an operation successfully.

According to these analysts, this situation would exist when the Soviet Union possessed a first strike nuclear force strong enough to destroy the United States nuclear retaliatory forces found primarily in the Strategic Air Command. These individuals believed that this was the ultimate goal of the Soviet Union and that Russia was pursuing this goal with all the technological and natural resources at its disposal. This alleged Russian doctrine was based on the belief that the Soviet Union was pursuing a "counterforce strategy." (See Counterforce in Glossary.) [1] Those who accepted this interpretation of the basic military philosophy of the Soviet Union tended to overestimate Soviet missile programs and to accept (or create) missile projection figures which appeared to substantiate their position.

In the early 1950s, well before the Soviet Union had a long-range bomber, American Air Force spokesmen made statements which cast doubts on the future ability of the United States Air Force to deter a Russian bomber attack on the United States.[2] The Soviet Air Show in May 1955 added credence to this American fear of possible Soviet strategic superiority. By flying the same squadron of ten Bison heavy bombers in a circle over the reviewing stand, the Russians created the impression of an extensive long-range nuclear delivery capability which was interpreted by many Americans to mean that the "bomber gap" had arrived. Later evidence revealed that the Soviet Union did possess the capability to produce enough Bisons to create a possible "bomber gap," but that the leaders of the

---

1. One of the major conclusions of this paper is that this evaluation of Soviet intent was incorrect and has not been proven by the production of Russian weapons systems during this period. (See below.)

2. See chapter 1. Also, statement by the Air Force Chief of Staff, General Hoyt C. Vandenburg, *Aviation Week*, vol. 54 (June 11, 1951), p. 11.

Soviet Union chose not to invest scarce Russian resources in the production of a large number of long-range bombers.[3] As a matter of fact, the Soviet Union never possessed more than 200 bombers capable of reaching the United States, while the American strategic bomber force numbered almost 2000.[4] When the "bomber gap" did appear, it appeared in reverse and favored the United States.

Once it became evident that the Soviet Union had not engaged in the production of a large strategic bomber force and that the "bomber gap" was not going to develop, the proposition was put forth that the Russians had tricked the United States into thinking that they were producing bombers, when in actuality the Soviet Union was engaged in a "crash" missile production program.[5] There does not appear to be much doubt that the United States was tricked by the Soviet Union into believing that Russia was engaged in the mass production of long-range bombers, but this was not because the Soviet Union had engaged in a "crash" missile production program. It seems more likely that the Soviet Union was diverting some resources to missile development (but not necessarily programmed missile production), and used the Air Show in 1955 to create the impression of a massive Russian bomber force which did not exist.[6] This American willingness to overestimate the predicted Soviet production of nuclear delivery vehicles continued until the "missile gap" was recognized as a myth.

The belief that the Soviet Union was preparing for a surprise attack on the United States did not die a quick death, but the fact remains that at no time during the period under consideration did the Soviet Union fully

---

3. Dulles, *The Craft of Intelligence*, p. 27.
4. See Appendix A.
5. *The New York Times*, "Air Manual Hints Soviet Tricked U.S.," April 28, 1960.
6. The "Fly-by" itself was apparently done deliberately, although the exact reasons for this Soviet move are not certain. See: Dulles, *The Craft of Intelligence*, pp. 164–165.

mobilize its production capacity for bombers or missiles. The Soviet Union apparently produced only those weapons it felt were needed to deter a United States attack on Russia.

An analysis of the estimated weapons production of the Soviet Union (including some actual "official" Pentagon figures; see Appendix A), indicates that the leaders of the Soviet Union, for reasons of their own, decided to follow a "minimum deterrent" strategy to deter an American attack.[7] The Soviet Union possessed a limited number of long-range bombers (and later of ICBMs) and a large conventional military force to meet less than all-out nuclear aggression. With these conventional and nuclear forces, the Soviet Union could protect its large land mass from a conventional attack and deter a United States nuclear attack by possessing a large enough nuclear striking force to threaten the *possible* destruction of American population centers. The Soviet Union did not have to possess enough deliverable nuclear weapons to create the *absolute certainty* that it could destroy major American metropolitan areas; it only had to create among high Amer-

---

7. Soviet budgetary figures on national defense are notoriously difficult, if not impossible, to analyze. However, one of the best efforts at this type of analysis was made by Mr. Abraham S. Becker of the Rand Corporation. Mr. Becker's analysis showed that the Soviet military budget had been reduced from 1955 to 1959, and then, following a rather drastic increase in 1959, it was again reduced in 1960 and possibly in 1962. Mr. Becker's figures are given below and are in billions of rubles. The figures represent the "estimate total high" spending in the Soviet Union for defense purposes.

Year	1955	1956	1957	1958	1959	1960	1961	1962
Number of Rubles in billions	15.00	14.81	14.39	14.63	18.00	17.15	17.0 to 26.1	16.6 to 23.4

See: Abraham S. Becker, *Soviet Military Outlays Since 1955* (Santa Monica, California: The Rand Corporation, 1964) (Memorandum RM-3886-PR), p. 91.

If Mr. Becker's figures are correct, they offer additional evidence to the belief that the Soviet Union was pursuing a policy of "minimum deterrence" during this period.

ican officials an element of *uncertainty* that this might be done, to prevent an American attack on the Soviet Union.[8]

Apparently, the leaders of the Soviet Union believed that this strategy not only guaranteed Russian military security, but also offered an additional advantage. By not building a large operational nuclear delivery system, the Soviet Union could wait for the development of the next, more sophisticated weapons generation before large-scale production began (if needed), and therefore scarce Russian resources could be channeled into other facets of the Soviet economy.[9]

However, as will be seen below, in the long run this Soviet advantage was reduced, if not completely destroyed. The Russian leaders, particularly Premier Khrushchev, attempted to take maximum diplomatic advantage of the belief by many Americans in the possible missile gap. The Russian boasts of missile superiority and "rocket rattling" served to reinforce this American belief and resulted in a massive American missile buildup which substantially escalated the arms race—an escalation which the Russian leaders were either unwilling or unable to compete with on equal terms.

Soviet statements on their rocket development tended to conceal the fact that they were essentially following a minimum deterrent strategy. Thus, the fact that the Soviet Union had adopted this strategy was either not known or not understood by those Americans responsible for formu-

---

8. The 25 largest cities in the United States had a combined population of 60.8 million persons according to the 1960 United States Census. (Emphasis added.)

9. The question legitimately can be asked "Why did the Soviet Union bother with missile development at all?" The answer appears to be that the Soviet Union continued missile development and production for at least two basic reasons: (1) In order to avoid a future technological gap in missile development that could not be closed (either with the United States or China), and (2) the increased effectiveness of antibomber surface-to-air-missiles raised the possibility that an almost perfect bomber defense might be developed by an adversary at some future date.

lating military policy. With this kind of verbal assistance from the leaders of the Soviet Union, it was not difficult for many American leaders to remain solidly frozen in the earlier assumptions of the "cold war" vis-à-vis accepted Soviet hostility and aggressive intent. Therefore, the basic assumption of those accepting the "missile gap" was the belief that the Russians were utilizing the "maximum capability" credited to them by United States intelligence. This assumption was changed only when "hard" intelligence information became available which indicated that the Soviet Union was not using its maximum capability; and even this was not accepted by all agencies of the American intelligence community (e.g. the Air Force).

The implications of the threatened "bomber gap" and the successful Soviet ICBM test and Sputnik earth satellite caused many American officials to raise their estimates of Soviet capabilities and added a strong element of uncertainty within government circles in the calculation of Soviet strategic nuclear power. Obviously, this American lack of certainty caused serious alarm, and efforts were made by the United States government to obtain accurate information on Soviet missile and bomber programs. The exact extent of these intelligence efforts by the United States were not known. However, numerous public reports have reflected an awareness of at least two of the major sources of information on Soviet missiles available to the American intelligence community.

Knowledge of the first intelligence source appeared in various public reports indicating that in July 1955 the United States had installed missile tracking stations in Turkey which could monitor Russian long-range missile tests. These radar stations reportedly could track Russian missiles up to a range of 4000 miles.[10]

---

10. Harry Howe Ransom, *Can American Democracy Survive Cold War?* (this report originally appeared in *Aviation Week*, October 21, 1957), p. 209. Also reported in *The New York Times*, November 21, 1957; *Ibid.*, November 24, 1957.

The second major source of American intelligence information was not known to the public until May 1960. The U-2 photo reconnaissance aircraft began flying its high altitude photographic missions in June 1956, and was reported to have found the Soviet ICBM testing center at Trura Tam (near the Aral Sea) before the first Soviet ICBM test in August 1957.[11]

At the time, the most authoritative statement made on the value of the U-2 photographs was made by Secretary of Defense Thomas Gates:

> From these flights we got information on airfields, aircraft, missiles, missile testings and training, special weapons storage, submarine production, atomic production and aircraft deployment. . . . These results were considered in formulating our military programs.[12]

Later, Allen Dulles stated that the U-2 photos had given "hard" intelligence to American analysts and he claimed: "The Intelligence collected on Soviet missiles has been excellent as to the nature and quality of the potential threat."[13]

Various other claims have been made with respect to the accuracy and value of the U-2 photographs, but perhaps the strongest, and if true the most substantial, was the claim that the U-2 airplane could photograph all of the operational first generation Soviet ICBMs due to the fact that they were strung out along the Trans-Siberian Railroad since their large and cumbersome nature prevented their emplacement far from a major railroad.[14] If this was the case, then all the U-2 had to do was fly along this railroad periodically to photograph the new missile sites

---

11. *The New York Times*, news article on the C.I.A. by Tom Wicker, John W. Finney, Max Frankel, E. W. Kentworthy, and others, April 27, 1966; also reported in: Murphy, "Khrushchev's Paper Bear," pp. 225–227.

12. Dulles, quoting Secretary of Defense Gates in 1960, *The Craft of Intelligence* p. 67.

13. *Ibid.*, p. 65.

14. Murphy, "Khrushchev's Paper Bear," pp. 58–59.

or those under construction, and then return with the valuable information on Soviet operational ICBM strength.

However, the classified nature of the American Turkish radar stations and the U-2 photographs did not allow the concerned elements of the American public to determine the comprehensiveness and accuracy of the intelligence sources available to the United States government. The possibility also existed that the Eisenhower Administration had other sources of intelligence information which still have not been made public.[15]

The fact remains that from the published information on United States intelligence efforts during the missile gap period, the Eisenhower Administration apparently had valuable intelligence sources upon which to base the American estimates of Soviet strategic delivery means.

The debate over the missile gap constantly reverted to the confusing question of the numerous intelligence figures that appeared, indicating that a number of different assessments existed on projected Soviet missile strength. The reasons for the confusion on intelligence estimates within the United State were numerous and this confusion

---

15. The possibility remains that President Eisenhower had highly sensitive intelligence sources known to only a few government officials, although the existence of such sources has never been proven. The rumor that President Kennedy had intelligence sources (or a source) inside the Kremlin during the 1962 Cuban missile crises certainly would indicate the possibility that President Eisenhower had the same type of source. See the Reports on the activities and trial of Oleg V. Penkovsky (former Colonel in the Soviet Army) who was accused of passing Russian rocket information to Western intelligence sources. *The New York Times*, May 8, 1963; *Ibid.*, November 2, 1965; *Ibid.*, January 7, 1961; and *The Penkovsky Papers* (New York: Doubleday & Company, 1965). Allegedly, Colonel Penkovsky passed valuable military intelligence information to Western Intelligence sources from April 1961 to August 1962. Colonel Penkovsky was officially arrested on October 22, 1962, was tried and executed as a spy. Edward Crankshaw (wrote the foreword to *The Penkovsky Papers*) accepted the "papers" authenticity beyond question (page 4 in the book), while the Central Intelligence Agency claimed that they were a forgery (*The New York Times*, November 2, 1965.

could not be traced to one single source. However, three major factors appeared to have caused this situation. These factors were: (1) the lack of decisiveness of the Executive Branch of the Government of the United States and the resulting lack of certainty caused by different statements on intelligence matters by military and Administration officials; (2) the fact that the individual military services, along with the Central Intelligence Agency and the United States Intelligence Board, prepared their own intelligence estimates of Soviet missile strength; and, (3) the unofficial "leaks" of information from government officials to friendly politicians and journalists.

Initially, the Central Intelligence Agency had resisted the pressure from the Department of Defense to produce intelligence projections on Soviet missile strength. In the past, when intelligence estimates had proven faulty the CIA had borne the brunt of public criticism, and it was not eager to assume the rather precarious position of being responsible for predicted Russian missile development and production. But the Department of Defense persisted, based on the fact that United States planning for American missile development and production had to have this information on Russian missiles to compensate for the long "lead times" needed to produce a given missile system (at least 18 to 30 months). Finally, the CIA admitted that they were the agency that should do this job and began work on this project.[16]

The CIA believed that the Soviet ICBM test in 1957 had shown a high degree of Russian competence in this field. But the basic question that faced these intelligence experts was to determine as closely as possible how the Soviet Union would allocate its total military effort. Obviously, Russian emphasis on heavy bombers, fighter planes, or conventional weapons would cut down on the funds available for missile programs. Therefore the early

---

16. Dulles, *The Craft of Intelligence,* p. 164.

CIA estimates on projected Russian missile strength were based on a combination of proven Russian capabilities, "our view of their intentions," and an overall assessment of Russian strategy.[17]

With these essential guidelines established, the CIA began to collect information on the Soviet missile effort (presumably from the U-2 flights and the Turkish radar stations). As "hard" facts became available, these intelligence experts attempted to estimate the actual programming of the Russian missile system. As more evidence continued to be produced, the CIA estimates of existing and projected Soviet ICBM strength were revised downward since "hard" intelligence indicated that the Soviet Union had not engaged in a "crash" missile production program. However, the continued existence of the earlier, more pessimistic estimates for a given year meant that there were several different missile projections in existence, produced at different times, but for the same year in the future. As will be seen below, these downward revisions by the CIA were not necessarily accepted by the Air Force or by spokesmen friendly to this military service. The resulting confusion deserves some attention.

The first evidence during the missile gap period of at least a limited amount of confusion within the United States intelligence community apparently occurred in 1957 concerning the so-called "Gaither Report."[18] In 1965, President Eisenhower admitted that this report indicated that United States retaliatory forces would become vulnerable to Soviet missile attack by about 1959, but said that he had "other information" on American Strategic posture and therefore did not accept the conclusions of the Gaither Committee.[19] The former President never explained the

---

17. *Ibid.*

18. See Chapter 2.

19. Eisenhower, *Waging the Peace*, p. 221. A writer in the *Boston Globe* claimed that the Gaither report estimated what the Russians *could* do rather than what they *would* do (capability versus intent). *The Boston Globe*, "Ike Discloses Gaither 'Missile Gap' Report," article by David Wise, September 26, 1965.

source of his "other information" or what it was. In view
of the fact that the Gaither Committee supposedly had
access to all essential classified information needed to conduct their study, it appears that intelligence information
existed that was not turned over to this Committee (possibly the U-2 interpreted photographs or an even more
sensitive source).

This early confusion within the United States government was the first of many such situations that arose under
the Eisenhower Administration and that probably could
have been avoided with better Executive coordination and
control of American intelligence information. The un-
favorable report made by the Gaither Committee gave the
initial impetus to the missile gap debate in 1957. If this
report on American strategic vulnerability could have
been avoided by presidential action, it would have saved
President Eisenhower a great deal of trouble in the years
to come.

In the summer of 1958, Senator Symington offered the
first concrete evidence that there was more than one set
of intelligence figures on Soviet missile programs in circulation within the United States government. He sent a
letter to President Eisenhower and charged that the United
States was lagging unjustifiably behind the Soviet Union
in missile development and gave "as his authority his own
intelligence sources." He further claimed that the full
extent of the danger had not been accurately estimated
by the Central Intelligence Agency.[20] Senator Symington's
"own intelligence sources" were never disclosed; but before the missile gap debate was over evidence had appeared
to indicate the possibility that his source of information
was the Air Force.[21]

This secret Symington letter to President Eisenhower
was not made public until 1959 when it became apparent
that the Central Intelligence Agency had made its first
downward revision of projected Russian missile strength.

20. Eisenhower, *Waging the Peace*, pp. 389–390.
21. See below.

No definitive evidence was found as to exactly when the CIA made its first downward revision of Soviet missile production. However, when the public statement was made early in 1959, it appeared to be based on the assumption that the United States and the Soviet Union had both reached the same negative conclusion concerning the value and efficacy of mass-producing large numbers of first generation intercontinental ballistic missiles.[22]

By 1959 at the latest the United States government had decided that the first generation liquid fuel ICBMs were not worth the investment of resources it would take to produce them in large numbers. The *Atlas* missile was a heavy, cumbersome and expensive weapon. In addition, it took 30 minutes to prepare (fuel) and launch, making it highly vulnerable to enemy surprise attack and therefore primarily a first strike weapon. The basic decision was made to produce a limited number of this weapons system and to move on to the development and production of the more sophisticated and cheaper second generation *Minuteman* system. (The same reasoning applied to the substitution of the *Polaris* system for the *Regulus* system.)[23]

The United States Government had decided to rely, temporarily, on the efficacy of its superiority in manned-bombers plus a limited number of first generation ICBM and IRBM missiles to deter a Soviet attack until the second generation of American missiles became operational.[24]

Secretary of Defense McElroy appeared to confirm this American policy when he testified early in 1959 that:

22. See Appendix A.

23. "Next Generation Seen as Missile Race Key," quoting General Bernard Schriever, p. 35. Although at one time the United States programmed about 230 first generation ICBMs (a small number compared to the final production of second generation missiles), in reality the United States produced fewer than 200 first generation missiles, counting both the *Titan* and *Atlas* systems. In all probability, both the programmed and produced number of first generation missiles would have been less if the Eisenhower Administration had not been under such heavy pressure to produce more missiles because of the feared missile gap.

24. The *Minuteman* attained operational status in 1962, while the *Polaris* was operational in 1960.

It is not our intention or policy to try and match missile for missile in the ICBM category of Russian capability *in the next couple of years.* Our position . . . is that our diversified capability to deliver the big weapons [nuclear warheads and bombs] is what we are going to count on as our ability to deter general war.[25]

The Secretary of Defense also admitted that in a year or two Russia could have more ICBMs than the United States.[26]

Evidently, early in 1959 the leaders of the Soviet Union also had decided not to produce first generation ICBMs in large numbers. As with the American decision, it was not possible to determine exactly when this became Soviet policy. However, according to the United States Defense Department, by 1961 the Soviet Union had produced only a "handful" of ICBMs and even by 1964 the Soviet Union was credited officially with less than 200 ICBMs.[27] If the Soviet leaders had embarked on a "crash" missile production program in 1959, the Soviet Union certainly would have had more than a "handful" of ICBMs in 1961 and far more than 200 by 1964 (in 1964 the United States had 750 operational ICBMs and 192 *Polaris* missiles). In spite of the claim by Premier Khrushchev that Russia was producing missiles in "serial production" and that one factory produced 250 missiles per year, the Soviet Union decided upon a very limited production program for first generation ICBMs.[28]

Early in 1959, the Central Intelligence Agency accepted the possibility that the Soviet Union was not engaged in a large build-up of first generation ICBMs. Therefore, the

25. *Joint Hearings, 1959*, p. 46. (emphasis added)
26. *Ibid.*, pp. 46, 49. During this same testimony, Secretary McElroy indicated that the reduced budget request for missile development in 1960 was due to the fact that the United States had stopped the development of the first generation *Snark* and *Regulus* missiles.
27. *The New York Times*, official Pentagon figures for January, 1961 and April, 1964, April 15, 1964. See Appendix A.
28. American intelligence sources publicly claimed this limited Soviet missile production program in 1960, see: *Joint Hearings, 1960*, p. 142. See below.

first downward revision of United States intelligence estimates of projected Soviet missile strength was made. This
fact came out during the *Joint Hearings, 1959,* when Senator Symington stated that during 1958 he had been
briefed by the CIA four times, and that although he disagreed with their estimates based on "other information I
had," the CIA figures had been the same all four times.
Then he claimed that even lower estimates allegedly from
the CIA had been given by Secretary of Defense McElroy
in an earlier secret hearing before a different Congressional committee.[29]

Simultaneously, the United States government purposely
produced two sets of figures in the National Intelligence
Estimate based upon different assessments of the number
of ICBMs the Soviet Union *could* produce. Due to a lack
of certainty on the part of the intelligence community as
to exactly what programs were being pursued by Russia,
the National Intelligence Estimate for 1959 attempted to
cover two possible contingencies. The smaller projected
number represented an "orderly" Soviet missile program
based on the missile production capacity credited to the
Soviet Union. The larger second figure attempted to cover
the possibility that the Soviet Union might use this capability to engage in a "crash" missile program.[30]

Later in 1959, Secretary of Defense McElroy publicly
implied for the first time the possibility of two sets of
United States figures. He stated that the "missile gap"
arose only when the number of missiles the United States
actually planned to produce was compared to the number
the Soviet Union "could" produce. The Secretary of Defense further stated that it was impossible to overempha-
size the importance of the word "could" in this "type of
estimate," and that United States estimates were not intended to mean that the Soviet Union actually would

29. *Joint Hearings, 1959,* pp. 26–27.
30. *Joint Hearings, 1960,* p. 442. (These two sets of estimates made
in 1959 were not made public until 1960.)

produce this large number of missiles. To support his argument, he referred to the "bomber gap" and the fact that at the time of this supposed "gap," the American estimates said the Soviet Union could produce 600 to 700 Bisons, but it chose not to do so.[31]

The existence of two official sets of intelligence figures produced in 1959 did not become public until 1960. When they were openly discussed they caused a great deal of confusion, even after it had been explained that official American estimates had rejected a "crash" Russian production program and believed that the Soviet Union had adopted an "orderly" program.[32]

By the end of January 1959, there was a real possibility that there were three sets of secret intelligence figures being discussed within United States government circles— the two sets in the National Intelligence Estimates ("orderly" versus "crash" production programs) and Senator Symington's "other information."[33]

But the confusion did not stop with this situation. At the same time that the "revised" intelligence estimates were being given to Congressional leaders, Secretary of Defense McElroy apparently admitted that by the early 1960s, the Soviet Union would have a three-to-one advantage over the United States in operational long-range ballistic missiles. The transcript of the Congressional hearing where he allegedly made this statement was never released, but a vast number of reports of this statement were made and it was never denied by Secretary McElroy.[34]

31. U.S. Congress, Senate, Committee on Appropriations, Department of Defense Appropriations for 1960, *Hearings*, 86th Cong., 1st sess., Vol. 4 (May 1959), p. 5.

32. *Joint Hearings, 1960*, p. 442. It was impossible to determine which set of figures had upset Senator Symington when presented by Secretary of Defense McElroy, or if Senator Symington had seen both sets and still disagreed.

33. It was possible that Senator Symington's other information came from the "crash" set of figures, but this seems unlikely.

34. As seen above, this statement in books by Mr. Schlesinger, Mr. Sorensen, Mr. Spanier, Mr. Huntington, and in the *Joint Hearings, 1960*.

The public was never told which set of intelligence figures was used by Secretary McElroy in arriving at this prediction.

Politically, which set of figures used by the Secretary of Defense was not relevant. This alleged statement gave the partisan critics of the Eisenhower Administration an "official confirmation" of the existence of a future "missile gap."

This episode served as a good example of two very important contributory factors in the creation of the missile gap and the almost perpetual confusion that surrounded this question. The first factor was President Eisenhower's failure to give strong leadership in controlling Administration statements on intelligence matters and his failure to set up a coordinated method for arriving at a single intelligence "policy line" to be followed by these spokesmen. The second factor, and an essential corollary to the first, was the almost undeniable fact that there were officials within the United States government who "leaked" classified information to friendly public sources, and that there were reporters who publicly disclosed sensitive information gained in supposedly secret "background briefings."[35]

The accuracy of the journalistic coverage of the missile gap controversy is certainly open to serious question. The claims of "leaks" and of the possession of "official estimates" could not be certified, and even if these claims were true, this could not be admitted by the government officials concerned. Journalistic treatments of this question also represented many of the political biases and subjective opinions so often found in coverage of any controversial issue. In spite of these very real handicaps to objectivity, and the lack of objectivity in many of the articles that dealt with the missile controversy, an interesting pattern of reporting on the comparative strategic Ameri-

---

35. Both of these factors recurred throughout the missile gap debate and will be dealt with in more detail below.

can-Soviet power appeared in selected newspaper and periodical analyses.

The earliest public estimates of the missile gap for the year 1962 gave a projected ICBM lead of from 8 to 14 Soviet ICBMs to one ICBM for the United States. According to these earlier figures, by 1962 the Soviet Union was supposed to have between 1000 and 1500 ICBMs while the United States allegedly was programmed to have only 130. Following the first American downward revision of projected Soviet missile strength in 1959, the publicly predicted Russian strength was reduced accordingly to 500 ICBMs. Also, several of these new projections appeared to follow Secretary McElroy's predicted three-to-one Soviet advantage, rather than the earlier predictions of a Soviet advantage of roughly ten to one. It is impossible to determine with certainty whether these figures presented in the mass media were "leaks" from government officials. However, the fact remains that throughout the missile gap period many newspaper and periodical missile projections closely paralleled the later figures claimed by the United States government to be the "official intelligence estimates."[36]

The confusion of American intelligence estimates that occurred in 1959 took place for the most part in secret; it was not until early 1960 that the almost chaotic situation within the United States intelligence community became apparent in public sources. This confusion, which continued through 1960 and for most of 1961, was never cleared up in public sources and only disappeared when the missile gap illusion itself disappeared in late 1961.[37]

---

36. See Appendix A. The one exception to the 1959 "revision" was found in an article by Joseph Alsop (October 7, 1959, Appendix A). By the end of 1959, the projected number of Soviet missiles for 1962 was reduced to 400 ICBMs. It is worthy of note that the public estimates that appeared accurate lagged from three to five months behind the changes made in official estimates.

37. The situation in 1960 has been dealt with in some detail in chapters 5 and 6. Therefore, only summary conclusions on this period will be presented here.

General Power's controversial speech in January 1960 served as a strong catalyst to the "numbers game" being played with missile projections on comparative United States-Soviet Union strengths. In spite of his foreboding prediction of the ability of 300 Soviet ICBMs and IRBMs to destroy the American retaliatory forces, the fact remains that in 1960, the Soviet Union did not have anywhere near 300 missiles (at the most they had 10 ICBMs) and had only 150 long-range bombers. Arrayed against this force was a large, diversified American deterrent force which even General Power called "the most powerful retaliatory force in the world."[38] The American deterrent force consisted of almost 600 B-52s, 1200 B-47s (with in-flight refueling), and over 200 carrier-based aircraft dispersed on 14 American attack carriers (plus an unknown number of American fighter-bombers with a nuclear capability stationed at various American bases throughout the world). No one, not even General Power, questioned existing American security, but the debate continued to revolve around the estimates of future comparative missile strength.

The most interesting aspect of General Power's speech was that he was allowed to make it in the first place. He claimed that the speech had been cleared by the "Air Staff, by the Department of Defense, by the Joint Chiefs of Staff, and by the State Department."[39] Since this claim was never directly contradicted, it must have been true. However, the fact that Secretary of Defense Gates called General Power's analysis "unrealistic" and "oversimplified" indicates that the Secretary of Defense had not seen the speech beforehand, and it does not appear logical that President Eisenhower would have allowed such a speech to be made if he had known the content.

Once again, President Eisenhower's failure to maintain closer control over the public statements of the military

38. *Joint Hearings, 1960*, p. 23.
39. *Joint Hearings, 1960*, p. 13.

and political leaders of his Administration allowed potent arguments for the missile gap thesis to emerge from within the Administration itself.[40] The alarm caused by General Power's speech was demonstrated during the *Joint Hearings, 1960*. According to General Power, the predicted missile gap would arrive when the Soviet Union had 150 ICBMs and 150 IRBMs. At this time, the Strategic Air Command could be destroyed as an effective retaliatory force. Therefore, the *Joint Hearings, 1960* concentrated on the question of the predicted Soviet missile strength. This question had to be answered by the American intelligence community, but this community offered "several" conflicting and contradictory answers.

During 1959, a series of unconfirmed reports indicated that the Soviet Union had run into difficulty in its ICBM testing and development programs. There were also indications that the Russian missile program had placed a serious strain on the Russian economy. These reports presaged the second major downward revision, in 1960, of American intelligence estimates of projected Soviet missile strength.[41]

This revision occurred early in 1960 when Thomas Gates, the new Secretary of Defense, stated that the Russians had engaged in an "orderly" missile production program and therefore earlier estimates based on a "crash" Soviet missile program were too high.[42] Simultaneously,

---

40. This point brings up the delicate question of how much "censorship" should be exercised by political leaders over military statements, and if the military leaders should be made to conform to political considerations on matters concerning national defense.

41. *The New York Times*, "Washington Finds No Proof Moscow had Capability to Launch ICBMs," by Hanson W. Baldwin, March 25, 1959; *Ibid.*, "McElroy Reports U.S. and Russians Lag on Missiles," news article by Jack Raymond, June 28, 1959; Murphy, "The Embattled Mr. McElroy," p. 242; "Missiles: Ours and Russia's," (this article reported the alleged strain on the Soviet Economy), *Newsweek*, Vol. 54 (July 13, 1959), p. 52.

42. This downward revision also raised the question of whether United States intelligence estimates were based on Soviet "intent" or "capability." (See chapter 5 for a detailed analysis of this problem.)

CIA director Allen Dulles produced a less optimistic set of intelligence figures and the Air Force came up with a third set which was higher than either of the first two estimates. The exact figures used in these estimates were never made public, nor were the reasons for the confusion publicly stated.

It now appears that three factors combined to produce the chaotic situation within the United States intelligence community in 1960 and early 1961. These three factors were: (1) In spite of the continued downward revision of projected Soviet missile strength, several individuals within the Administration apparently continued to accept the earlier, more pessimistic projections; (2) The existence of at least two official sets of figures in the National Intelligence Estimates ("orderly" versus "crash" Soviet programs) until 1960 gave some spokesmen the supposed option of accepting either a "high" or a "low" set; and, (3) The fact that the military services continued to produce their own estimates of future Soviet missile strength gave rise to at least two additional possible sets of figures— one set from the Air Force and one from the Army-Navy coalition.[43]

In considering these three factors within the intelligence community, logic would indicate the possibility of at least six different sets of figures in 1960 purporting to be the projected number of Soviet missiles for a given

---

43. In 1964, one author claimed that after the CIA's success with the U-2 Photo reconnaissance aircraft, the U.S. Air Force bought its own U-2 planes and began to fly "spy" missions over the Soviet Union. (See: Murphy, "Khrushchev's Paper Bear," p. 224. Two other authors hinted that the Air Force might have had its own U-2 photographs and stated flatly that the Air Force did use its own photo interpreters to come up with diffierent conclusions than the Central Intelligence Agency held on Russian missile programs. See: David Wise and Thomas B. Ross, *The Invisible Government* (New York: Bantam Books, published by arrangement with Random House, Inc., 1964), p. 226. Neither of these reports could be substantiated by official documents. However, there does not appear to be much doubt that the Air Force did have its own photo interpreters analyzing U-2 Photographs.

year. However, this does not appear to be the case. The real possibility exists that there was a great deal of overlap and duplication within American intelligence circles. For example, the "crash" estimates rejected by the Department of Defense could have been the same as the "high" Air Force estimates, while the "low" Army-Navy estimates could have been the same as the "orderly" Department of Defense figures. By 1970, the reasons for this confusion still had not been clarified for the American public.

The almost unbelievable confusion in the American intelligence community apparently continued until the fall of 1961. At that time, President Kennedy managed to combine the various intelligence estimates of the military services under the control of the Secretary of Defense and the newly-created Defense Intelligence Agency (DIA). Once this was done, the Air Force apparently accepted the lower figures of the Army-Navy estimates and the military services finally agreed upon one set of projected Soviet ICBM figures.[44]

Once again the mass media appear to have reflected the downward revisions of the United States Government. The 1960 downward revision by Secretary of Defense Gates was represented in many periodicals and showed the Soviet Union with a maximum missile advantage over the United States of three to one by 1961-1962.[45] In early 1961 the published projections still showed a Soviet ICBM lead, but a reduced lead compared to earlier projections; and by the end of 1961 most published reports claimed either missile parity between the two super powers or a slight United States lead.[46]

---

44. Once this was done, the number of intelligence figures was reduced considerably. (The "crash" estimates had been dropped in early 1960.) However, the Strategic Air Command did not accept the lower figures, so two sets of possible figures were still in existence.

45. See Appendix A.

46. During this period, there were reports of "leaks" of intelligence information: see the *Joint Hearings, 1960* and the reports of the alleged McNamara "background briefing" of February 1961. See above.

Surprisingly, there have not been many published reports that attempt to explain "Where the Missile Gap Went," or to assess the blame for its creation. Spokesmen for the Kennedy Administration attempted to blame statements made by President Eisenhower and his Administration for creating the missile gap illusion.[47] Others claimed that Mr. Kennedy's statements were made in "good faith."[48] Still other sources blamed American "politicians," "sensation seeking journalists," "the Military-Industrial complex," and in some cases the blame was placed almost entirely on the "bravado" of the Soviet Union.[49]

It has become apparent that any attempt to discover a single cause for the creation of the missile gap illusion would result in the oversimplification of an extremely complex situation. Nonetheless, it is doubtful that the missile gap controversy would have assumed its intense and confusing nature had it not been for the lack of coordination and duplication that occurred within the United States intelligence community.

One of the major personalities involved in the creation of the missile gap myth, Senator Stuart Symington, came up with his own interesting version of "how" the missile gap was created and "where it went," although he did not deal with "why" it was created.[50] Senator Symington blamed the Central Intelligence Agency and its constant downward revision of national intelligence figures based

47. Schlesinger, *A Thousand Days*, p. 317; McGeorge Bundy, "The President and the Peace," *Foreign Affairs*, Vol. 42 (April 1964), p. 354.

48. Alsop, "McNamara Thinks about the Unthinkable," p. 18.

49. Rush and Horelick, *Strategic Power and Soviet Foreign Policy*. (This was one of the major themes developed in this book.)

50. In the process of explaining the missile gap, Senator Symington attempted to justify his own role in its development and also implied that he was not certain it had really disappeared. U.S. Congress, Senate, Armed Service Committee, *Hearings*, Military Procurement Authorization for Fiscal Year 1963, 87th Cong., 2nd., sess., Vol. 10 (January-February 1962), pp. 49–50; Senator Stuart Symington, "Where the Missile Gap Went," *The Reporter*, Vol. 26 (February 15, 1962), pp. 21–22.

on Soviet "intent" rather than the Russian "capability" to produce missiles as the major cause of the missile gap myth. To prove his point, Senator Symington quoted alleged official United States intelligence figures for projected Soviet missile production for the years 1961-1962. In order to avoid going into the classified number of missiles involved in these secret projections, he used the percentage of predicted Russian missile production as of 1959 as compared with the new percentage used in 1961. (See Tables I and II.) According to the figures used by Senator Symington, the official United States government estimates of Russian missile production had been reduced by 96.5 percent from December 1959 to September 1961, so that as of September 1961, the Soviet Union only was given credit for the production of 3.5 percent of the missiles that the United States had said in 1959 that the Russians would produce.[51]

When Senator Symington confronted Secretary of Defense McNamara with these figures, Secretary McNamara answered rather lamely that those who had discussed the missile gap had based their comments on national intelligence estimates and "were speaking of the missile gap in good faith."[52]

Table I
Total High Estimated Soviet Missile Production
For 1961–1962**

	100%			
100%	(1500 ICBMs)			
80%				
60%				
40%		34% (512 ICBMs)		
20%			30% (450 ICBMs)	
				15% (225 ICBMs)
0%				3.5% (52 ICBMs)
	December 1959	February 1960	August 1960	June 1961	September 1961

51. U.S. Congress, Senate, Armed Services Committee, *Hearings on Procurement for 1963*, 8th Cong., pp. 49–50.
52. *Ibid.*

The figures in parentheses represent the number of Soviet ICBMs projected by public sources for late 1961-early 1962. The 1959 prediction is used as the base year. The December 1959 figure of a projected 1500 ICBMs was used here to present the most pessimistic public estimate used at the time.

Table II
Lower Estimated Soviet Missile Production
For 1961–1962**

	December 1959	February 1960	August 1960	June 1961	September 1961
100%	100% (1000 ICBMs)				
80%					
60%					
40%		34% (340 ICBMs)			
			30% (300 ICBMs)		
20%				15% (150 ICBMs)	
0%					3.5% (35 ICBMs)

The figures in parentheses represent the number of Soviet ICBMs projected in public sources using a lower base number of ICBMs (1000 ICBMs).

** The projected number of Soviet ICBMs can be found in Appendix A. Both sets of percentage figures were given by Senator Symington in place of classified missile figures. See: U.S. Congress Senate, Military Procurement Authorization for Fiscal Year 1963, Hearings, 87th Congress, 2nd session, Vol. 19 (January–February 1962), p. 49; Senator Stuart Symington, "Where the Missile Gap Went," p. 22.

Due to the fact that Senator Symington had been a major protagonist in the missile gap debate, it was logical that he would attempt to find an explanation for its creation that did not damage his own reputation or political image. Nonetheless, his rationalization of the missile gap appears to be one of the few *public* statements made by one of the individuals who had access to classified information and was connected closely with the development of the missile gap.

If Senator Symington's percentages are analyzed in an attempt to gain a picture of how the missile gap appeared to those who accepted its existence, the following picture emerges.[53] By using the highest 1959 Soviet ICBM projection for 1962 (1500 ICBMs) as a base figure and then reducing the number of projected missiles as the estimates were revised downward (according to Senator Symington's percentages), the most pessimistic view of the missile gap seen by those who accepted the downward revision is discernible.[54] (Table I) If the lower 1959 prediction of 1000 Soviet ICBMs for 1962 is used (Table II), then the potential gap is reduced but remains substantial.

From this analysis an interesting observation can be made. A check on the figures presented in Appendix A reveals that the figures in Table II (in parentheses) resemble many of the public estimates presented from 1958 to 1961 in the popular journalistic treatments of the missile controversy.

A comparison of Senator Symington's figures and those presented to the public gives rise to two tentative conclusions. First, the possibility existed that Senator Symington's percentage projections offer enough evidence to create a relatively accurate reconstruction of at least one set of intelligence figures found in the United States government during the missile gap controversy. And, second, the apparent accuracy of some of the newspaper and journalistic reporting on at least this set of missile projections offers strong evidence that classified information was being revealed by government sources to some representatives of the mass media. These two conclusions are tenuous, but there is enough evidence to warrant their serious consideration as a valid reconstruction of how the missile gap appeared to those who accepted a substantial United States missile inferiority. If, in fact, the Soviet

---

53. It was not possible to determine which set of figures or whose estimates Senator Symington based his percentages on, although it is safe to speculate that he used one of the higher sets of intelligence figures available (probably either the "crash" figures or those of the Air Force, if they were different).

54. For those who did not accept the downward revisions, the projected 1500 Soviet ICBM's by 1962 remained a possible reality.

Union had possessed between 1000 and 1500 ICBMs by late 1961, the "missile gap" would have been a reality; but the fact remains that at this time the Soviet Union was credited with the possession of less than 100 ICBMs.

At the same time that Senator Symington attempted to explain the missile gap, an Air Force spokesman admitted that the Russians had the "capability" to create the gap, but "they [the Russians] did not do what our intelligence people thought they would do."[55]

The evidence available indicated that the United States government was fairly accurate in determining the Soviet "capability" to produce long-range ballistic missiles, but misinterpreted and overexaggerated the "intent" of Russian policy makers in assuming that they would use this capability to its fullest possible extent.

The acceptance of the missile gap by many individuals in the United States had a definite impact on American domestic policies and this question deserves considerable analysis.

Budgetary, Partisan and Military Effects of the Missile Gap

The domestic impact of the missile controversy on the United States can be divided into three general, inter-related categories:

1. Defense expenditures and interservice rivalry.
2. Partisan politics and the missile gap.
3. American military strategy and missiles.[56]

The budgetary procedures of the United States government are extremely difficult to analyze, even for those

---

55. U.S. Congress, House, Appropriations Committee, Department of Defense Appropriations Subcommittee, *Hearings for Fiscal 1963*, testimony by General Frederick H. Smith, Jr., Vice Chief of Staff, U. S. Air Force, 87th Cong., 2nd sess., pt. 2 (February 1962), p. 489. Stewart Alsop later admitted to the same conclusion: Stewart Alsop, "The Alternative to Total War," *Saturday Evening Post*, Vol. 236 (December 1, 1962), p. 16.

56. Some of the major aspects of these three factors have been dealt with in the text of this study and will not be repeated here.

with access to the classified details on the process of defense appropriations and expenditures.[57] The budget categories conceal the nature of American preparedness for various military contingencies and the figures available are "written in a jargon that defies comprehension."[58] In addition to these handicaps, the increasing complexity of technological developments in the defense field make the whole process of defense appropriations extremely difficult to understand. As a result, Congress usually allows the major budgetary decisions to be made in the Executive Branch and contents itself with minor revisions or at most dramatic proposals that still are left to the White House for final action.[59]

These serious difficulties, inherent in American budgetary procedures, complicate tremendously the task of analyzing United States defense expenditures during the period of the missile gap and lead to conclusions that, for the most part, are general in nature.

The prime ingredient of the struggle among the United States military services was the constant fight for a higher budgetary appropriation for a given service so that it could carry out the mission the service visualized for itself. In order to justify the requests for these appropriations and to maximize the future role of a given military service, military doctrines on limited and all-out war were articulated and defined by the military services and their allies. It would not be accurate to attribute the entire debate over American strategic doctrine since World War II to the selfish demands of the military services for larger appropriations; but neither can it be denied that this was a significant aspect of interservice rivalry which played an important part in the missile gap controversy. The Air

57. Senator Henry M. Jackson, "Organizing for National Survival," *Foreign Affairs*, Vol. 38 (April 1960), p. 446.

58. *Ibid.*, pp. 455–456.

59. Bernard K. Gordon, "The Military Budget: Congressional Phase," *Journal of Politics*, Vol. 23 (November 1961), p. 692.

Force's belief in a counterforce doctrine (or a variation on this doctrine) and the Army-Navy acceptance of a form of a minimum deterrent strategy reflected, in part, a belief on the part of these services that these doctrines would best serve the military interests of the United States. However, whichever doctrine was accepted, the policy would require large expenditures for the weapons systems that would add appreciably to the appropriations for the military service advocating a given strategic approach.

Along with the constant statements on national security in support of a given doctrine and the weapons system needed to implement this doctrine, the military services also mobilized their "independent" organizations and publications to support their position. The Air Force, by far the strongest politically of the three services, presented its case through the Air Force Association and the Air Force's unofficial publication *Air Force* (later named *Air Force and Space Digest*).[60] The politically weaker, but still potent, Army and Navy arguments were presented by the Association of the United States Army (*Army Magazine*) and by the Navy League (*Navy: The Magazine of Sea Power*), respectively.[61]

The military services also found valuable allies in those industries engaged in the production of weapons systems for national defense and among the Congressmen who represented the districts (or states) in which these industries were located. These industries advertised in the service periodicals as well as in national periodicals with a broader circulation. With huge defense contracts at stake, it was to an industry's advantage to do everything in its power to see that the funds were obtained for the develop-

---

60. Also, *Air University Quarterly* could be counted on for support of the Air Force position.

61. Also *Military Review* represented the point of view of the Army, while the *U.S. Naval Institute Proceedings* represented the Navy. See: Samuel P. Huntington, "The Military Lobby: Its Impact on Congress, Nation." *Congressional Quarterly Review*, Vol. 14 (March 24, 1961), p. 466.

ment and production of a weapons system in which it was involved. Therefore, for example, in the *Thor-Jupiter* struggle, the Chysler Corporation, under contract to develop the Army's *Jupiter* and with major plants in Alabama, heralded the ability of the Army *Jupiter* and was joined by the Alabama Congressional delegation. Simultaneously, Douglas Aircraft supported the *Thor* missile and was joined by the California delegation.[62]

This coalition of military and industrial interests led to President Eisenhower's warning of the potential threat of the "military-industrial complex." This same theme has been dramatized and expanded by several authors who came to the conclusion that the pressures for increased defense spending can be traced almost exclusively to this "military-industrial complex."[63]

There does not appear to be much doubt that the military and industrial interests in the United States played an extremely significant role in the determination of the allocation of resources for defense purposes. But to claim that these were the only sources of pressure for the increased expenditures is to overlook such important aspects of Defense Department appropriations as domestic in-

62. The same picture emerged from the conflict between the Army's *Nike-Zeus* versus the Air Force's *Bomarc* systems. (Western Electric supported the *Nike* system and Boeing Aircraft backed the *Bomarc* system.) An excellent analysis of this problem can be found in Samuel Huntington's article listed above. *Ibid.,* pp. 40–52. A Congressional Committee investigated the connection between the military and industry in a series of special hearings in 1959. See: U.S. Congress, House, Committee on Armed Services, Subcommittee for Special Investigation, *Hearings,* Employment of Retired Military and Civilian Personnel by Defense Industries, 86th Cong., 1st sess., Vol. 8 (July-August-September 1959). The so-called *Hebert Hearings.*

63. See: Cook, *The Warfare State,* pp. 12–15; Victor Perlo, *Militarism and Industry: Arms Profiteering in the Missile Age.* (New York: International Publishers, 1963), pp. 161–170. Mr. Perlo attempted to prove there was (and is) a direct political and financial connection between many of the key personalities in the missile gap controversy and the business community. (Senator Stuart Symington, p. 161; Senator Henry Jackson, p. 161; Mr. Robert C. Sprague, Co-chairman of the Gaither Report, p. 170).

flation, fluctuating tensions of the "cold war," spiraling weapons costs, straight partisan politics, and a large number of other significant factors-

Therefore, in spite of the sustained effort by the different military services and their allies during the missile gap period to gain a larger share of the defense budget, the services continued to obtain about the same percentage of the defense budget they had received before the missile crisis arose. Throughout the missile gap period, the Air Force received roughly 46 percent of the defense budget, while the Navy maintained 28 percent and the Army 23 percent.[64] The one possible major exception to this unwritten budgetary rule occurred in 1957, when the Air Force received a rather substantial budgetary increase over the Army and the Navy.[65]

The crises atmosphere created by the missile controversy, along with the above-mentioned factors, did lead to an annual overall increase in the United States defense budget from 1956 to 1959. When American defense expenditures were reduced in 1960, this reduction apparently was the result of three factors. First, 1960 was an election year and the Republican Administration attempted to create what it believed would be viewed as a favorable economic climate in the United States for this election. Secondly, this decrease in defense spending reflected the

Table III
National Security Expenditures for the Army, Navy, and Air Force
1956–1962*
(in millions of dollars) **

---

64. *Joint Hearings, 1960* (Senate), testimony by General Maxwell D. Taylor (U.S. Army, retired), pp. 190–191; Huntington, *The Common Defense,* pp. 446–456. Mr. Huntington used the figures: Air Force 47 percent, Army 22 percent, and Navy 29 percent. For actual service expenditures see Table III and Appendix B.

65. This was the year of the Soviet ICBM and Sputnik and a recession in the United States. See Table III for actual expenditures in 1957.

	1956	1957	1958	1959	1960	1961	1962
ARMY	8,702	9,063	9,051	9,468	9,392	10,332	11,559
NAVY	9,744	10,398	10,906	11,728	11,642	12,313	13,193
AIR FORCE	16,749	18,363	18,435	19,084	19,066	19,816	20,883
TOTAL DEFENSE BUDGET:	40,641	43,270	44,142	46,426	45,627	47,494	51,107

* "United States Defense Policies in 1964," The Library of Congress, Legislative Reference Service (Washington, D.C.: U.S. Government Printing Office, June 4, 1965), 89th Congress, 1st sess., House Document No. 285, p. 179.
** Not included in total expenditures: Direction and coordination of defense, other central defense activities, civil defense, military assistance, development and control of nuclear energy, stockpiling and other defense-related activities. For complete figures see Appendix B.

earlier decision by American leaders not to mass-produce first generation missiles, but to wait for the more sophisticated, cheaper, second generation. And, finally, the Eisenhower Administration's willingness to cut the defense budget must have reflected President Eisenhower's personal belief that United States security would not be seriously affected by this move.[66]

In 1961, the American defense expenditures began to increase once again. But before these additional funds could have any significant impact on United States deterrent posture, President Kennedy had successfully convinced the American people that there was no missile gap.

The fact that the defense expenditures of the United States did increase during the period of the missile gap is indisputable and there does not appear to be much doubt that the pressures of the alleged missile gap added to defense costs. However, numerous other factors were working simultaneously to increase the appropriations the American Congress and Executive branch allocated for United States security.

66. In reality, this defense reduction hit the Air Force much harder than either the Army or the Navy. See Table III.

One of these "other factors" which created pressure for additional funds was the substantial role played by partisan politics in the missile gap controversy. By definition, a two-party democracy should have a party of the "opposition" and in this case the party of opposition was the Democratic Party. At the national party level, the conflict between the Democratic and Republican National Committees continued throughout the missile debate, and the Democratic Advisory Council was the constant critic of the defense policies of the Eisenhower Administration. But the most interesting aspect of this partisanship was found in the actions and statements of the individuals involved.

The politicians who propagated the missile gap thesis appeared to be reacting to at least three interrelated stimuli: prospects for partisan advantage; loyalty to a military service, to a strategic concept, or to an industrial friend; and a sincere concern for the defense posture of the United States. The exact make-up of any single individual's motivation cannot be determined and any conclusions on this question would depend upon the source accepted as valid and a subjective assessment of individual motivation.

The missile debate was not sufficiently developed in 1958 to play a major role in the Congressional elections of that year. When the debate did become an issue in the 1960 Presidential elections, it was transformed from the question of a "missile gap" to one of American prestige based on United States military and space achievements. The Democratic Presidential nominee, Senator John F. Kennedy, attempted to exploit this "prestige" issue in October 1960, and during this period the public opinion polls showed definite gains in his vote-getting ability. However, with the multitude of issues involved and the impact of the "great debate," it cannot be claimed that the transformed missile gap question proved decisive, but only that it was a factor.

The most interesting observation on the long-run

partisan effects of the missile gap debate is the fact that none of the major participants were seriously damaged politically by their mistaken advocacy of this myth. Senators Symington and Jackson have since been reelected and Senator Johnson became President of the United States in a "landslide" election in 1964, with hardly a murmur about his past activities in connection with this critical issue on national defense.[67]

President Kennedy, after limited political difficulty due to Secretary McNamara's "background briefing" in February 1960, handled the missile gap question with a great deal of finesse and skill. By the time he finally denied its existence in November 1961, he not only escaped any major blame for its creation, but at least one writer credited him with single-handedly closing the missile gap.[68]

Several "quasi-official" biographies of President Kennedy's campaign and Adminstration have been written by individuals who had high positions in the Kennedy Organization. In the biographies an attempt was made to defend Senator Kennedy's role in the development of the missile gap. One of these sources stated that the intelligence information gained from the U-2 reconnaissance missions had demonstrated that Premier Khrushchev was bluffing and that the Soviet Union had not engaged in the large scale production of first generation missiles. However, this same author contended that the Democratic presidential nominee had not been permitted to see this intelligence data and that the intelligence information the Eisenhower Administration did make available indicated that the United States faced a "dangerous situation" militarily in the years to come.[69]

---

67. It also appeared as though the Alsop brothers, who had done a great deal to create the impression of the missile gap in journalistic writings, escaped any serious damage to their reputation as reporters.

68. Andre Beaufre, *Introduction to Strategy* (New York: Frederick A. Praeger, 1965) , pp. 95–96.

69. Theodore C. Sorensen, *Kennedy*, pp. 611–612. This information was not corroborated by other sources. Mr. Schlesinger in *A Thousand Days*

Once the missile gap controversy ceased in early 1962, the issue did not appear again politically until 1964. Then, when it was discussed by the Republican Presidential nominee, Senator Goldwater, he did not attack the earlier creation of this myth. Instead he attempted to create a new "deterrent gap" based on his belief that American missiles were not reliable and therefore the United States should rely more on the manned bomber than on missiles that had not been tested in combat.

Any assessment of the total impact of the missile gap debate on partisan politics in the United States is by definition a subjective matter. Although the missile debate raged for over four years and at times assumed an almost completely partisan nature, most of the evidence indicated that it played an important but not a lasting role in the American political process. As a political issue, it helped Senator Kennedy get elected and in view of the very close nature of the 1960 presidential election, a case could be made for the fact that it was one of the important factors in President Kennedy's election.

By 1966 the original missile gap had disappeared and the "new" missile gap was in favor of the United States. The political figures involved in the earlier debate were concerned with other problems of national defense planning and did not seem inclined to discuss this old issue any more than they discussed the "bomber gap" of an earlier period.

Obviously, the partisan and budgetary effects of the acceptance of the missile gap were closely related to the

---

does not indicate whether President Kennedy had access to the U-2 intelligence. However, he does state that Senator Kennedy was not fully briefed during the 1960 campaign on the proposed Bay of Pigs invasion until after he became President-elect (he was told on November 17, 1960). See: Schlesinger, *A Thousand Days*: pp. 232–233. On March 19, 1962 President Kennedy made the same claim on the failure of the Eisenhower Administration to brief him on the proposed Bay of Pigs invasion. See: *The New York Times*, March 20, 1962.

impact of this possible United States missile inferiority on the development of American military strategy.

An attempt to isolate the missile gap and attribute any basic shifts of American military strategy exclusively to this question would misrepresent the development of American strategy during this period. Such factors as the growing number of nuclear weapons available to both sides, changing concepts of the nature of the "cold war," the growth of American economic capacity, shifts in military strategy only indirectly related to the strategic uses of nuclear power, and many other factors played an important part in the calculation of American strategy. Nonetheless, an analysis of the missile gap debate in conjunction with these factors does offer some significant insights into the formulation of American military policy during this period.

Once the missile gap illusion was destroyed, the following basic question legitimately was asked by many observers: "Was the United States, at anytime during the missile controversy (1957-1961), in danger of having the American retaliatory forces destroyed by a surprise Russian attack?" The answer to this question is an unqualified "No." At no time during this period did any major military or political leader claim that at that moment the Soviet Union could destroy American nuclear power. The "period of maximum danger" of the missile gap always was placed sometime in the future and when such a date arrived, a new period of "maximum danger" was defined. It became apparent that during the ICBM controversy the United States consistently possessed a nuclear delivery system far superior to that of the Soviet Union.

Until early 1961, the United States nuclear superiority was based primarily on the fact that the United States had many more long-range and medium-range bombers (with in-flight refueling) than Russia. As ICBMs became operational, the United States relied on the mixed-forces concept of using missiles and bombers to provide the superior American retaliatory force. By late 1961, it be-

came apparent that the United States possessed a superiority over the Soviet Union in long-range bombers and in
intercontinental ballistic missiles.

From 1957 to 1961, officials of the Eisenhower Administration claimed that there was no "deterrent gap" and
all of the available evidence indicates the truth of this
contention.[70]

The United States had entered the period of the threatened missile gap with a strategic military approach to deterrence that had evolved from the earlier concept of massive retaliation. As nuclear weapons became more plentiful
and their delivery means more sophisticated, this doctrine
had been so modified that many observers believed that it
was obsolete as a strategic concept to meet less than an all-
out nuclear attack on the United States. By the time the
new Kennedy Administration revised American strategic
doctrine, it was admitted that the United States had a
rather substantial superiority over the Soviet Union in
both missiles and bombers, but even this superiority did
not make the doctrine of massive retaliation an effective
instrument for preventing limited aggression. A detailed
analysis of Secretary of Defense McNamara's "second strike
counterforce doctrine" goes far beyond the scope of this
paper, but it will suffice to say that this new doctrine rejected the doctrine of massive retaliation and would have
been impossible without a recognized United States
strategic superiority.[71]

---

70. Even if at some time during the 1957–1961 period the Soviet Union
had possessed more ICBMs than the United States, a successful surprise
attack by the Soviet Union on American retaliatory forces would have been
extremely difficult to coordinate. One group of experts estimated that it
would take from four to six Soviet ICBMs to destroy one American SAC
base (*Johns Hopkins Report, 1959*, p. 58) . The dispersal of about 100 SAC
bases with between 400 and 600 aircraft on "ground alert" further complicated the Russian task. The Soviet Union also would have had to find
and destroy 12 to 14 American attack aircraft carriers with a nuclear capability.

71. For a detailed analysis of this new doctrine see: *The New York
Times*, text of a major address by Secretary of Defense Robert McNamara

The American nuclear superiority over the Soviet Union was the result of numerous interrelated factors. Certainly, the pressures exerted on behalf of the expected missile gap led to an acceleration of the United States missile program. President Eisenhower decided to produce only a limited number of first generation ICBMs, but the defense critics of his Administration caused the number of these missiles actually produced to be increased. Concurrently with the decision to limit first generation missile production, President Eisenhower assigned the highest priority to the development and production of the more sophisticated second generation of United States ICBMs and *Polaris* IRBMs. Therefore, when President Kennedy was inaugurated, the second generation *Polaris* already was operational and the *Minuteman* ICBM was less than a year from being operational. The new President's decision to accelerate these two missile programs assured continued American superiority over the Soviet Union in the number of warheads that the American military forces could deliver on the Russian targets.

Militarily, probably the greatest irony of the missile gap debate is the fact that while many American governmental officials questioned the nonexistent strategic military inferiority of the United States, the real American inferiority was found in its restricted ability to fight a conventional limited war. United States Army and Navy spokesmen had emphasized this fundamental American weakness for several years, but no decisive action was taken by the Eisenhower Administration to correct this deficiency.

When President Kennedy assumed office he found that the United States had a scant 11 combat-ready Army and Marine divisions. In spite of the heated public discussions still going on in 1961 over the strategic military posture of

at Ann Arbor, Michigan, June 17, 1962; and U.S. Congress, House, Committee on Armed Services, *Hearings on Military Posture*, 88th Cong., 1st sess., Vol. 2 (January 30, 1963) .

the United States and the President's acceleration of the missile program, the Kennedy Administration immediately began to strengthen the ability of the United States to engage in a limited military conflict.[72] This new emphasis on the ability to fight a limited war was reflected in the final budgetary expenditures for the various services from 1961 through 1964. During this period the Army and the Navy received roughly two billion dollars each in additional funds for the three year period, while the Air Force received less than a billion dollar increase.[73] This evidence tended to substantiate the belief of Army-Navy spokesmen that while the United States was involved in the missile gap debate, the American ability to fight a limited war had been seriously neglected to the extent that this weakness had to be compensated for and corrected at a later time.

The total impact of the missile gap controversy on the budgetary, political, and military situation in the United States proved to be rather large in its scope. The missile debate was a factor in the increased American defense spending, the election of President Kennedy, and the misallocation of resources among the military services of the United States. In this sense, it was almost an all-encompassing consideration in the development of American policies during this period. However, the impact of the missile gap was greatly diluted due to the large number of other equally powerful interacting forces at work on the same processes in American policy formation.

The Impact of the Missile Gap Abroad

It would be easy to overestimate the impact of the alleged missile gap on American policy and the policies of the other major world powers. Just as different individuals within the United States accepted or refused to accept this gap, so various nations (or national leaders) adopted their

---

72. Schlesinger, *A Thousand Days*, pp. 315–316.
73. See Appendix B.

own attitudes toward this critical question. Also, the distinction should be made between the public attitudes expressed by these leaders and their personal knowledges of existing and future American power and the United States willingness to use this power. Nonetheless, there were three general areas in which the missile gap illusion figured rather prominently: (1) Soviet policy toward Western Europe and the partial fragmentation of the NATO alliance; (2) the Cuban missile crisis; and (3) the Sino-Soviet dispute.[74]

The fundamental question posed by a possible missile gap to the Western European allies of the United States was: "Does the United States deterrent remain credible in the face of Soviet strategic superiority?" Or, as was later asked, even if there was no missile gap, could the United States be relied upon to deter a Soviet attack on Western Europe in the "age of nuclear parity." The doubts created by the missile gap among Western European leaders hastened the process of questioning American nuclear credibility, but it would appear that even if there had been no missile gap illusion, the increasingly plentiful supply of American and Soviet nuclear weapons and their delivery systems would have created similar attitudes.

Concurrent with the supposed weakened posture of the American strategic deterrent capability in Western Europe was the growing realization on the part of many military experts that tactical nuclear weapons probably would aid a Russian military offense in Western Europe more than NATO defense of this area. And in any case, a tactical

---

74. The question of the United States nuclear credibility and the NATO Alliance has been dealt with in Chapter 3 and only will receive brief treatment here. In addition, the American strategic nuclear superiority during this period decreased the possibilities of fruitful disarmament discussions between the Soviet Union and the United States. Any arms limitation agreement between the two super powers would have required some sort of mutual inspection system. The Russian strategic inferiority was not a fact that the leaders of the Soviet Union could have allowed to be divulged by American or neutral inspection teams.

nuclear war in Europe probably would destroy the very area defended.[75]

If this was the case, then Western Europe would have to be defended with conventional armed forces and this was a capability that few western leaders believed the NATO Alliance possessed. America's European allies had never met the conventional force requirements agreed upon by the Alliance, and the United States possessed a very limited capability to fight a conventional war.

Thus, the credibility of the American nuclear deterrent to prevent an attack on Western Europe was weakened at the same time that many observers doubted the ability of the armed forces of the NATO Alliance to defend this area without destroying it in the process.

The Eisenhower Administration had been too pre-occupied with the strategic nuclear balance and increased national defense costs to provide the funds essential for a large number of combat-ready conventional divisions. The Kennedy Administration recognized this weakness, began to expand the limited war capability of the United States, and made an attempt to redefine its military policies toward NATO in 1962-1963.[76]

The situation during the alleged missile gap presented the Soviet Union with an opportunity that it did not pass up. On numerous occasions, the leaders of the Soviet Union attempted to exploit the unanswered questions that surrounded "deterrence and defense" for Western Europe. The American IRBM bases in Europe, the United States presence in Berlin, and the past firmness of the Alliance

---

75. Numerous writers have expounded this belief and it would seem to be based on sound reasoning. See: Liddell Hart, *Deterrence or Defense* (New York: Frederick A. Praeger, 1958); F. O. Miksche, *The Failure of Atomic Strategy* (New York: Frederick A. Praeger, 1958). Snyder, *Deterrence and Defense.*

76. *The New York Times,* text of Speech by Secretary McNamara at Ann Arbor, Michigan, June 17, 1962; U.S. Congress, House, Committee on Armed Services, *Hearings on Military Posture,* 88th Cong., 1st sess., Vol. 2 (January 30, 1963), pp. 428–435.

were all situations that Soviet diplomacy wanted to change. When the opportunity presented itself, the leaders of the Soviet Union had no compunction about threatening America's NATO Allies with "nuclear blackmail" based on the alleged Soviet strategic superiority.[77]

The period of the alleged missile gap had occurred simultaneously with other military, economic and political changes that led inevitably to a crisis within the NATO Alliance. The role of the missile gap in this crisis appears to be twofold: (1) In Europe, the doubts created by the missile gap helped to reduce the credibility of the American deterrent posture, and (2) In the United States the possibility of a missile gap encouraged the military misallocation of American resources for the development of strategic weapons at the expense of a conventional capability. The former gave rise to the demand for an independent nuclear force by at least one European ally, while the latter eventually led to an increased American emphasis under the Kennedy Administration on the development of the capability to fight limited war (both conventional and unconventional).[78]

A second area in which the events surrounding the missile gap appear to have been an important factor was the Soviet decision to place intermediate-range ballistic missiles and medium-range bombers in Cuba in October 1962.[79]

By the fall of 1962, the United States had achieved a

77. In a book published in 1966, the authors develop this point as one of the major themes of their book; see: Horelick and Rush, *Strategic Power and Soviet Foreign Policy.*

78. Neither of these problems has been resolved by 1970 and the NATO Alliance remains in a state of flux. In the above analysis, the assumption of aggressive Soviet intentions in Western Europe has been taken for granted, even though a case can be made that such was not the case.

79. The reports on the exact number of Russian bombers and missiles placed in Cuba vary, but apparently the Soviet Union placed between 42 and 64 medium-range ballistic missiles and about 30 medium-range jet bombers in Cuba during the fall of 1962. See: Schlesinger, *A Thousand Days,* p. 796; *The New York Times,* November 12, 1962.

position of recognized strategic superiority over the Soviet Union.[80] The uncertainty that arose from the possibility of the missile gap had caused the United States to increase the number of strategic aircraft capable of reaching the Soviet Union and to accelerate the American missile program. At the same time the Soviet Union apparently felt that Russian security could be maintained with less than 200 long range bombers and less than 100 ICBMs.[81]

After the Cuban missile crisis, there were many reports on "why" Premier Khrushchev had risked the emplacement of Russian bombers and missiles so close to the continental United States. Some observers contended that his move was intended to prevent another attempted American invasion of Cuba, while others believed that this move by the Soviet Union once again demonstrated the highly aggressive nature of the Soviet Union and its desire to upset the balance of power and threaten a first strike on the United States.[82] However, a more logical explanation is rooted in the fact that the United States, with its large strategic nuclear superiority, had upset what Premier Khrushchev believed was the balance of terror between the United States and the Soviet Union. In order to redress this American nuclear superiority, the Soviet Union placed nuclear delivery vehicles on Cuban soil and gambled on a passive American reaction to this act.[83]

When the leaders of the Soviet Union were confronted with the firm American demand for the removal of these weapons, they had no alternative but to withdraw the

---

80. *The New York Times*, Statement by Roswell L. Gilpatric, Deputy Secretary of Defense, November 12, 1962.

81. See Appendix A.

82. Thomas S. Power, *Design For Power*, p. 21; Alsop, "The Alternative to Total War," p. 15.

83. The most authoritative source for this information is: Dulles, *The Craft of Intelligence*, p. 165; however, a number of other authors have accepted this same reasoning, see: Wolfe, *Soviet Strategy at the Crossroads*, pp. 24, 33; Beaufre, *An Introduction to Strategy*, p. 96; Horelick and Rush, *Strategic Power and Soviet Foreign Policy*, pp. 141–158.

missiles and bombers from Cuba or risk an all-out war at a time when the United States had a large nuclear strategic superiority.

The final major area in which the alleged missile gap played an important, though very limited role, was in the field of Sino-Soviet relations. A detailed study of this dispute is far beyond the scope of this paper. Nonetheless, the missile gap controversy evidently added an additional element of friction to the developing split between these two Communist nations.

The acceptance of the missile gap thesis by many Americans and the Russian claims of missile superiority caused the leadership of Communist China to believe in the existence of a missile gap favoring the Soviet Union. Apparently, Mao Tse Tung incorrectly assumed that the Soviet development of the ICBM in 1957 had brought about a decisive change in the balance of strategic power in favor of the Soviet Union. Based on this belief, the Chinese leader embarked upon a more militant foreign policy in an attempt to achieve the elimination, or at least the reduction, of American power in Asia. When the Soviet Union did not appear to exploit sufficiently this supposed military advantage, the Communist Chinese resented the cautious foreign policy pursued by the Soviet Union and accused Russia of ceasing to be a revolutionary power.[84]

As has been seen above, the Soviet Union itself added credence to the belief in the existence of the missile gap whenever possible. The boasts and bravado of Premier Khrushchev had been *one* of the fundamental causes of the creation of the missile gap. However, viewed in retrospect, it appears as though the Soviet Union paid a high price for very little, if any, temporary gains in its attempt to militarily bluff the United States. Diplomatically, during the period of the missile gap (1957-1961), the leaders of the

84. Donald S. Zagoria, "China's Crisis of Foreign Policy," *The New York Times Magazine*, May 1, 1966.

Soviet Union made no solid gains, although negatively it was possible that the Soviet Union had managed to keep the diplomatic initiative. Soviet leadership eventually had to face the consequences for their willingness to exploit the possible missile gap. The Russian statements on Soviet missile strength had added strong impetus to the the belief in the missile gap in the United States and therefore helped to encourage an escalation in the arms race which the Soviet Union could ill afford. Soviet claims and diplomacy managed to disillusion Communist China and led to a major diplomatic defeat in the Caribbean in October 1962. Finally, Soviet statements on missile strength and the threats of "nuclear blackmail" did nothing to increase the desired image of the Soviet Union as a peace-loving, progressive nation dedicated to the goals of a Marxian utopia.

GLOSSARY

This glossary is intended to help the reader decipher some of the jargon used in any defense policy study. Where there is basic disagreement on the accepted definitions of some of the words found in the glossary, this writer has attempted to set down the definition of a given term as it is used in the text of this book. No attempt was made to give final authoritative definitions.

AICBM (ABM): Anti-ballistic missile. A weapons system including detection, tracking, and calculation of the extended trajectory of incoming missiles, and the launching of a guided missile which will destroy the attacking missile.

Airborne Alert: An alert system in which a certain number of long-range bombers are kept in the air constantly, ready to retaliate in case of an enemy surprise attack.

Background Briefing: A briefing given by an American governmental official to the press. The information in this type of briefing is intended for "background" only. The identity of the briefer is supposedly secret and in many cases the information given in the briefing is not supposed to be made public. (This same type of briefing can be given to Congressional leaders.)

BMEWS: Ballistic Missile Early Warning System, designed to give the United States fifteen minutes warning of an impending missile attack.

BOMARC: United States Air Force surface-to-air (anti-

bomber) missile. The Army's NIKE system was
adopted instead.

Bombers (Russian):

TU-4:   An early Russian bomber, operational about
1950, roughly equivalent to the American
B-29, with a range of 2000 miles. Incapable
of striking the United States.

TU-16 (Badger): Medium-range bomber, operational about 1954, range about 4000 miles.
Capable of making a one-way strike on the
United States, but lacking any in-flight refueling capability.

TU-20 (Bear): First Soviet long-range bomber,
roughly comparable to the American B-36,
with a range of 7000 miles. Operational about
1954.

Myasishchev 500 (Bison): A bomber comparable to
the American B-52 with a range of 6000 miles.
This bomber appeared in the Soviet Air Show
in 1955 and was supposedly the plane that
created the alleged "bomber gap."

CIA: Central Intelligence Agency, United States Government. Responsible for the overall assimilation of
American intelligence efforts. Under the directorship
of Allen Dulles during the period of the missile gap.

Circular Probability Error (CEP): An indicator of the
accuracy of a missile's ability to strike within a certain
distance of a designated target. Also used as a factor
in determining probable damage to a target. The
abbreviation CEP reflects an earlier phrase reading,
Circular Error Probability.

Counterforce Doctrine: Essentially a first-strike doctrine
aimed at the destruction of the enemy's nuclear capability to prevent effective retaliation. Once this was
accomplished, the enemy's cities could be held as
hostages with the remaining nuclear power, and the

war could be won. (See also second strike counterforce.)

Deterrence: Convincing a potential aggressor, in advance, that it can and will be made to suffer more by aggression than can be gained by it.

DEW: Distant Early Warning system to warn of an impending enemy bomber attack.

Explorer I: First United States satellite. Placed into orbit on January 1, 1958 by a United States Army JUPITER C missile. (Satellite weighed 30.8 pounds.)

First Strike: The attempted surprise delivery of nuclear warheads on the enemy's nuclear delivery systems in an attempt to destroy the enemy's ability to retaliate.

Ground Alert: An alert system in which a certain number of long-range bombers are kept in constant readiness on the ground. These bombers could be airborne, fifteen minutes after the warning of an impending enemy attack was received.

Hardened Operational Missile Site: A missile launch site in which missiles are stored in underground silos from which they can be fired, and which are protected against all but very close strikes by nuclear weapons.

ICBM: Intercontinental ballistic missile. A surface-to-surface missile with ballistic-type trajectory and a range of 5000 miles or more.

IRBM: Intermediate-range ballistic missile. A surface-to-surface missile with ballistic-type trajectory and a range of about 1500 miles.

Jupiter: Army IRBM with a range of more than 1500 miles.

Midas: An earth satellite designed to give early warning to the United States in case of enemy missile attack. The first operational MIDAS was launched in the fall of 1961.

Minimum Deterrent: A nuclear striking force to be used against an enemy's cities in the event of nuclear war.

A limited striking force designed to deter an enemy attack by threatening the destruction of its population centers, essentially a second-strike doctrine. An essential corollary to this doctrine is the capability to fight a limited war, so that limited aggression can be met with less than an all-out nuclear response.

Minuteman: A hardened, solid-propellant ICBM which serves as one of the principle United States deterrent weapons. Range over 6500 miles. More than 1000 Minutemen are now operational.

Missiles (Russian):

> T-1: A short-range liquid fuel missile. Accurate up to 400 miles, 78,000 pounds of thrust.
>
> T-2: Intermediate-range ballistic missile. Range 1800 miles, 265,000 pounds of thrust.
>
> T-3: A liquid fuel ICBM. Range over 5000 miles, 500,000 pounds of thrust.

MRBM: Medium-range ballistic missile. A surface-to-surface missile with ballistic-type trajectory and a range of about 950 miles.

Nike-Zeus: Army antimissile system.

NATO: The North Atlantic Treaty Organization.

Pad: A missile load-bearing surface, constructed or laid on the ground (or underground) upon which a permanent or mobile catapult or launcher can be placed.

Passive Defense: Features of a weapons system that enable it to survive damage resulting from enemy action. Armor plate, strategic location, and hardened underground missile silos are examples of such features.

Polaris: Navy underwater-to-surface, or surface-to-surface solid-propellant fleet ballistic missiles, range 1380 miles. "B" version has a range of 1725 miles, "C" a range of 2875 miles.

Pre-emptive war: The launching of a first-strike nuclear attack by a nation when it feels that an enemy attack is imminent and its retaliatory forces are in danger of being destroyed. A nation with a *sure* second-strike capability is much less vulnerable to this type of pressure than one with only a vulnerable first-strike capability .

Preventive war: The launching of a first-strike nuclear attack by a nation when it feels that war is inevitable some day in the future, i.e., not imminent. This sort of attack would be based on the nation's belief that a nuclear war today would be more favorable to its national interests than one in the future when its enemy's strength had increased.

Regulus Missile: A first-generation, slow, airbreathing, submarine surface-launched missile. Replaced by the Polaris.

SAC: The Strategic Air Command, commanded by General Thomas Power during the period of the missile gap, and then by General Curtis LeMay. Units of the US Air Force assigned the mission of deterring a strategic attack on the United States. Made up of long-range and medium-range bombers, and ICBMs and IRBMs.

Samos Satellite: An earth satellite designed to take reconnaissance intelligence photographs. The SAMOS became operational in 1961.

Second Strike Counterforce: Defined by Secretary of Defense McNamara in a speech at Ann Arbor, Michigan, June 16, 1962 (though he was not the first to define it) . This doctrine rules out surprise nuclear attack as a rational act. Instead, if nuclear war is initiated against the United States, American retaliatory power would respond in a controlled fashion after the enemy's first strike. The United States retaliatory forces would attack all Soviet nuclear installations, but not its cities, and then see if war can be stopped. City strike against the Soviet Union would be used last. The goal is to stabilize the "balance of terror," but the implied superiority needed to follow the doctrine could be seen as a first strike nuclear force.

Snark: Early Air Force air-breathing, subsonic guided intercontinental cruise missile weapon system.

Sputnik I: The world's first earth satellite, launched by the Soviet Union, October 4, 1957.

Strategic Delivery Vehicle: A bomber or missile which is capable of striking the homeland of an enemy with a nuclear warhead.

Targeting: In missile warfare, the plotting the correct trajectory for a designated target.

Thor: Early U.S. Air Force IRBM, range around 1750 miles, payload 1500 pounds.

Titan I: Two stage liquid propellant ICBM, must be raised from silo before launching. Range over 6300 miles.

Titan II: A two stage liquid propellant ICBM which can be silo-launched employing storable propellants, and can be launched in less than a minute. It has greater thrust, range, and payload than any other American ICBM. Range over 9000 miles. 10 megaton.

USIA: United States Information Agency.

USIB: United States Intelligence Board; submits national intelligence estimates to the President or the National Security Council. Membership consists of: Representatives of the United States Air Force (A-2), Navy (Office of Naval Intelligence), and Army (G-2), the director of intelligence of the Atomic Energy Commission, State Department (Assistant Secretary of State), Federal Bureau of Investigation, National Security Agency, and the director of the Defense Intelligence Agency. The director of the CIA is chairman of the USIB.

Weapons System: Entity consisting of an instrument of combat, such as a bomber or missile together with all related equipment, support facilities, and services required to bring the instrument upon its target.

APPENDIX A

COMPARATIVE WEAPONS SYSTEMS OF THE UNITED STATES AND THE SOVIET UNION 1949-1966

This appendix is an attempt to present the reported comparative strategic military power of the United States and the Soviet Union from 1949 to 1966, with special emphasis on the "missile gap" period of 1958–1961. Although all of the information in this appendix came from unclassified sources, most of these estimates allegedly came from an "official source" or supposedly represented some "official intelligence estimate."

The information contained in this appendix serves a rather paradoxical purpose. First, it will show the large and diversified amount of information available to the public during the "missile gap" period. But, at the same time, a close examination of this information shows an amazing amount of consistency and similarity of the figures presented to the American public (with some notable exceptions). A summary of the significance of these figures can be found in the conclusions of this book (Chapter 7).

The final reason for this appendix is to provide an easily accessible listing of the existing and projected strategic power balance between the United States and the Soviet Union.

The figures listed in this Appendix are listed chronologically as they appeared publicly.

Comparative Weapon Systems

1949:   The Soviet Union explodes its first atomic device in August 1949.

Weapons:

United States—Atomic stockpile in three figures.

Soviet Union—unknown.

Delivery Means:

United States—with a quantitative and qualitative lead.

Soviet Union—making a surprisingly fast start.[1]

---

1. *The New York Times,* October 2, 1949.

1950:   *Weapons:*
United States—stockpile in three figures.
Soviet Union—in low two figures.
Delivery Means:
United States—using the B-29.
Soviet Union—using TU-4, Soviet equivalent of United States B-29. (Neither of these planes capable of long range strategic strike, limited range to around 2000 miles.) [2]

1951—November 1952: United States explodes the first hydrogen bomb.
Weapons:
United States—stockpile in four figures (also has developed 5-kiloton tactical weapon.) [3]
Soviet Union—30 to 80 atomic bombs.[4]
Delivery Means:
United States—using the B-29 and introducing the B-36 and B-47.
Soviet Union—still using the TU-4.[5]

1953:   Soviet Union explodes its first Hydrogen bomb in August.
Weapons:
United States—over 1000 atomic or hydrogen weapons.
Soviet Union—100 to 200.[6]
Delivery Means:
United States—B-36 and B-47 operational.[7]
Soviet Union—over 1,000 TU-4s, doubtful that they could be of any strike value other than as decoys.[8]

1954:   *Weapons:*
United States—2000 to 3000 weapons stockpile.
Soviet Union—300 to 400.[9]

---

2. *The New York Times,* May 7, 1950.

3. *The New York Times,* October 5, 1951.

4. *The New York Times,* June 7, 1951.

5. Leonard Bridgeman, ed., *Jane's All The World's Aircraft* (London: Sampson Low, Marston & Company Ltd., 1952), p. 18.

6. *The New York Times,* December 10, 1953.

7. "Weapons," *Air Force,* Vol. 40, No. 8 (August, 1957), p. 353.

8. Asher Lee, *The Soviet Air Force* (New York: The John Day Company, 1962), pp. 132–134.

9. *The New York Times,* February 13, 1954.

Delivery Means:
United States—using B-36, B-47 and the B-52 being phased in.[10]
Soviet Union—
> TU-4: over 1000 (still doubtful long range capability, no inflight refueling).
> TU-16: (Badger) Operational, with a range of over 4000 miles (one way strike to part of the United States).[11]
> TU-20: (Bear) Compares very favorably with United States B-36; possesses less than 100 of these aircraft.[12] Range of over 7,000 miles.[13] TU-20 even given credit for matching the B-52 in many important areas of performance.[14]
> 500: Myasishchev (Bison) comparable to B-52. Range of 6,000 miles. In production.[15]

1955:   *Weapons:*
United States—stockpile of over 5000.
Soviet Union—over 500.[16]
Delivery Means:
Both sides with about the same as above, only with an increase in operational aircraft.[17]

1956–1957: August 1957 the Soviet Union announced the first successful firing of an ICBM.[18]
Weapons:
United States—stockpile of 7000 to 10,000 weapons.
Soviet Union—over 2000.
Delivery Means:

10. "Weapons," *Air Force,* Vol. 40, No. 8 (August, 1957), p. 353.

11. Lee, *The Soviet Air Force,* p. 133.

12. "Reds put Muscle in Strategic Air Arm," *Aviation Week,* Vol. 60, No. 11 (March 5, 1954), p. 91.

13. *Communist Bloc and the Western Alliances: The Military Balance 1961–1962* (published by the Institute for Strategic Studies, London), p. 3.

14. "How Good is Russia's Long-Range Turboprop Bear Bomber?" *Air: Air Intelligence Training Bulletin* (published by the United States Air Force), Vol. 9, No. 9 (September 1957), p. 39.

15. "Reds Put Muscle in Strategic Air Arm," *Aviation Week,* Vol. 60, No. 1 (March 5, 1954), p. 92.

16. *The New York Times,* February 13, 1955.

17. Lee, *The Soviet Air Force,* p. 234.

18. *The New York Times,* August 27, 1957.

Both systems still growing along the same lines, with the exception of the addition of the B-58 to the United States system.[19]

1958: *Weapons:*
Both sides with sizeable stockpiles by this time.
Delivery Means:
United States—250 B-52s, 1800 B-47s, and an unknown number of B-58s. (Hanson Baldwin set the figure at 4000 to 5000 aircraft capable of carrying megaton range weapons to the Soviet Union.[20]

Soviet Union—The predicted 500 Bison bombers mentioned here, reflected the belief in the "bomber gap" and was later contradicted and the figure was lowered to around 200 long-range Bison.

500 Bisons and 1000 Badgers.[21] Unknown number of T-3 ICBMs with over 5,000 miles range.[22]

July 1958 (as reported in Thomas R. Phillips, "The Growing Missile Gap," *The Reporter,* Vol. 20 (January 8, 1959), p. 11. The figures below were attributed to Joseph Alsop as of July 1958.

	United States (ICBMs)	Soviet Union (ICBMs)
1959	0	100
1960	30	500
1961	70	1000
1962	130	1500
1963	130	2000

1959

January 8, 1959 (Ibid., same figures reproduced in *The New York Times*).

---

19. "Weapons," *Air Force* (August, 1957), p. 353.

20. Baldwin, *The Great Arms Race,* p. 39.

21. "Military Strengths" (unpublished Air Force mimeographed material obtained from Professor of Air Science Lt. Col. Stephen Bull, Tufts University, AROTC).

22. *The Soviet Union and the NATO Powers—The Military Balance, 1959* (now known as *The Communist Bloc and the Western Alliances: The Military Balance),* published by the Institute for Strategic Studies, London, p. 5.

January 12, 1959 (The New York Times, "U.S. Raising Goals as Critics foresee Gap," news article by Richard Witkin).

United States (ICBMs)	Soviet Union (ICBMs)
1960	30	100
1961	70	500
1962	130	1000
1963	130	1500
1964	130	2000

February 9, 1959 (Missile Gap—How Perilous?" *Newsweek,* Vol. 53 p. 23.)

United States (ICBMs)	Soviet Union (ICBMs)
1963	300	1000 to 1500

February 16, 1959 ("Arms, McElroy, and Menace," *Newsweek,* Vol. 53 p. 28).

United States (bombers)	Soviet Union (bombers)
1000 B-47 (medium range)	350–850
500 B-52's (long range)	100–150

No ICBMs for either side

March 9, 1959 ("Soviets Study Military Aspects of Space," *Aviation Week,* Vol. 70, p. 314. Russia reported to be building 15 ICBMs per month, based on a "conservative" estimate).

1959 Soviet Union with 100 ICBMs
1962 Soviet Union with 600 ICBMs

March 9, 1959 (James R. Shipley, "Life and Death Debate over Missile Program," *Life,* Vol. 46, p. 119. Figures below were claimed to represent the National Intelligence Estimate, revised).

United States (ICBMs)		Soviet Union (ICBMs)	
July 1960	10	March 1959	10
December 1961	80	March 1960	60
Mid-1963	400	1962	500

March 25, 1959 (The New York Times, news article by Hanson W. Baldwin).

1959   Today, Soviet Union with 150 long-range bombers.
1960   Soviet Union with 100 ICBMs.
1962   Soviet Union with 500 ICBMs.

April, 1959 (Charles J. V. Murphy, "The Embattled Mr. McElroy," *Fortune,* Vol. 59, p. 242. These estimates appear to represent the downgraded

United States estimates referred to earlier in 1959).

Earlier Estimates of Soviet ICBM strength

1959   10 ICBMs
1960   100 ICBMs
1961   500 ICBMs

"Downgraded" estimates of early 1959 of Soviet ICBMs

1961 60 to 100 ICBMs (Russian) mid-1962 or later 500 Russian ICBMs

April 28, 1959 (The New York Times, It was reported that the United States had 75,000 deliverable nuclear weapons).

May 16, 1959 (Stewart Alsop, "Our Gamble with Destiny," *Saturday Evening Post,* Vol. 231, pp. 116–117. Also quoting the downward revision of Secretary of Defense McElroy).

	United States	Soviet Union
1959	3 ICBMs	
	500 B-52s	
	1300 B-47s	
	100 B-58s	
1960		100 ICBMs
1961	30 ICBMs	300 ICBMs (some say 1000 ICBMs by this time)
1962		500 ICBMs (other reports of 1000 by this time)

July 30, 1959 (The New York Times, text of news conference by President Eisenhower, July 30, 1959).

	United States	Soviet Union
1959	Atlas operational by September 1, 1959	10 ICBMs

September 28, 1959 ("The U.S. is about even with the Soviet Union in Missiles," *U.S. News and World Report,* Vol. 47, p. 63).

	United States (ICBMs)	Soviet Union (ICBMs)
1959 (now)	10	10
		(concedes maybe 50 to 100, but said it didn't make any difference to U.S. "mixed force.")

October 7, 1959 (Washington Post and Times Herald, "After

Ike the Deluge," news article by Joseph Alsop).

United States (ICBMs)		Soviet Union (ICBMs)
1960	30	100
1961	70	500
1962	130	1000
1963	130	1500

"Missile gap" to disappear in 1965–1966 when second generation solid fuel missiles become operational.

December 5, 1959 ("In Missiles a Three-Year Gap Ahead," *Business Week*, p. 24).

United States
585 B-52s (13 wings with 45 planes each)
1260 B-47s (28 wings at 45 planes each)
Strategic Air Command with 44 United States bases and 20 overseas bases.

December 6, 1959 (*Developments in Military Technology and their Impact on United States Strategy and Foreign Policy, Study #8 (The Johns Hopkins Report, 1959)*, Washington Center of Foreign Policy Research, The Johns Hopkins University [Washington, D.C.: Government Printing Office, December 6, 1959], pp. 52–58).

by mid-1962 United States 100 ICBMs, Russia 400 ICBMs but admits these figures may be exaggerated.

Report also states that it would take an average of 4 to 6 Soviet ICBMs to destroy a SAC airfield, whereas it would take 30 to 40 ICBMs to destroy a hardened missile site.

1960

January 1960 (Frank Gibney, "The Missile Mess," *Harper's Magazine*, Vol. 220, p. 38).

Predicted a six to one Soviet advantage over the United States in ICBMs.

January 18, 1960 ("The Age of Damocles," *The New Republic* [editorial], Vol. 142, p. 4).

Predicted a three to one Soviet ICBM advantage until 1963.

January 28, 1960 (*The New York Times*, quoting Senator Stuart Symington's news conference, January 28, 1960).

Senator Symington stated that the period of the "missile gap" would give the Soviet Union a greater advantage than three to one over the United States in ICBMs.

February 2, 1960 (*The New York Times,* news article by John W. Finney, February 8, 1960) .

	United States (ICBMs)	Soviet Union (ICBMs)
1961	50	150 (3–1)

February 7, 1960 (*The New York Times,* [editorial]) .

United States (ICBMs)		Soviet Union (ICBMs)
February 1960	3	10
June 1960	18	38
June 1961	40–50	140–200
1963	200	500

February 8, 1960 ("The Coming Missile Gap," *Time,* Vol. 75, p. 18).

United States (ICBMs)		Soviet Union (ICBMs)
February 1960	3	10
1961	72	100
Revised 1963	200–250	400–500

February 8, 1960 (U.S. Congress, Senate, Committee on Armed Services [Preparedness Subcommittee] in conjunction with the Committee on Aeronautical and Space Sciences, *Hearings,* 86th Cong., 2nd sess. [February-March 1960], referred to as *The Joint Hearings, 1960,* testimony by the Chief of Naval Operations, Admiral Arleigh Burke, p. 320.

Admiral Burke added a new element to the public debate over the "missile gap" when he stated that the United States had 200 aircraft with a nuclear capability on 14 attack aircraft carriers.

February 18, 1960 (Thomas R. Philipps (United States Army General, retired), "The Great Guessing Game," *The Reporter,* Vol. 22, p. 26. Mr. Philipps reported that the Soviet Union was producing ICBMs at the rate of 50 per month) .

	United States (ICBMs)	Soviet Union (ICBMs)
1961	50	150
1962	200	600 (3–1)

February 29, 1960 ("The Truth about Missiles," *U.S. News and World Report*, Vol. 48, p. 42.

This periodical claimed that Russia might lead the United States in ICBMs by 100 to 200 missiles, but that this force was balanced by the strong "mixed force" of the United States deterrent power.

March 1960 to December 1960 (Interestingly, and inexplicably, during the Presidential campaign of 1960, those involved in the "missile gap" controversy refrained from making specific predictions as to the future of the missile gap.)

1961

January 1961 (*The New York Times*, official Pentagon figures on United States and Soviet strategic weapons as of January 1961, released April 16, 1964).

	United States	Soviet Union
Long-range bombers	500	about 190

Both sides with only a "handful" of ICBMs and missile launching submarines.

January 23, 1961 ("Is the World Balance in Missiles Shifting to U.S.?" *U.S. News and World Report*, Vol 59, pp. 65–66).

United States (existing strength)	Soviet Union
9 Atlas ICBMs	35 ICBMs
32 Polaris IRBMs	500–800 IRBMs (could not reach the U.S.)
60 Thor IRBMs	
20 Snark missiles	
600 Long-range bombers	150
1100 Medium-range bombers	1500—could not reach U.S.
400 Carrier-based bombers	none
2000 Air Force fighter bombers	could not reach U.S.
United States (projected strength)	Soviet Union

Mid-1961	50 ICBMs	150–200 ICBMs
	48 Polaris	
Mid-1962	100 ICBMs	500 ICBMs
	144 Polaris	
Mid-1963	300 ICBMs	1000 ICBMs
	240 Polaris	
Mid-1964	870 ICBMs	1500 ICBMs
	336 Polaris	

January 25, 1961 (*The New York Times,* report by the House Republican Policy Committee reported on February 9, 1961).

United States	Soviet Union
16 Atlas	35 ICBMs
32 Polaris	none
600 Long-range	200
bombers	

February 1, 1961 (*The New York Times,* "Kennedy's Defense Study," news article by Hanson W. Baldwin, February 1, 1961).

United States (retaliatory force in missiles)
48 Polaris
60 Thor missiles in Britain—range 1725 miles
30 Jupiters in Italy
15 Jupiters enroute to Turkey
12 Atlas

February 12, 1961 (*The New York Times*). Air Force estimated the Soviet Union with 150 ICBMs on launching pads, while the National Intelligence estimates gave the Soviet Union a lower number.

United States	Soviet Union
9 Atlas	50–150
48 Polaris	32–64 submarine launched missiles, from surface, 500 mile range

1500 SAC bombers

February 13, 1961 (James Barr [Military Affairs Editor], "Latest Reports say Missile Gap Continues," *Missiles and Rockets,* Vol. 8, p. 14).

Russia continues to enjoy a three to one advantage over the United States in ICBMs.

February 17, 1961 ("Defense: The Missile Gap Flap," *Time*,
          Vol. 77, p. 12).

United States	Soviet Union
10 Atlas	50 ICBMs
60 Thor	
30 Jupiter in Italy	
15 Jupiter in Turkey	
32 Polaris	

February 20, 1961 ("The Ammo was Political," *Newsweek*,
          Vol. 57, p. 24).

United States	Soviet Union
by mid-June 1961	
6 Atlas	50–70 ICBMs
48 Polaris	

February 27, 1961 ("The Truth about the Missile Gap," *U.S.
          News and World Report*, Vol. 50, p. 41. "Gap"
          favors the United States).

United States	Soviet Union
124—missile deliv- ered warheads	—23–50
3500—bombers with range to reach enemy's homeland.	—200–300

March 8, 1961 (*The New York Times*, speech by Representa-
          tive Francis Bolton (Rep.-Ohio), March 8, 1961,
          in which Mr. Bolton presented the same figures
          given for February 27, 1961).

May 16, 1961 (*The New York Times*, March 16, 1961).

United States	Soviet Union
27 Atlas	25–50 ICBMs
32 Polaris	

July 9, 1961 (*The New York Times*, article by Hanson W.
          Baldwin).

United States	Soviet Union
100 Atlas	less than 50 ICBMs
48 Polaris	

September 18, 1961 ("Is U.S. Ahead in Arms Race?" *U.S. News
          and World Report*, Vol. 51, p. 44. U.S. with a
          35–1 advantage over the Soviet Union in bomb-
          ers that can reach the other's homeland.

United States	Soviet Union
24 Atlas	50–100 ICBMs
60 Thor	not reach the U.S.
30 Jupiter	not reach the U.S.
80 Polaris	none
500 B-52s and B-58s	150–200
1100 B-47s (with in-flight refueling)	none
2000 fighter bombers	not reach the U.S.
1500 carrier based bombers	none

November 13, 1961 ("Was there ever a Missile Gap or just an Intelligence Gap?" *Newsweek*, Vol. 58, p. 23).

United States	Soviet Union
45 ICBMs	35–50 ICBMs

These figures supposedly came from The National Intelligence Estimate.

November 19, 1961 (*The New York Times*, "U.S. Missile Lead Claimed in Study," news article by Jack Raymond.)

United States	Soviet Union
48 Atlas	50 ICBMs
80 Polaris	
60 Thor	
45 Jupiter	

1962

March 26, 1962 (*The New York Times.*)

United States	Soviet Union
54 Atlas	50–75 ICBMs
9 Titans (April 1962)	
96 Polaris	

December 20, 1962 (*The New York Times.*)

United States	Soviet Union
126 Atlas	75–100 ICBMs
54 Titan	
20 Minutemen	
over 100 Polaris	

1962 (The Communist Bloc and the Western Alliance: The

Military Balance, 1962–1963 [London: The Institute for Strategic Studies], p. 5).

United States	Soviet Union
650 B-52s with "hound-dog" air-to-air missiles	70 Bear long-range bombers
1000 B-47s	1000 Badgers (medium-range)
55 B-58s	50–100 ICBMs
Atlas Operational	
Titan Operational	
80 Polaris	unknown number of Bisons (B-52)

1963

January 10, 1963 (*The New York Times,* "The Soviets' need for a Super-bomb," news article by Hanson W. Baldwin.)

United States	Soviet Union
200 ICBMs	75–100 ICBMs
	Approximately 60 submarine
144 Polaris (9 subs)	launched missiles
45 Jupiter	
60 Thor	

1964

April 15, 1964 (*The New York Times,* the Pentagon released its official figures on comparative United States Soviet Military strength to avoid another "missile gap" debate in the 1964 presidential election, April 15, 1964).

United States	Soviet Union
540 Long-range bombers	270
750 ICBMs	below 200
192 Polaris	substantially fewer with only a 500 mile range

1966

July 14, 1966 (*The New York Times,* "U.S. Lead in ICBMs

is said to be Reduced by Build-up in Soviet
Union," news article by Hanson W. Baldwin.)

United States	Soviet Union
800 Minutemen	300 ICBMs with one-half hardened
54 Titan II	
80 Minutemen II	
Total ICBMs 934	Total 300
400 Polaris with	150 short range missiles
656 operational by the end of 1966	
25,000 stored megatons	12,000 stored megatons

United States still far ahead of the Soviet Union in number
of long-range bombers and carrier naval aircraft capable of
delivering a nuclear weapon.

APPENDIX B

TOTAL UNITED STATES
MILITARY EXPENDITURES
1950-1964

Major national security expenditures, actual for fiscal years 1951–1963
(Discrepancies in totals due to rounding)
(In millions of dollars)

Description	1951	1952	1953	1954	1955	1956	1957	1958	1959	1960	1961	1962	1963
Direction and coordination of defense	12	13	15	12	13	14	14						
Other central defense activities	353	379	394	452	481	582	602	669	853	1,115	1,066	1,189	2,146
Army defense activities	7,469	15,635	16,242	12,910	8,899	8,702	9,063	9,051	9,468	9,393	10,332	11,559	11,963
Navy defense activities	5,582	10,162	11,875	11,293	9,733	9,744	10,398	10,906	11,728	11,642	12,313	13,193	14,746
Air Force defense activities	6,349	12,709	15,085	15,668	16,407	16,749	18,363	18,435	19,084	19,066	19,816	20,883	20,594
Subtotal, military functions	19,764	38,899	43,611	40,336	35,532	35,791	38,439	39,062	41,233	41,215	43,227	46,725	48,048
Civil defense													
Military assistance	991	2,442	3,954	3,629	2,292	2,611	2,353	2,187	2,340	1,609	1,449	1,390	1,721
Development and control of atomic energy	897	1,670	1,791	1,895	1,857	1,651	1,990	2,268	2,541	2,623	2,713	2,806	2,758
Stockpiling and other defense-related activities	793	966	1,008	1,045	994	588	490	625	312	180	106	92	24
Total, major national security	22,444	43,976	50,363	46,904	40,626	40,641	43,270	44,142	46,426	45,627	47,494	51,103	52,755

"United States Defense Policies in 1964," The Library of Congress (Washington, D.C.) June 4, 1965, 89th Cong., 1st sess., p. 179.

APPENDIX C

RELEVANT PUBLIC OPINION POLLS

Poll #1: United States Information Agency Poll, on British and French opinion on the comparative United States-Soviet military standing. (*The New York Times*, reprint of text of poll, October 27, 1960.) Question: "All things considered, do you think the United States or Russia is ahead in total military strength at the present time?" (Figures in percent.)

	Great Britain				France			
	Nov. 1957	Oct. 1958	Feb. 1960	May 1960	Nov. 1957	Oct. 1958	Feb. 1960	May 1960
U.S. considerably ahead	4%	7%	15%	12%	6%	3%	16%	25%
U.S. a little ahead	15	9	—	—	11	16	—	—
Russia a little ahead	31	22	59	25	13	21	37	40
Russia considerably ahead	19	19	—	—	12	8	—	—
Both equal	6	8	4	5	20	34	16	—
No opinion	25	25	22	28	38	18	31	35
Net U.S. ahead	−31	−15	−44	−43	−8	−10	−21	−15

"All things considered, which country do you think is ahead in space development at the present time—the United States or the Soviet Union?" (Figures in percent.)

	Great Britain		France	
	Feb. 1960	May 1960	Feb. 1960	May 1960
U.S. ahead	5%	7%	2%	7%
U.S.S.R. ahead	84	81	85	74
Neither ahead	2	4	3	11
No opinion	9	8	10	19
Net U.S. ahead	−79	−74	−83	−63

Poll #2: United States Information Agency, Office of Research and Intelligence, "Free World Views of the US-USSR Power Balance," (R-54-60, August 29, 1960). Figures in percent (page 22).

	West Germany Feb. 1960	Norway June 1960	Italy Feb. 1960
U.S. ahead	22	15	38
Soviet Union ahead	47	45	32
Both equal	8	17	5
No opinion	25	23	25

This quote appeared as part of the conclusion of this study:

While sophisticated political and press opinion tends to regard the current military situation as one of nuclear stalemate in which neither of the two super-powers has any material advantage over the other, the more impressionistic popular opinion seemingly concluded from Soviet boasts of superiority and American admissions of a temporary "missile gap" that the United States is not only currently militarily inferior to the USSR but will continue to be so for the next decade or two as well. (page 5)

Poll #3: *World Gallup Poll* (November, 1960), reprinted in: Hazel Gaudet Erskine (article editor), "Report from the Polls," *Public Opinion Quarterly,* Vol. 25 (Spring, 1961), p. 133.
"In the last year would you say that respect for the United States has increased or decreased?" (Figures in percent)

	Increased	Decreased	The Same	No Opinion
United States	22	45	23	10
Netherlands	18	44	16	22
Great Britain	19	36	29	16
Norway	20	36	30	14
France	7	34	43	16
West Germany	29	16	47	8

Poll #4: *Ibid.,* p. 129, *American Institute of Public Opinion* (August-November 7, 1960).
"If the election were being held today, which ticket would

you vote for—Nixon and Lodge or Kennedy and Johnson?"
(Percent for each ticket)

	Kennedy-Johnson	Nixon-Lodge
Early August (after convention)	47	53
Late August	50	50
Early September	51	49
Late September (before first T.V. debate)	49	51
Sept. 27 - Oct. 4 (after T.V. debate)	52	48
Early October	50	50
Late October	53	47
Early November	51	49
Election	50.1	49.9

Poll #5: *Ibid., American Institute of Public Opinion* July 27, 1960

"Which political party, the Democrats or Republicans, do you think can do the job of increasing respect for the United States throughout the world?" (Figures in percent), p. 22.

	Democrats	Republicans	No Difference—No Opinion
1956	26%	35%	39%
1960	41	25	34

BIBLIOGRAPHY

Note on Source Materials

In spite of the fact that much of the information on the missile gap debate was (and still is) classified, this writer found a voluminous amount of source material on the subject. The relative importance and accuracy of a particular source was very difficult to determine. The individual bias, or lack of it, was not always evident. It was only by the use of later evidence that a relatively clear picture of the importance of the different sources could be evaluated.

With very few exceptions, the popular periodical literature during the missile gap period appeared to reflect rather accurately the intelligence estimates of the various agencies of the United States Government, although there did appear to be about a four month period between the time the official estimate was made within the government and the time it appeared in the public press based on an "informed source." Most representatives of the press reflected the downward revisions of the United States Government as the government revised its earlier estimates on projected Soviet missile strength from estimates based on existing missile production capability to those based on "hard intelligence" on known missile production (see Appendix A). The existence of at least two sets of government intelligence figures of projected Soviet missile production appeared in the concerned press, depending on which "informed source" the periodical relied upon.

During the missile gap period, most of the periodical press (or its signed articles) at one time or another reflected the belief in the coming missile gap, or at least a serious missile lag. The major exceptions to this general statement were articles found in *The Nation, World Politics, The Atlantic*

Monthly, Fortune, and to a limited extent in *Newsweek.* In this book, the popular periodical literature was used mainly to demonstrate what the American people were being told and only to a limited extent to establish existing facts.

Both the so-called "liberal" and "conservative" periodicals tended to accept the missile gap. However, there was a noticeable tendency of several periodicals known to support the Republicans (and specifically President Eisenhower) to continue to support the Republican Administration on defense questions, especially when the debate centered on budgetary questions. Logically, the service and industrial publications were consistently found supporting whichever particular military strategy or weapons systems conformed to the service and industry's own beliefs and interests.

The most valuable source materials on this topic were the numerous Congressional hearings and investigations conducted on United States defense policy and spending. In spite of the closed nature of many of these hearings and the limited value of the censored versions that were later released, the testimony of these military and civilian officials proved an indispensable source of both factual information or the attitudes of the various sectors of the United States government that were in conflict over United States defense policy.

The New York Times and the various special studies mentioned in this bibliography also proved to be essential and valuable source material.

None of the books found by this writer dealt in any great detail with the problem of the missile gap. Therefore, the contribution of most of these studies was the excellent background information they offered. The books written by individuals who had been high ranking military or civilian leaders offered considerable insight and occasionally possessed a high degree of exact knowledge on specific events that surrounded the missile gap debate.

Certain nongovernmental individuals appeared to have a firm and realistic grasp of United States defense problems and deterrent posture, although they allegedly had no access to classified material. This was especially true of men like Hanson Baldwin, Military Editor of *The New York Times* and

Charles J. V. Murphy writing in *Fortune* magazine. At the time they wrote, it was impossible to ascertain the accuracy of their knowledge; but later events tended to confirm their earlier predictions.

Finally, the almost undisputable fact that there were numerous "leaks" from officials with access to classified knowledge proved indispensable in this study. In spite of the legal and ethical question concerning government security regulations, this writer owes a tremendous debt to those unknown individuals who divulged segments of classified information for eventual publication. Without these sources it is doubtful that this book could have been written.

Books

Almond, Gabriel A., *The American People and Foreign Policy* (New York: Frederick A. Praeger, 1950).

Baldwin, Hanson H., *The Great Arms Race: A Comparison of U.S. and Soviet Power* (New York: Frederick A. Praeger, 1958).

Beaufre, André, *An Introduction to Strategy* (New York: Frederick A. Praeger, 1965).

Becker, Abraham, *Soviet Military Outlays Since 1955* (Santa Monica, California: The Rand Corporation, 1964).

Berkowitz, Morton, and Block, P. G. (Eds.), *American National Security: A Reader in Theory and Policy* (New York: The Free Press, 1965).

Blackett, P. M. S., *Studies of War* (New York: Hill and Wang, 1962).

Bobrow, Davis B., ed., *Components of Defense Policy* (Chicago: Rand McNally and Company, 1965).

Boulding, Kenneth E., *Conflict and Defense* (New York: Harper and Row, Publishers, 1962).

Brennan, Donald G., ed., *Arms Control, Disarmament, and National Security* (New York: George Braziller, 1961).

Bridgeman, Leonard, ed., *Jane's All the World's Aircraft* (London: Sampson Low, Marston and Company Ltd., 1952).

Brodie, Bernard, *Strategy in the Missile Age* (Princeton, New Jersey: Princeton University Press, 1959).

Chase, Harold W., and Lerman, Allen H. (Eds.), *Kennedy and the Press* (New York: Thomas Y. Crowell Company, 1965).

Chase, Stuart, *American Credos* (New York: Harper Brothers, Publishers, 1962).

Childs, Harwood L., *Public Opinion: Nature, Formation, and Role* (Princeton, New Jersey: D. Van Nostrand, Inc., 1965).

Conquest, Robert, *Power and Policy in the USSR* (New York: St. Martin's Press, 1961).

Cook, Fred J., *The Warfare State* (New York: The Macmillan Company, 1962).

Dinerstein, H. S., *War and the Soviet Union* (rev. ed., New York: Frederick A. Praeger, Publishers, 1962).

Dulles, Allen, *The Craft of Intelligence* (New York: Harper and Row, Publishers, 1963).

Eisenhower, Dwight D., *The White House Years: Waging the Peace, 1956–1961* (Garden City, New York: Doubleday and Company, Inc., 1965).

Emme, Eugene M., *The Impact of Air Power: National Security and World Politics* (New York: D. Van Nostrand Company, Inc., 1959).

Fenton, John M., *Managing Editor of Gallup Polls Looks at Polls, Politics and the People from 1945 to 1960* (Boston: Little, Brown and Company, 1960).

Fromm, Erich, *May Man Prevail?* (Garden City, New York: Doubleday and Company, Inc., 1961).

Garthoff, Raymond, *Soviet Strategy in the Nuclear Age* (New York: Frederick A. Praeger, Publishers, 1958). Also rev. ed., 1962.

———, *The Soviet Image of Future War* (Washington, D.C.: Public Affairs Press, 1959).

Gavin, James M., *War and Peace in the Space Age* (New York: Harper and Brothers, Publishers, 1958).

Gilpin, Robert, *American Scientists and Nuclear Weapons Policy* (Princeton, New Jersey: Princeton University Press, 1962).

Hilsman, Roger, *Strategic Intelligence and National Security* (New York: The Free Press, 1965).

Horelick, Arnold L., and Rush, Myron, *Strategic Power and*

Soviet Foreign Policy (Chicago: The University of Chicago Press, 1966).

Huntington, Samuel P., ed., *Changing Patterns of Military Politics* (New York: The Free Press, 1962).

———, *The Common Defense: Strategic Programs in National Politics* (New York: Columbia University Press, 1961).

Kahn, Herman, *On Thermonuclear War* (second edition, Princeton, New Jersey: Princeton University Press, 1961).

———, *Thinking about the Unthinkable* (New York: Horizons Press, 1962).

Kaufman, William W., *Military Policy and National Security* (Princeton, New Jersey: Princeton University Press, 1956).

Kennan, George F., *Russia, the Atom and the West* (New York: Harper Brothers, 1957).

Khrushchev, N. S., *New York: Documents on Trip* (New York: Concurrent Press, 1960).

———, *World Without Arms: World Without Wars* (Moscow: Foreign Language Publishing House, 1959).

Kilmarx, Robert A., *A History of Soviet Air Power* (London: Faber & Faber, 1962).

Kissinger, Henry A., *Nuclear Weapons and Foreign Policy* (Garden City, New York: Doubleday and Company, Inc., 1957).

———, *The Necessity for Choice: Prospects of American Foreign Policy* (Garden City, New York: Doubleday and Company, Inc., 1962).

———, Henry A., ed., *Problems of National Strategy* (New York: Frederick A. Praeger, Publishers, 1965).

Knorr, Klaus, ed., *NATO and American Security* (Princeton, New Jersey: Princeton University Press, 1959).

Lee, Asher, *Air Power* (New York: Frederick A. Praeger, 1955).

———, *The Soviet Air Force* (New York: The John Day Company, 1962).

Lerner, Max, *The Age of Overkill: A Preface to World Politics* (New York: Simon and Schuster, 1963).

Liddell Hart, B. H., *Deterrent or Defense* (New York: Frederick A. Praeger, 1960).

Loosbrock, John F. (Ed., with other editors of *Air Force* magazine), *Space Weapons: A Handbook of Military*

Astronautics (New York: Frederick A. Praeger, 1959).

McBride, James H., and Eales, John I. W., *Military Posture: Fourteen Issues Before Congress*, 1964 (Washington, D.C.: The Center for Strategic Studies, Georgetown University, 1965).

McClelland, Charles A., *Nuclear Weapons, Missiles and Future War* (New York: Chandler Publishing Company, 1960).

McGovern, William M., *Strategic Intelligence and the Shape of Tomorrow* (Chicago: Henry Regnery Co., 1961. Published in cooperation with the Foundation for Foreign Affairs, Inc., Foundation of Foreign Affairs Series Number 5).

Medaris, John B., *Countdown for Decision* (New York: G. P. Putnam's Sons, 1960).

Miksche, F. O., *The Failure of Atomic Strategy* (New York: Frederick A. Praeger, 1958).

Morgenstern, Oskar, *The Question of National Defense* (New York: Random House, 1959).

Nogee, Joseph L., and Spanier, John W., *The Politics of Disarmament* (New York: Frederick A. Praeger, 1963).

Osgood, Robert Endicott, *Limited War: The Challenge to American Strategy* (Chicago: The University of Chicago Press, 1957).

———, *NATO: The Entangling Alliance* (Chicago: The University of Chicago Press, 1962).

Parsons, Nels A., Jr., *Missiles and the Revolution in Warfare* (Cambridge, Massachusetts: Harvard University Press, 1962).

Pearson, Drew and Anderson, Jack, *U.S.A.—Second Class Power?* (New York: Simon and Schuster, 1958).

Peeters, Paul, *Massive Retaliation: The Policy and its Critics* (Chicago: Henry Regnery Company, 1959).

Penkovskiy, Oleg (Translated by Peter Debiabin), *The Penkovskiy Papers* (Garden City, New York: Doubleday and Company, 1965).

Perlo, Victor, *Militarism and Industry: Arms Profiteering in the Missile Age* (New York: International Publishers, 1962).

Pokrovsky, G. I., *Science and Technology in Contemporary*

War (trans. by Raymond Garthoff, New York: Frederick A. Praeger, 1959).

Power, Thomas S. (General, USAF, retired), *Design for Survival* (New York: Coward-McCann, Inc., 1964).

Powers, Lieutenant Colonel Patrick W., *A Guide to National Defense: The Organization and Operations of the U.S. Military Establishment* (New York: Frederick A. Praeger, 1964).

Quade, E. S., *Analysis for Military Decisions* (Chicago: Rand McNally and Company, 1964).

Ransom, Harry Howe, *Government Secrecy and National Security, An Analysis* (Harvard University Defense Policy Seminar, Serial No. 123, January 1958).

——, *Central Intelligence and National Security* (Cambridge, Massachusetts: Harvard University Press, 1958).

——, *Can American Democracy Survive Cold War?* (Garden City, New York: Doubleday and Company, 1963).

Ross, Thomas B., and Wise, David, *The Invisible Government* (New York: Random House, Inc., 1964).

Schelling, Thomas, *The Strategy of Conflict* (Cambridge, Massachusetts: Harvard University Press, 1960).

——, *Strategy and Arms Control* (New York: The Twentieth Century Fund, 1961).

Schlesinger, Arthur M., Jr., *A Thousand Days: John F. Kennedy in the White House* (Boston: Houghton Mifflin Company, The Riverside Press, Cambridge, 1965).

Schwiebert, Ernest G., *A History of the U.S. Air Force Ballistic Missiles* (New York: Frederick A. Praeger, 1964).

Snyder, Glenn H., *Deterrence and Defense: Toward a Theory of National Security* (Princeton, New Jersey: Princeton University Press, 1961).

Sokolovsky, Marshal V. D. (Ed.), *Military Strategy: Soviet Doctrine and Concepts* (New York: Frederick A. Praeger, 1963). Minor revision of translation by Translation Service Branch, Foreign Technology Division, Wright Paterson Air Force Base, Ohio; minor changes made by Richard Rockingham Gill.

Sorensen, Theodore C., *Kennedy* (New York: Harper and Row, Publishers, 1965).

Spanier, John W., *The Truman-MacArthur Controversy* (Cambridge, Massachusetts: The Belknap Press of Harvard University Press, 1959).

———, *American Foreign Policy Since World War II* (rev. ed., New York: Frederick A. Praeger, 1962).

Taylor, Maxwell D. (General, U.S. Army, retired), *The Uncertain Trumpet* (New York: Harper and Brothers, 1959).

Tully, Andrew, *The CIA* (New York: William Morrow and Co., Inc., 1962).

Wise, David, and Ross, Thomas B., *The Invisible Government* (New York: Bantam Books, published by agreement with Random House, Inc., 1964).

Witze, Claude (Senior Editor of *Air Force* magazine), *Space Weapons: A Handbook of Military Astronautics* (New York: Frederick A. Praeger, Publishers, 1959).

Wolfe, Thomas W., *Soviet Strategy at the Crossroads* (Cambridge, Massachusetts: Harvard University Press, 1964).

Newspapers

The Boston Globe
The New York Herald Tribune
The New York Times
The New Statesman
The St. Louis Post Dispatch
The Washington Post

Periodicals

Air Force and Space Digest
Air University Quarterly
American Political Science Review
Annals of the American Academy of Political and Social Science
Armed Forces
Army
Atlantic Monthly
Aviation Week
Bulletin of the Atomic Scientists
Business Week
Current History

Daedalus
Encounter
Foreign Affairs
Fortune
Harper's
International Affairs
Journal of the American Academy of Political and Social Sciences
Journal of Conflict Resolution
Journal of International Affairs
Journal of Politics
Life
Look
Military Review
Missiles and Rockets
The Nation
Navy—The Magazine of Sea Power
The New Republic
New Yorker
Newsweek
Orbis
Political Science Quarterly
Public Opinion Quarterly
The Reporter
The Saturday Evening Post
Scientific American
Survival
Time
U. S. Naval Institute Proceedings
U. S. News and World Report
World Affairs
World Politics

Articles

"Air Force Covers Up," *The New Republic*, Vol. 13 (May 29, 1957).

Albrook, Rober C., "How Good Are Our Missiles?" *The Reporter*, Vol. 18 (February 19, 1959).

Alsop, Stewart, "How Can We Catch Up?" *The Saturday Evening Post*, Vol. 230 (December 14, 1957).

————, "Our Gamble with Destiny," *The Saturday Evening Post*, Vol. 231 (May 15, 1959).

————, "Kennedy's Grand Strategy," (Interview with President John F. Kennedy), *The Saturday Evening Post*, Vol. 235 (March 31, 1962).

————, "McNamara Thinks about the Unthinkable," *The Saturday Evening Post*, Vol. 236 (December 1, 1962).

————, "The Alternative to Total War," *The Saturday Evening Post*, Vol. 236 (December 1, 1962).

Alsop, Stewart, and Bartlett, Charles, "In Time of Crisis," *The Saturday Evening Post*, Vol. 235 (December 8, 1962).

"Arms, McElroy and the Menace," *Newsweek*, Vol. 53 (February 16, 1959).

Aron, Raymond, "The Future of Western Deterrent Power, I, A View from France," *The Bulletin of the Atomic Scientists*, Vol. 16 (September 1960).

Aviation Week (Text of Premier Khrushchev's speech to the All Union Congress of Soviet Journalists), Vol. 71 (November 30, 1959).

Aviation Week, Vol. 54 (June 1, 1951).

Aviation Week, Vol. 58 (January 5, 1953).

Baar, James (Editor of Military Affairs), "Will Time Run Out for Kennedy's Build-up of U.S. ICBM's?" *Missiles and Rockets*, Vol. 18 (June 19, 1961).

————, (Editor of Military Affairs), "Latest Report Says Missile Gap Continues," *Missiles and Rockets*, Vol. 8 (February 13, 1961).

"Ballistic Missile Program Moves Forward," *Aviation Week*, Vol. 75 (September 25, 1961).

"Beaten to the Missile Punch?" *Aviation Week*, Vol. 66 (May 20, 1957).

Bernstein, Bart, and Hagan, Roger, "Military Value of Missiles in Cuba," *Bulletin of the Atomic Scientists*, Vol. 19 (February 1963).

"Big Cut in U.S. Defense Spending," *U.S. News and World Report*, Vol. 47 (December 14, 1959).

"Big Fuss about Missiles—These are the Facts," *U.S. News and World Report*, Vol. 46 (February 20, 1959).

Blackett, P. M. S., "Critque of Some Contemporary Defense Thinking," *Encounter*, Vol. 16 (April 1961).

————, "Steps Toward Disarmament," *Scientific American,* Vol. 9 (April 1962).

Brodie, Bernard, "The Atomic Bomb as a Policy Maker," *Foreign Affairs,* Vol. 27 (October 1948).

————, "Unlimited Weapons—Limited War," *The Reporter,* Vol. 11 (November 18, 1954).

————, "The Anatomy of Deterrence," *World Politics,* Vol. 11 (January 1959).

Buchan, Alastair, "The Future of Western Deterrent Power, III, A View from the United Kingdom," *The Bulletin of the Atomic Scientists,* Vol. 16 (September 1960).

Bundy, McGeorge, "The President and the Peace, *"Foreign Affairs,* Vol. 42 (April 1964).

Burns, Arthur Lee, "The International Consequences of Expecting Surprise," *World Politics,* Vol. 10 (July 1958).

Butz, J. S., Jr., "How Far is the Red Air Force Ahead?" *Air Force and Space Digest,* Vol. 44 (September 1961). (Published by the Air Force Association, formerly *Air Force* magazine).

"Can the United States Still Win the Missile Race?" *U.S. News and World Report* (Interview with Theodore von Karmen, Senior Missile Advisor to NATO, and Dr. Walter R. Dornberger), Vol. 43 (November 15, 1957).

"Congress Starts Digging," *Business Week* (November 30, 1957).

"Debate Over Missiles," *Commonweal,* Vol. 69 (February 20, 1959).

"Defense: Atlas at the Gap," *Time,* Vol. 73 (February 23, 1959).

"Defense Facts and Fancy," *The New Republic,* Vol. 142 (February 1, 1960).

"Defense: The Missile Gap Flap," *Time,* Vol. 77 (February 17, 1961).

Dinerstein, Herbert S., "The Revolution in Soviet Strategic Thinking," *Foreign Affairs,* Vol. 36 (January 1958).

"Dollars and Defense," *Commonweal,* Vol. 71 (February 5, 1960).

Drummond, Roscoe, "Our Strength in Being," *Reader's Digest,* Vol. 77 (July 1960).

Dubinin, M. M., "Potentialities of Chemical Warfare," *Bulletin of Atomic Scientists,* Vol.16 (June 1960).

DuBridge, Lee A., "Let's Stop Being Defeatists about Defense," *Reader's Digest*, Vol. 77 (July 1960).

Dulles, John F., "Policy for Security and Peace," *Foreign Affairs*, Vol. 32 (April 1954).

——, "Challenge and Response in U.S. Policy," *Foreign Affairs*, Vol. 36 (October 1957).

Dupuy, T. N., "Can America Fight a Limited War?" (Reprinted from *Orbis*, Spring, 1961), *Survival*, Vol. 3 (September-October 1961).

Eastman, Ford, "Senate Unit to View Space Status," *Aviation Week*, Vol. 70 (February 2, 1959).

——, "Gates Defend New Intelligence Concept," *Aviation Week*, Vol. 72 (February 1, 1960).

Erskine, Hazel Gaudet (editor), "Report from the Polls," (Reprint of World Gallup Poll conducted by American Institute of Public Opinion), *Public Opinion Quarterly*, Vol. 25 (Spring 1961).

Fellers, Bonner (United States Air Force Brigadier General), *Air Force*, Vol. 42 (March 1959).

Gallois, Pierre, "Nuclear Aggression and National Suicide," *The Reporter*, Vol. 19 (September 18, 1959).

Gardner, Trevor, "U.S. Tries to Catch Up," *Life*, Vol. 43 (November 4, 1957).

Garthoff, Raymond L., "Missiles in Soviet Strategy," *Air Force*, Vol. 41 (July 1958).

"Getting Back into the Missile Race," *Business Week* (November 16, 1957).

Gibney, Frank, "The Missile Mess," *Harpers Magazine*, Vol. 20 (January 1960).

Gordon, Bernard K., "The Military Budget: Congressional Phase," *Journal of Politics*, Vol. 23 (November 1961).

Gordon, Lincoln, "NATO in the Nuclear Age," *Survival*, Vol. 1 (May-June 1959) (From the *Yale Law Review*, 1959).

Halperin, Morton, "The Gaither Committee and the Policy Process," *World Politics*, Vol. 13 (April 1961).

——, "The Military Problem—Choosing Our Weapons," *The New Republic*, Vol. 145 (October 2, 1961).

Hazlitt, Henry, "The Economic Consequence of the ICBM," *Newsweek*, Vol. 59 (October 21, 1957).

Hoag, Malcomb W., "Some Complexities in Military Planning," *World Politics*, Vol. 11 (July 1959).

———, "Strains on the Alliance," *Foreign Affairs*, Vol. 41 (January 1963).

Hoiffding, Aleg, "Strategy and Economics: A Soviet View," reviewing a book by A. N. Lagouski published September 1957, *World Politics*, Vol. 11 (January 1959).

Hotze, Robert, "Fact and Fiction on the ICBM," *Aviation Week*, Vol. 67 (September 2, 1957).

———, "Missile Misinformation," *Aviation Week*, Vol. 67 (September 9, 1957).

———, "The Missile Industry Myth," *Aviation Week*, Vol. 67 (September 16, 1957).

"How Defense Planners Size up the Missile Race," *U.S. News and World Report*, Vol. 43 (November 15, 1957).

"How Much Time is Left?" *Air Force*, Vol. 40 (December 1957).

"How the U.S. Will Block Russia's Missiles," *U.S. News and World Report*, Vol. 43 (September 13, 1957).

Huntington, Samuel P., "Interservice Competition and the Political Role of the Armed Services," *American Political Science Review*, Vol. 55 (March 1961).

"ICBM's Speed-up Bring U.S. Gain in Missile Race," *Business Week* (July 2, 1960).

"In Missiles: A Three-Year Gap Ahead," *Business Week* (December 5, 1959).

"Intercontinental Missiles," *The New Republic* (editorial), Vol. 137 (September 9, 1957).

"Is the World Balance in Missiles Shifting to the U.S.?" *U.S. News and World Report*, Vol. 59 (January 23, 1961).

"Is the U.S. Ahead in the Arms Race?" *U.S. News and World Report*, Vol. 44 (January 10, 1958).

"It's Russia's Turn to Worry About the Missile Gap," *U.S. News and World Report*, Vol. 48 (February 22, 1960).

Jackson, Henry M. (United States Senator, Democrat, Washington, Chairman of Senate Sub-committee on Nuclear Weapons), "Senator Jackson on Missiles," *News Week*, Vol. 50 (September 9, 1957).

———, (United States Senator, Democrat, Washington), Organizing for National Defense," *Foreign Affairs*, Vol. 38 (April 1960).

"Johns Hopkins Report," *U.S. News and World Report*, Vol. 44 (January 31, 1958).

Kaplan, Morton A., "The Calculus of Nuclear Deterrence," *World Politics*, Vol. 11 (October 1958) .

Katzenbach, Edward L., Jr., "The United States Missile Muddle," *The Reporter*, Vol. 17 (October 3, 1957).

Kennedy, John F., "Disarmament Can Be Won," *The Bulletin of the Atomic Scientists*, Vol. 16 (June 1960) .

——, (President-elect), "What Kind of Defense?" *The New Republic*, Vol. 144 (January 9, 1961) .

King, James E., Jr., "Arms and Man in the Nuclear-Rocket Era," *The New Republic*, Vol. 139 (September 1, 1958) .

Kissinger, Henry A., "Missiles and the Western Alliance," *Foreign Affairs*, Vol. 36 (April 1958).

——, "The Search for Stability," *Foreign Affairs*, Vol. 37 (July 4, 1959) .

——, "The Unsolved Problems of European Defense," *Foreign Affairs*, Vol. 40 (July 1962).

——, "Strains on the Alliance," *Foreign Affairs*, Vol. 41 (January 1963) .

——, "NATO's Nuclear Dilemma," *The Reporter*, Vol. 28 (March 28, 1963) .

Knorr, Klaus, "The Future of Western Deterrent Power, II, A View from the United States," *The Bulletin of the Atomic Scientists*, Vol. 16 (September 1960).

Lapp, Ralph E., "Nuclear Weapons Systems," *The Bulletin of the Atomic Scientists*, Vol. 17 (March 1961) .

Leghorn, Colonel Richard S., "No Need to Bomb Cities to Win War," *U.S. News and World Report*, Vol. 38 (January 28, 1955).

Lemnitzer, Lyman L., "Forward Strategy Re-appraised," *Survival*, Vol. 3 (January-February 1961) . (Message to Annual Meeting of the Association of the U.S. Army, August 8, 1960) .

"Letting Down our Defenses," *The New Republic*, Vol. 140 (July 5, 1959).

Lippman, Walter, "Only One Driver Can Sit at the Wheel," *The New Republic*, Vol. 147 (December 22, 1962) .

Loosbrock, John F., "Minimum Deterrent is a Phony," *Survival*, Vol. 3 (March-April 1961). From *Air Force and Space Digest*, December 1960.

"McElroy and Missiles," *The New Republic*, Vol. 140 (February 9, 1959) .

Marshall, R. E., "The Nature of the Soviet Challenge," *The Bulletin of the Atomic Scientists,* Vol. 14 (February 1958).

Milburn, Thomas W., "What Constitutes Effective Deterrence?" *The Journal of Conflict Resolution,* Vol. 3, (June 2, 1959).

"Missile Gap—How Perilous?" *Newsweek,* Vol. 53 (February 9, 1959).

"Missiles on the Firing Line," *U.S. News and World Report,* Vol. 44 (January 31, 1958).

"Missiles: Ours and Russia's," *Newsweek,* Vol. 54 (July 13, 1959).

Murphy, Charles J. V., "America's Widening Military Margin," *Fortune,* Vol. 56 (August 8, 1957).

————, "The Embattled Mr. McElroy," *Fortune,* Vol. 59 (April 1959).

————, "Khrushchev's Paper Bear," *Fortune,* Vol. 70 (December 1964).

"Needed: A Mightier Sword," *Life,* Vol. 48 (February 18, 1960).

"News Digest," *Aviation Week,* Vol. (November 23, 1959).

"Next Generation Seen as Missile Race Key," *Aviation Week,* Vol. 68 (January 27, 1958).

Osgood, Charles E., "A Case for Unilateral Graduated Disarmament," *The Bulletin of Atomic Scientists,* Vol. 16 (April 1960).

Phillips, Thomas R. (United States Army, retired), "Air Force Covers Up," *The New Republic,* Vol. 137 (July 29, 1957).

————, "The Growing Missile Gap," *The Reporter,* Vol 20, (January 8, 1958).

————, "Mr. McElroy's Maginot Line," *The Reporter,* Vol. 20 (February 19, 1959).

————, "We Can't Buy the Time That Has Been Lost," *The New Republic,* Vol. 140 (January 19, 1959).

————, "The Great Guessing Game," *The Reporter,* Vol. 22 (February 28, 1960).

"Platforms," *The New Republic,* Vol. 143 (August 8, 1960). Texts of the defense sections of the 1960 Republican and Democratic national platforms.

Power, Thomas S. (Commanding Officer, SAC), "A Look at SAC's Future," *Air Force,* Vol. 41 (June 1958).

Price, George C., "Arguing the Case for Being Panicky," *Life,* Vol. 43 (November 8, 1957).

Rabinowitch, Eugene, "Accidental War, Missiles, and the World Community," *The Bulletin of the Atomic Scientists,* Vol. 14 (June 1958).

Rathjens, George W., Jr., "Deterrence and Defense," *The Bulletin of the Atomic Scientists,* Vol. 14 (June 1958).

"Reds Put Muscle in Strategic Air Arm," *Aviation Week,* Vol. 60 (March 1964).

Rovere, Richard H., "Letter from Washington," *The New Yorker,* Vol. 34 (February 14, 1959).

————, "Letter from Washington," *The New Yorker,* Vol. 36 (January 31, 1961).

"Scientists Explain U.S. Technological Lag," *Aviation Week,* Vol. 67 (December 30, 1957).

Shipley, James R. (Chief of *Time-Life* Correspondents), "Life and Death Debate over the Missile Program," *Life,* Vol. 46 (March 9, 1959).

Shulman, Marshall D., "Changing Appreciation of the Soviet Problem," *World Politics,* Vol. 10 (July 1958).

"Soviet Study-Military Aspects of Space," *Aviation Week,* Vol. 70 (March 9, 1959).

Stehling, Kurt, "The Missile Experts," *The New Republic,* Vol. 137 (December 23, 1957).

"Superweapons Race: Balance of Power Shifts to the U.S.," *U.S. News and World Report,* Vol. 43 (December 12, 1958).

Symington, Stuart, "Where the Missile Gap Went," *The Reporter,* Vol. 26 (February 15, 1962).

"TRB from Washington," *The New Republic,* Vol. 142 (February 15, 1960).

Taylor, Maxwell (General, United States Army, retired), "Security Will Not Wait." *Foreign Affairs,* Vol. 39 (January 1961).

"The Age of Damocles," *The New Republic,* Vol. 142 (January 18, 1960). (editorial)

"The Ammo was Political," *Newsweek,* Vol. 57 (February 20, 1961).

"The Coming Missile Gap," *Time,* Vol. 75 (February 8, 1960).

"The High Price of Ike," (by TRB from Washington), *The New Republic*, Vol. 144 (January 30, 1961).

"The Imbalance of Terror," (editorial), *The New Republic*, Vol. 145 (September 18, 1961).

"The Military Lobby: Its Impact on Congress, Nation," *Congressional Quarterly Report*, Vol. 14 (March 24, 1961).

"The Missile Bogey," *The Nation*, Vol. 188 (February 18, 1959).

The New Republic, Henry Brandon Interviewing Dr. Werhner von Braun, Vol. 139 (October 20, 1958).

"The Pentagon in Politics," *Commonweal*, Vol. 71 (June 22, 1960).

"The Pushbutton Comes of Age," *Newsweek*, Vol. 52 (December 1, 1959).

"The Soviet Air and Rocket Forces," *U.S. News and World Report*, Vol. 47 (July 20, 1959).

"The Soviet ICBM Announcement," (text), *Current History*, Vol. 34 (January 1958).

"The Truth about the Missile Gap," *U.S. News and World Report*, Vol. 50 (February 27, 1961).

"The Truth about the Missiles," *U.S. News and World Report*, Vol. 48 (February 29, 1960).

"The U.S. is about Even with Soviet Russia in Military Missiles," *U.S. News and World Report*, Vol. 47 (September 28, 1959).

U. S. News and World Report, interview with Secretary of Defense Neil McElroy, Vol. 44 (April 25, 1958).

U. S. News and World Report, partial text of speech by Senator John F. Kennedy before the United States Senate, June 14, 1960, Vol. 148 (June 27, 1960).

"United States Planned Delivery Systems," *The Bulletin of the Atomic Scientists*, Vol. 19 (April 1963).

"United States Prestige Abroad: What the Polls Show," *U.S. News and World Report*, reprint of the full text of an editorial in the *London Daily Telegram* of October 28, 1960, Vol. 49 (November 7, 1960).

"U. S. Taking Lead in Missiles," *U.S. News and World Report*, Vol. 42 (November 1, 1957).

Walkowicz, T. F., "Strategic Concepts for the Nuclear Age," *The Annals of the American Academy of Political and Social Science*, Vol. 299 (May 1955).

"Was There Ever a 'Missile Gap'—Or Just an Intelligence Gap?" *Newsweek*, Vol. 58 (November 13 1961).

Wasserman, Benno, "The Failure of Intelligence Predictions," *Political Studies*, Vol. 8 (June 1960).

"Weapons," *Air Force*, Vol. 40 (August 1957).

"What's New in Red Air Power?" *Air Force*, Vol. 41 (February 1958).

White, Theodore W., *Look*, Vol. 27 (April 23, 1963).

White, Thomas D. (Chief of Staff, United States Air Force), "The Air Force and How We are Doing It," *Air Force*, Vol. 41 (August 1958).

Witze, Claude, "Can the Airborne Alert Prevent a Space Age Pearl Harbor?" *Air Force*, Vol. 42 (March 11, 1960).

———, "Airpower and the News," *Air Force*, Vol. 44 (March 1961).

Wohlstetter, Albert, "The Delicate Balance of Terror," *Foreign Affairs*, Vol. 37 (January 1959).

Wolfers, Arnold, " 'National Security' as an Ambiguous Symbol," *Political Science Quarterly*, Vol. 67 (December 1952).

United States Government Documents

U. S. *Congressional Record*, 83rd Cong., 2nd sess., Vol. 100, pt. 1.

U. S. Library of Congress, Legislative Reference Service, *United States Defense Policies in 1957*, 85th Cong., 2nd sess., House Document 436.

U. S. Library of Congress, Legislative Reference Service, *United States Defense Policies 1958*, 86th Cong., 1st sess., House Document 227.

U. S. Library of Congress, Legislative Reference Service, *United States Defense Policies 1961*, 87th Cong., 2nd sess., House Document 502.

U. S. Library of Congress, Legislative Reference Service, *United States Defense Policies 1962*, 88th Cong., 1st sess., House Document 155.

U. S. Library of Congress, Legislative Reference Service, *United States Defense Policies 1964*, 89th Cong., 1st sess., House Document 285.

U. S. Congress, House, Committee on Armed Services, *Hearings*, Investigation of National Defense and Missiles, 85th Cong., 2nd sess., Vol. 4, hearings for fiscal year 1959 (January-February, 1958).

U. S. Congress, House, Committee on Armed Services, Subcommittee for Special Investigations, *Hearings*, Employment of Retired Military and Civilian Personnel by Defense Industries (called the Hébert Hearings), 86th Cong., 1st sess., Vol. 8 (July-September, 1959).

U. S. Congress, House Committee on Armed Services, *Hearings*, Military Posture Briefings, 87th Cong., 1st sess., Vol. 2 (February-March, 1961).

U. S. Congress, House, Committee on Armed Services, *Hearings on Military Posture*, 87th Cong., 2nd sess., Vol. 4 (January-February 1962).

U. S. Congress, Senate, Committee on Armed Services, Preparedness Subcommittee, *Hearings*, 85th Cong., 1st sess., Vol. 2, pt. 1 (November 25 to December 17, 1957).

U. S. Congress, Senate, Committee on Armed Services, Preparedness Subcommittee, *Hearings*, 85th Cong., 2nd sess., Vol. 3, pt. 2 (January 1958).

U. S. Congress, Senate, Committee on Armed Services and the Committee on Aeronautical and Space Sciences, Preparedness Investigating Subcommittee, *Joint Hearings* on Missiles, Space, and other Major Defense Matters (referred to as *Joint Hearings, 1959*), 86th Cong., 1st sess., (January 29 and 30, 1959).

U. S. Congress, Senate, Committee on Armed Services and the Committee on Aeronautical and Space Sciences, Preparedness Investigating Subcommittee, *Joint Hearings* on Missiles, Space, and other Major Defense Matters (referred to as *Joint Hearings, 1960*), 86th Cong., 2nd sess. (February-March, 1960).

U. S. Congress, Senate, Committee on Armed Services, *Hearings*, Military Procurement for Fiscal Year 1962 Authorization, 87th Cong., 1st sess., Vol. 10 (April, 1960).

U. S. Congress, Senate, Committee on Armed Services, *Hear-*

ings, Military Procurement for Fiscal Year 1963 Authorization, 87th Cong., 2nd sess., Vol. 10 (January-February, 1962).

U. S. Congress, House, Committee on Appropriations, Department of Defense Appropriations for 1958, *Hearings,* 85th Cong., 1st sess., Vol. 9, pt. 2 (February, 1957).

U. S. Congress, House, Committee on Appropriations, Department of Defense, *Hearings,* The Ballistic Missile Programs, 85th Cong., 1st sess., Vol. 8 (November 20 and 21, 1957).

U. S. Congress, House, Committee on Appropriations, Department of Defense Appropriations for 1959, *Hearings,* Department of the Air Force, 85th Cong., 2nd sess., Vol. 11 (March, 1958).

U. S. Congress, House, Committee on Appropriations, Department of Defense Appropriations for 1959, *Hearings,* Department of the Navy, 85th Cong., 2nd sess., Vol. 12 (February, 1958).

U. S. Congress, House, Committee on Appropriations, *Hearings* on Fiscal Year 1960 Defense Budget, 86th Cong., 1st sess., Vol. 9, pt. 1 (February 18, 1959).

U. S. Congress, House, Committee on Appropriations, *Hearings,* Department of Defense Appropriations for 1961, 86th Cong., 2nd sess., pt. 1 (January, 1960).

U. S. Congress, House, Committee on Appropriations, *Hearings,* Department of Defense Appropriations for 1962, 87th Cong., 1st sess., pt. 3 (April, 1961).

U. S. Congress, House, Committee on Appropriations, *Hearings,* Department of Defense Appropriations for 1963, 87th Cong., 2nd sess., pt. 2 (February, 1962).

U. S. Congress, Senate, Committee on Appropriations, *Hearings,* Department of Defense Appropriations for 1958, 85th Cong., 1st sess., Vol. 4 (May, 1957).

U. S. Congress, Senate, Committee on Appropriations, *Hearings,* Department of Defense Appropriations for 1959, 85th Cong., 2nd sess., Vol. 5 (June, 1958).

U. S. Congress, Senate, Committee on Appropriations, *Hearings,* Department of Defense Appropriations for 1960, 86th Cong., 1st sess., Vol. 4 (May, 1959).

U. S. Congress, Senate, Committee on Appropriations, *Hearings*, Department of Defense Appropriations for 1961, 86th Cong., 2nd sess., Vol. 6 (March, 1960).

U. S. Congress, Senate, Committee on Appropriations, *Hearings*, Department of Defense Appropriations for 1962, 87th Cong., 1st sess., Vol. 3 (April, 1961).

U. S. Congress, House, Committee on Government Operations, *Organization and Management of Missile Programs*, House Report 1121, 86th Cong., 1st sess. (1959).

U. S. Congress, Senate, Committee on Government Operations, Subcommittee on National Policy Machinery, *Hearings*, 86th Cong., 2nd sess., pt. 2 (1960).

Special Reports

International Security: The Military Aspect (done under the auspices of the Special Studies Project of the Rockefeller Fund, Inc. (Garden City, New York: Doubleday and Company, Inc., 1958) (referred to as the *Rockefeller Report*).

The Soviet Union and the NATO Powers: The Military Balance, 1959) London: Institute for Strategic Studies, 1959).

Communist Bloc and the Western Alliance: The Military Balance, 1961–1962 (London: The Institute for Strategic Studies, 1962).

Communist Bloc and the Western Alliance: The Military Balance, 1962–1963 (London: The Institute for Strategic Studies, 1963).

Developments in Military Technology and their Impact on United States Strategy and Foreign Policy, Study #8 (prepared at the request of the Committee on Foreign Relations, United States Senate) (Washington, D.C.: Washington Center of Foreign Policy Research, The Johns Hopkins University, 1959). (Referred to as the *Johns Hopkins Report, 1959*).

Other Documents

American Foreign Policy Current Documents (1957–1961),

United States Department of State (Washington, D.C.: Department of State Historical Office).

Zinner, Paul E., *Documents of American Foreign Relations* (1957–1961), (New York: Published for the Council on Foreign Relations by Harper and Brothers).

The Current Digest of the Soviet Press.

Unpublished Manuscripts

Roy E. Licklider, "Defense, Intelligence and the Political Process," "The Missile Gap Controversy" (unpublished M. A. Seminar Paper, Yale University, March 31, 1964).

Martin Cyril McGuire, "Information and the Arms Race" (unpublished Ph.D. thesis, Harvard University, December, 1963).

"Military Strengths" (unpublished Air Force mimeographed material obtained from Professor of Air Science, L. Lieutenant Colonel Stephen Bull, Tufts University, ARTOC, Spring, 1963).

Bruce Lee Raymond Smith, "The Rand Corporation: A Case Study of a Non-profit Advisory Corporation" (Ph.D. thesis, Harvard University, 1964; later published by the Harvard University Press).

INDEX

263

Pravda, 34
Preemptive war, 70
Prestige (American), 116
Preventative war, 70

Quarles, Donald A., 29n., 43, 49n., 57n.

Radford, Arthur W. (Admiral), 19, 53n.
Regulus Missile, 95, 182
Republican National Committee, 132
Republican Party, 144, 152, 202
Reston, James, 44
Rockefeller, Nelson, 137
Rockefeller Report, 47–48

Saltonstall, Leverett (Senator), 133
Samos Satellite, 130
Schriever, Bernard (General), 77n., 91n., 94n., 96n., 111, 129–30, 148
Second strike counterforce, 206
Serial missile production (Soviet Union), 183
Sharp, Dudley C., 121
Sides, John H. (Admiral), 43n.
Sino-Soviet dispute, 209, 213
Skybolt Missile, 169
Snark Missile, 95
Sokolovsky, Vasily (Marshall), 73
Space race, 141
Sprague, Robert C., 48n.
Sputnik, 101, 176
Stalin, Joseph, 70–72
Stevenson, Adlai, 41, 115–16
Strategic Air Command (SAC), 35–36, 45–46, 54, 57–59, 63, 90–91, 93–94, 104–6, 112, 118–19, 128–29, 137, 162, 172, 189

Strauss, Lewis, 28n.
Suez Crises (1956), 64, 75
Symington, Stuart (Senator), 37–38, 40, 78–81, 87n., 91–92, 97–99, 115–16, 121–22, 125, 132–34, 152, 181, 184, 192–96, 203

Tactical nuclear weapons, 23, 27–28, 33, 209–210
Taylor, Maxwell D. (General), 31n., 53n., 110, 131n.
The Nation, 99
The New York Herald Tribune, 117
The New York Times, 88, 117, 131, 138, 141–143, 148, 151, 154–155, 167–169, 199
Thor Missile, 31–32, 40, 43, 64, 85–86, 157
Titan Missile, 94n., 105–106
Trans Siberian Railroad, 177
Truman, Harry S., 17, 22, 41, 59, 82–83, 132
Turkey, 176, 180
Twining, Nathan (General), 54, 60n., 66–67, 123–125, 127, 129

U-2 Aircraft, 130n., 135–137, 177–178, 180–181, 203
United States Information Agency (USIA), 141–143

Vandenburg, Hoyt (General), 21
von Braun, Wernher, 33n., 55–56
von Karmen, Theodore, 55n.

White, Thomas D. (General), 35n., 54, 78n., 91, 92n., 96n., 113n., 129
Wilson, Charles E., 29n., 31–32, 40, 43, 64